Behavioural Problems in Adolescent Period

(Psychology of Adolescence)

Behavioural Problems in Adolescent Period

(Psychology of Adolescence)

M. Rajamanickam

AUTHORSPRESS
Publishers of Creative & Scholarly Books

Worldwide Circulation through Authorspress Global Network
First Published in 2006
by
Authorspress
Q-2A Hauz Khas Enclave, New Delhi-110 016 (India)
Phone: (0) 9818049852
E-mail: authorspressgroup@gmail.com
Website: www.authorspressbooks.com

Behavioural Problems in Adolescent Period

(Psychology of Adolescence)

ISBN 978-81-7273-324-7

Printed in India at Kensington Press

Preface

Our aim in bringing out this book in this form is to present a broad and selective survey of what is known about the behavioural problems of the adolescent boys and girls. The necessity is felt, because psychology of adolescence mainly deal with that part of human life which lies in between the childhood and the adulthood periods. Though the study of adolescence is a apart of the developmental psychology, it is given an independent status for dealing with the subject matter in detail. Only in the adolescent period several important changes in human life take place. The physical changes can be easily seen with the physical changes, and there is also mental development. Since it is a period of rapid growth and development, changes in social behaviour and emotional experiences also occur. The individual goes through puberty and maturity and becomes a youth. But certain specific developmental and the behavioural problems of the adolescent are not dealt with either in developmental or in the adolescence areas. The adolescent period is a crucial period of human life, and the various problems that arise in this period should be adequately dealt with.

The adolescent period has definite age range. It is a transitory period between childhood and adulthood. It begins with puberty, the onset of physical changes at around the age of 13 and approximately ends in maturity at the age of 19 years. But it varies in individuals and also in cultures. During this period they are full of energy and wild imaginations. The adolescent period is generally characterised by conflict between impulses such as sensitivity versus cruelty, selfishness versus altruism and radicalism versus conservatism. It is a period of storm and stress.

In the ongoing physical changes some of the adolescents may behave aggressively and violently. There is both a general growth of tissues such as muscles and bones and vigorously accelerated maturation of the reproductive system. Some physical changes are not noticed, but the growth in height and weight and the body build are easily apparent. The adolescent, apart from some unavoidable activities, has to adjust to an evolving new self, but also to the reactions of the members of the society. The level of physical growth and development vary from individual to individual and the cultural backgrounds. The physical maturity in the case of girls takes place more rapidly than in the case of boys. At the same time the behaviour of boys and girls change differently and varied types of problems emerge among them. The boys are interested in adventurous activities and the girls are interested in fine arts and domestic activities.

The traditional textbooks in developmental psychology do not deal with the problems that adolescents encounter in their life. Therefore separate studies on specific problems are to be made. We come to understand the problem only when an incident occurs. Psychologists have explored all such areas where the adolescents, behaviour creates problems. In the studies presented here we find that parents also are responsible for their children's problems. The adolescents mostly get into the grip of emotional maladjustments. Therefore most of their problems are based upon adjustment and academic achievements, perceptual processes and development of personality. Studies on these areas bring out valuable results and solutions may be sought for resolving them. The materials presented here may be of some use for those who are interested in adolescent problems.

Kcherry Sudarshan deserves all appreciation for publishing this book in an attractive manner.

M. Rajamanickam

Contents

Preface 5

PART 1 ADJUSTMENT PROBLEMS DURING ADOLESCENCE

1. Behavioural Problems during the Adolescent Period 13
   M. Rajamanickam
2. Adjustment Problems of Adolescent Students in Relation to their Achievements 32
   M. Rajamanickam and R. Vasanthal
3. Adjustment Problems in Relation to Psychosomatic Disorders among Adolescent Girls 59
   M. Rajamanickam and Mercy Arunmozhi
4. Adjustment Problems of High and Low Aspirant Adolescents 92
   Ravi Sandhu
5. Adjustment and Creativity among Adolescents through High School Years 103
   C.B. Asha
6. Criminality and Adjustment Problems of High School Students 112
   Vijayalaxmi A. Aminabhavi
7. Adjustment Pattern of Discriminated Girls of the Twenty-first Century: An Empirical Study 123
   Swatantra Jain
8. Parent-Child Relationship, School Achievement and Adjustment of Adolescent Boys 130
   Paromita Roychaudhury and Jayanti Basu

PART II INTELLIGENCE, ACADEMIC ACHIEVEMENTS AND SKILLS

9. Intelligence and N-Achievement of Adolesent Girls and Their Attitudes towards the Status of Women 143
   Ira Das

10. Family Background and Scholastic Achievements of Secondary School Students 148
M. Sarada Devi and Kavitha Kiran

11. Influence of Family Socio-economic Status on Educational and Occupational Aspirations of High and Low Achieving Adolescents 154
Mahmood S. Khan and Tsehaie Jemberu

12. Self-Concept and Scholastic Achievement of the Girls of Working and Non-working Mothers 161
Sadhna Mittal

13. Adolescent Students' Achievement in Science Subjects in Secondary Schools— A Factor Analytical Study 166
Nimai Charan Das and M. Rajamanickam

14. Relative Efficiency of Piagetian Conservation Abilities and Academic Achievement in Science 178
H.M. Kasinath

PART III ADOLESCENTS' PERCEPTION OF ISSUES AND PROBLEMS

15. Adolescent's Perception of Child-rearing Practices of the Parents and Delinquency Proneness 189
Kanwal Nalwa and Vidhu Mohan

16. Perception of Child-rearing Practices of Deprived and Non-deprived Adolescent Students 206
Vidhu Mohan and Kanwal Nalwa

17. Personal Problem Solving: The Perception and Strategies of the Adolescent Girls 221
Mukul Bhalla and Pallavi Bhatnagar

18. Adolescents' Perception of Indian Women's Position in Different Areas 238
Anjana Sharma, Ira Das, and S.P. Sinha

19. Perception of Feminine Worth and Its Relation to Fear of Success in Adolescents with Army and Civilian Backgrounds 243
Vidhu Mohan and Monica Bali

PART IV PERSONALITY PROBLEMS OF ADOLESCENT PERIOD

20. Root Personality Dimensions to Intelligence and Quality of Social Interaction among Adolescent Students 261
Sreekumar, E. and George Mathew V.

21. Personality Profile of Adolescent Delinquents 269
Uma Devi I. and Mayuri K.

22. Personality Traits of Adolescent Girl Students in Relation to their Parents 285
Swatantra Jain

23. School Achievement and Personality: A TAT Study 295
N. Hota

24. Effect of Inhabitance on Personality Traits of Scheduled Tribe and Scheduled Caste Adolescents in Comparison with Upper Caste 303
Kalpana Jain and V.L. Chouhan

PART 1
ADJUSTMENT PROBLEMS DURING ADOLESCENCE

The adolescent period is generally said to be as the period of problems in the human span of life. The reason for this is that it is the period in which the human individual is highly sensitive and emotional to the situation. It is the period in which the emotional development and personal adjustment to the situations are taking place. If these two aspects of human life, at the adolescent period, went on smoothly in a person then there is no problem. But these two aspects in many cases do not take place successfully. There are several different areas through which the adolescent boys and girls should go through successfully to achieve harmonious emotional development and adjustment. Some of the areas are the academic achievements in schools, developing emotionally well balanced motivation as the level of aspirations, developing creative skills, maintaining oneself free from delinquency, not getting maladjusted due to any discrimination by the parents, maintaining good relationship with parents, maintaining adjustment with peers and others in the school situation and in the play ground. Any impairment in any of these areas may cause some problem for the adolescent boys and girls. Adolescent boys and girls who have no problems appear cheerful and pleasant in all situations. But if they have any problem they appear in a tensional state which may impair their happiness. The inherent impulses in the adolescent period are always in conflict. If the conflict is not resolved then it may cause several problems like frustration, aggression, violence and personality disorganisation.

CHAPTER 1

Behavioural Problems during the Adolescent Period

M. Rajamanickam

Psychology is a behavioural science which studies human life right from the time of birth. Some scholars even go to the stage of embryonic state for studying the developmental processes. Of the various stages of human development the adolescent period is the most important one. Generally human beings plan the future prospects of a person only during the adolescent period. If a man fails to plan his future at this stage he is at a loss later on. Therefore the period of adolescence is the most crucial period of human life and he has to very carefully think and plan his future in the light of his family background and environmental and social conditions.

But it is also true that during the adolescent period a person will not have sufficient knowledge about his future. When he grows and develops his knowledge about various occupational chances he can plan and work out on the desired area. This stage may occur in the life of a person only at the early adulthood period. The parents may aspire that their son or daughter should get into some lucrative job. They may be providing all the facilities for their son or daughter and guiding him/her on the lines they wanted. But the parents' desires and the interests of the adolescent must syncharonze on the same idea. But even if the adolescent is not fully in agreement with the parents, they may persuade him/her to accept and to carry out their ambition.

Since the adolescents do not want to go against their parent' wishes they might have joined a particular professional course like medicine or engineering. But they might have desired to take up some biological science and specialise in it. This sort of problems often arise in families. Here the adolescent is facing some adjustment problem with regards to his/her academic achievement or the carrier he/she desired. This type of instances are occurring in the life of an adolescent. The adolescent is put into a conflicting situation he/she has to decide whether to follow the parents' desire or to go with his/her own idea. At this stage it is better that both the parents and their ward should have the psychological counselling to avoid the problem that may occur further. Adolescent students face not only this type of problem, but also other problems like emotional and social maladjustments. It is very difficult to assess correctly the type of problem the adolescent they face unless specific studies are conducted. There are quite number of studies made by trained investigators and psychologists in India on the adolescent students' problems.

Adjustment Problems during the Adolescent Period

Adjustment has to be made by individuals in all life situations. Every situation may need different type of adjustment. If an individual fails to adjust himself to the situation then the problem arises. It may be any one of the psychological consequences, like conflict, frustration, emotional maladjustment, aggression and violence. The adolescent sometimes does not withstand the severe emotional maladjustment to the situation. Adolescents even discard everything and run away from homes irrespective of the consequences. The mass media of communication report three or four cases every day of these adolescents disappearing from their homes. The television makes announcements with their photographs giving other particulars like age, height, complexion and other information. The parents report to the police who try to trace and hand them over them to the parents. Why are these instances occurring often?

One of the main reasons is that these adolescents are highly emotional and do not tolerate even a slight critical remark from their parents and from others, like their teachers and friends. It is rooted in the infant and childhood period and in the child rearing practices of the parents. Another important reason for these types of behaviour patterns of the adolescents is the themes of the motion pictures. Adolescents are very fond of movies. Sometimes they play truant from their classes to go to the movies. Another pastime they eagerly prefer is viewing television programmes everyday. Generally the present day motion pictures and the television series are packed with aggression, violence, fightings, quarrelling, eloping, use of vulgar words and indecent sexuality. The adolescents are easily influenced by these themes and engage themselves in all soots of fantastic imaginations. They try to imitate certain things which they like very much. Instances are often reported in newspapers where some adolescents wanted to see the cine stars and went round the cinema studios with a view to becoming cine stars. They were nabbed by the police and handed over to their parents. Such students do not concentrate on their studies. As result of it their their performances become very poor. When the their progress reports are given to them to get the signature of the parents, for fear of scolding and punishment they do not show them to their parents. Some of them run away from homes with the view of find job elsewhere. These are common occurrences in the behaviour of the adolescents these days.

In the lower socioeconomic-status families some of the adolescents do not take their educational career very seriously. They join with their peer groups and get involved in all sorts of undesirable activities. Their adjustment is very much impaired by their association with their peers. They generally are very much sensitive to things and events and they develop emotional maladjustment and become problematic. Psychological studies on the behavioural patterns of adolescents were made with special reference to personal, social, academic and environmental factors. Textbooks on psychology of adolescence mainly discuss the developmental processes and the causes of problems in general. Therefore, it is important to go in detail on the specific behavioural problems of the adolescents. We are discussing here several of the factors that have caused problems.

In the discussion on the problems of the adolescents we find that most of them were found to based on adjustment of the adolescents to the situations. Adjustment generally means an effective adaptation to the environment both internally and externally which also includes the full acceptance of the group norms, ideas and values. Mouly (1966) states that adjustment is the process by means of which an individual seems to maintain his physiological and psychological equilibrium and propels himself toward self-enhancement. Adjustment represents the quality of an individual's behaviour in relation to his interpersonal relations. A well-adjusted person, according to Cronbach (1954), is one who commits himself to socially desirable goals and uses his energies effectively in working toward them. The well adjusted have a sense of security and a feeling of adequacy.

The term 'adjustment' became very popular in psychological studies in the 1930s. It was Shaffer who has given strong emphasis in his classical work *The Psychology of Adjustment.* Shaffer (1956) emphasized the biological adaptation of the organism to its living environment. This is a mechanistic approach on the lines of Watson's behaviourism. But writers of other schools of psychology have stated that man not only adapts himself to the environment but also by using his intelligence, experience and imagination changes his environment for meeting his needs and demands. Lazarus (1976) discussed the process of adjustment in terms of accommodation and assimilation, but when man alludes to defence mechanisms he approaches adjustment as a process and not an end result that an individual accomplishes successful or unsuccessfully.

A well adjusted child, according to Feinberg (1953) is like a well adjusted adult, makes good social adjustment and has harmonious relationship with the people with whom he is associated, at home, at school and in the playground. The degree to which an adolescent adjusts to others is the indication of how well he is adjusted as a person. According to Eysenck (1953), the psychological process of adjustment is dynamic in nature rather than static in quality. He states that the psychology of adjustment is based on the quality of life.

Adjustment is a continuous process of action in the life of human beings right from the period of childhood, adolescence and adulthood with a definite purpose of meeting the needs of the self, the needs of the environment and the needs of the culture. The ultimate end of the process of action of adjustment is the successful survival of the organism. The failure of the process of adjustment may end in the extermination of the organism. In the adolescent's environment, adjustment is the combined influence of several forces that are operating to produce a well adjusted or poorly adjusted personality. There are several Indian studies on the adolescents adjustment problems. The study made by Rajamanickam and Vasanthal (1993) has brought out several interesting results. It was the study among the school students relating adjustment to their school achievements. It revealed that the better adjusted adolescent students showed very good achievements in their school performances and the students who had low adjustment showed poor achievements in their studies. It was also observed in this study that the number of siblings in the family had adverse effects in the school performance of the adolescent students' achievements. The more number of siblings there are, the poorer the achievements. A family with one or two siblings showed very good achievements in the adolescents boys and girls.

In another study made by Rajamanickam and Mercy Arunmozhi (1992) among adolescent girls, it was tested whether adjustment was influenced by factors like psychosomatic problems. The girls' age ranged from 15 to 19 years and were from different socioeconomic backgrounds. It was observed in this study that the girls who were free from psychosomatic problems were well adjusted and those who had psychosomatic symptoms and were found to be poorly adjusted. The girls from affluent families were found having the least psychosomatic symptoms to be well adjusted; the girls from lower socioeconomic families had high symptoms of psychosomatism and were poorly adjusted. Psychosomatic disorders had a definite influence on the adjustment problems of the adolescent girls.

An attempt was made to test whether adjustment problems had any influence in the creative abilities of the adolescents. Asha (1988) tested this hypothesis. The results showed that the better adjusted boys and girls had high creative abilities. There were three levels of creativity: highly creative, moderately creative and low creative. The well adjusted boys were found to be superior in creativity than the well adjusted girls and others.

Ravi Sandhu (1997) studied the adjustment problems of high and low aspirant adolescents. There were 150 school students in this study. It is generally believed that adolescents will have a high level of aspirations. Everyone may claim that he/she can achieve the said goal, irrespective whether he/she could do it or not. Aspiration is an ego involved goal seeking desire that a person sets for himself. The more ego an individual has the higher aspiration he sets in and the more it relates to the areas of behaviour. But it sometimes affects his adjustment. Thus the adjustment is affected by the ego one sets for oneself. This was what the investigator had observed in her study.

There are several studies made in the past relating to adjustment problems and criminality. Criminality is a behaviour pattern that has been classified as antisocial and delinquent behaviour in society. Generally, antisocial behaviour like delinquency, theft, cheating, homicide, adultery and forceful rape and other similar behavioural patterns are prevailing more among the persons of emotionally maladjusted. But how an individual becomes a delinquent and develops criminal tendencies has become a subject matter for the psychologists to investigate as several of the psychosocial factors are found to be having an influence on the criminal and antisocial behaviour of the individual. Whether such tendencies originate at the adolescent level or they are situational incidences has been investigated and tested by Vijayalaxmi A. Aminabhavi (1997) among the adolescent boys and girls. The results of this study show that the adolescent students' adjustment problems had positive relationship with the criminal tendencies of the students. The adolescents who were poorly adjusted had a higher level of criminal tendencies than the well adjusted students. Other factors that have an influencing effect on the criminal tendencies are poor adjustment at home, poor health, poor social adjustment, poor and emotional adjustment and the birth order. The adolescent boys had higher criminal tendencies than the girls.

In the Indian culture children of different gender are not treated in the same manner by the parents. There is a general tendency among the parents to give more importance to male children and little or no importance to female children. Thus children are put into differential treatment and thereby the discriminated female child develops a sense of insecurity, helplessness and maladjustment in the family situation. Female children are put into severe ordeal and hard work all through life, while the male children enjoy the favours of the parents.

It is very unfortunate that the parents of the twenty-first century expect that their daughters should be docile, submissive, accept differential treatment and carry out more works. But if a female child questions the differential treatment of her parents she is put into severe stress which results in maladjustment, depression and other emotional problems. The adjustment of such girls is very much affected by this type of differential treatment. This problem was studied by Swatantra Jain (1998) among 300 adolescent girls. He has taken much efforts in bringing out the intricacies of the problem.

The type of parent-child relationship and the adolescent students' achievements seem to have some effect on the adjustment problems of the adolescents. This problem was investigated and tested by Poramita Chaudhury and Jayanti Basu (1998) in their studies. It was observed that the type of relationship the mothers have with children significantly influence the school adjustment of the adolescent boys which also determine their school achievements.

Intelligence, Academic Achievements and Skills of Adolescents

Psychologists and educationists have studied intelligence very extensively under different themes, like development, assessment and nature of intelligence. They have also indicated how it functions and helps to solve problems. Intelligence is related to the performance of some activities and in behavioural patterns. In some individuals intelligence may function effectively in the very early years of life and in some it functions successfully only in the later years of life. For example, John Stuart Mill (1806-1871) and Sir Francis Galton (1826-1911) were rated as geniuses at the age of five and six. Mill was a political philosopher and an economist and Galton was a great scientist. Their intelligence quotients were assessed as above 180 at the age of six.

But there were persons who revealed their excellence and great achievements only at the adult age. For example, Abraham Lincoln (1809-1866) was a woodcutter in the early years of his life. Only at the adult age he started his education and became an eminent lawyer and great orator who also became the president of the United States. Louis Armstrong was a neglected child whose father deserted the family and whose mother was usually out of town. He was caught and placed in coloured wall home for his antisocial activities, where he was taught to play a musical instrument and he became the genius of the time in USA. It is a simple fact of jazz music, the only art form America ever wholly originated, that virtually all that is played today comes from Louis Armstrong. Thus intelligence depends upon how well one manipulates one's mental abilities and exercises it. A person may exercise his intelligence in action at varied times. It may be at the early years or at the later years. This is what takes place in the case of school students also. Some may show achievements earlier and some make it at the later years.

In the studies made by psychologists it is observed that some students made better achievements in the early period. Several factors were found to have influence on results. The level of intelligence of the individual, the family school background, the interest the teacher shows in teaching the subject and the treatment of the students — all may have influence on the academic achievements of the students. In one of the studies made by Ira Das (2001), it was tested whether intelligence had anything to do with N-achievement in the case of adolescent girls and also the attitudes they had towards the status of women. It was found that those who were highly intelligent had N-achievement and also a positive attitudes towards the status of women. But some of them had low N-achievement but high positive attitudes towards the status of women.

In this study it was observed that girls with low intelligence level had low N-achievement and they accepted the low status of women. Thus the level of intelligence determines some of the aspects of the adolescent girls' life. Adolescents are drawn to schools from different types of families and each type of family has certain disadvantages and influence upon the academic achievements of the students. In the study made by Sarada Devi and Kavitha Kiran (2002) it is observed that large family size, low educational level of the parents, low parental involvement and low parental motivation were the major factors found to be having an influence upon the scholastic backwardness of the adolescent students.

The socioeconomic status of the family was found to be another important factor to influence educational and occupational aspirations of the adolescent students who showed high and low achievements in schools. This problem was investigated by Khan and Tschaie Jembery (2002). The authors observed that many of the adolescent students were from nuclear families. Most of the mothers of the students had only primary education and few of them were illiterates. The main cause of the low achievement of the students was large family size. Another reason seemed to be the low education of the mothers. It is observed that the educational status of the parents determine their involvement and motivation of their children's educational levels.

The family in every culture functions as the primary institution in inculcating the socio-cultural norms and values, discipline and other aspects of behavioural patterns on the children. All these characteristics are induced in the child by the process of socialisation. The child is made to learn the best lessons of citizenship both from the father and mother. As the child grows into an adolescent several problems arise due to various changes in the environmental conditions.

The adolescent period is a critical period of human life as it mostly determines a person's future. The present generation is highly competitive and each one in the family has to earn his/her bread. Women with adequate qualifications get employed in some organisation in the interest of their children's education and welfare.

The adolescents try to develop confidence in their children, the adolescent boy/gird should have some self-esteem about himself/ herself and have confidence that he/she can make best scholastic achievements. Studies in this area have conflicting views. Some of the investigators tried to clarify this issue. Sadhana Mittal (1997) had conducted a study among adolescent girl students of working and non-working mothers. The results showed that the children of working mothers have made better scholastic achievements and also had the self-concept than the children of non-working mothers. This shows that the children of working mothers have developed more of self-concept and they also wanted to be like their mothers, make better school achievements, get into a job and earn, whereas the children of nonworking mothers did not develop such self-confidence and aspiration.

Adolescent students' academic achievements in some specific areas were also tested. Since many of the adolescent students were found to be very backward in some subjects it has aroused the curiosity of some investigators to find out the causes behind it. Nimai Charan Das and Rajamanickam (2002) have tried to find out the cause of continuous death in the performance of the students in science subjects. The factorial analysis of their study indicated several causes such as the emotional maladjustment, lack of study materials, disinterested teachers, short of teachers in the school, unsympathetic teachers, improper examination system, defective teaching methods and undesirable home conditions of the students. It is for the school and educational authorities to alleviate the defects and create interest in the subjects among the students.

The adolescent students' academic achievement in science subjects was also related to cognitive development in the studies made by (2002) Kasinath (2002). The author tested this issue through piagetian conservation abilities on a group of 198 adolescent students studying in 8th standard. The results of his study showed that the best predictors of academic achievement in science were conservation of length, number, classification and solid. Among the boys the best predictors of academic achievement in science were conservation of classification, length and solid and among the girls the predictors were conservation of length, number, weight and classification. It was also found that in understanding the science concepts actions on concrete objects were very essential.

Adolescent Students' Perception of Various Problems

Perception is a basic psychological process which serves as the means of acquiring experience and knowledge about the world. It is the response to the external stimulation. Right from the time of birth the human beings respond to the stimulations that are attracting the sense organs. Perception takes place in an organism through the sense organs. If the sense organs are in sound condition and respond to the internal and external environmental stimulations, then the organism experiences and understands the meanings of the stimuli. Therefore sensations are the gateways to perception and perception involves sensation, experience and knowledge.

Perception originally discussed only in philosophy. Philosophically perception means insight or keen understanding of persons, objects and events. It is the mental grasping of objects, events and persons through senses. Psychologically perception mainly refers to the experience one gains through sense organs. Perception includes learning and thinking. How the adolescent boys and girls perceive the world in their every day life experiences? Psychological studies were made on the problems of perception the adolescents face were brought out. First of all the adolescent boys and girls perceive their home situations. How they were reared and brought up by their parents when they were children, gets into their perceptual processes of these adolescent boys and girls.

The adolescent period is highly sensitive and critical one in which the adolescent boys and girls get easily frustrated and emotional and become maladjusted. The way in which children are reared and brought up becomes one of the main reasons for children becoming the delinquents in the later life. In every community and culture boys and girls at the adolescent period develop delinquency if they were not brought up properly. They become problems for-the parents and also for the community. This problem was investigated by Kanwal Nalwa and Vidhu Mohan (2001, 1996). The results of their studies showed how defective child rearing practices are causing serious problems in the adolescent period.

An individual could see his/her own problems and also evolve strategies for solving the problems. This assumption was tested by Mukul Bhalla and Pallavi Bhatnagar (1992) in their study. This study was conducted among adolescent girls studying in higher secondary schools, aged between 16.5 and 17.5 years. These girls were able to perceive their problems, but the solutions for the problems were not complete. Adolescent students' perception of the status of Indian women is an issue for study. The Indian women's status as perceived by the adolescent students was tested by Anjana Sharma, Ira Das and Sinha (1999) among adolescent boys and girls. The results indicated that the boys perceived the Indian women's status negatively while the girls perceived it positively. Students from lower socio-economic status families have perceived the women's status more negatively than the students from higher socio-economic status families. The authors are of the view that these students have not correctly understood the present status of women in India. They are in need of knowing the correct status prevailing in India.

A tradition is set up in the Indian culture that a female child is a financial burden on the parents and considered as inauspicious creature. There are occurrences of feticide, infanticide, neglect, physical violence and lack of medical care. All these result at higher mortality rates for girls than for boys. However there are indications that women perceive the birth of a female child is a welcome. Generally boys and girls are afraid of success in their life. There is also a tendency to perceive the worth of feminine in Indian culture. Vidhu Mohan and Monica Bali (1994) have investigated and tested this problem in their studies. It was observed that fear of success among females caused poor perception of the worth of women. This study brought out several interesting results.

Personality Problems of Adolescent Students

Psychological studies on personality are so numerous that it is very difficult to quote and enumerate them. Several experiments were conducted and many theories were evolved to explain the personality traits of the individuals. Personality studies were made mainly to trace the traits that are influencing the behavioural patterns of the individuals and also to classify individuals into different types and to predict the behaviour of an individual. Sreekumar and George Mathew (2003) have investigated the relationship of root personality dimension to intelligence and quality of social interaction. This study they have conducted among the adolescent boys and girls aged between 15 and 17 years, studying in higher secondary schools. The results of their study indicated that the personality trait inertia had negative correlation with intelligence. When inertia increased intelligence decreased and Inertia is characterized by fear, low adaptive ability. According to the results of this study personality traits do not highly correlate with intelligence.

Uma Devi and Mayuri (2001) have studied the personality profile of adolescent delinquents. These delinquents were staying in observation homes. These adolescent delinquents had very poor personality characteristics and had no future aspirations. The development of delinquency in these adolescents was found to be mainly due to the defective child rearing practices, disturbed family backgrounds, lack of proper care of their life aspects and bad social surroundings.

Swatantra Jain (1992) had attempted to assess the personality traits of adolescent girls in relation to their parents acceptability. The sample consisted of 250 adolescent girls of which 50 were low accepted and 46 were highly accepted. The observed result was that the parents had negative attitudes towards these girls which caused in these girls anxiety, low self-esteem, low self-confidence and seclusions. The negative attitudes of the parents towards the girls was the cause of the development of unpleasant personality traits in these girls. This also indicates that there might have been defective child rearing practices of these parents.

In one of the studies school achievements were related to the personality traits of the school students. In this study there were three cultural groups. Hota (1998) selected 108 tribal students, one hundred rural students and 92 urban students for his study. It was a cross cultural study. The results indicated that there was high degree of positive relationship between school achievements and self-assertiveness among the urban students. The tribal students had the positive relationship between aggressiveness and school achievements. The rural students had significant relationship between school achievement and affiliation. Thus all the three cultural groups had different types of personality traits. This might be due to the cultural variation. Cultural factors were found to be having influence in the development of personality traits of the adolescent school students. It is also found in this study that rural-urban backgrounds have influencing effect in the development of personality.

There are certain isolated unusual environmental conditions that are having influence in the development of personality traits. Some researchers had felt that people who are living in forest and hill areas are very much influenced by their inhabitance. This hypothesis was tested by Kalpana Jain and Chauhan (1990) in their studies. The investigation was conducted among the scheduled tribe and scheduled caste community adolescent students and among the upper caste adolescent students. The tribal people who were involved in this investigation, were living in forest and hill areas. Personality traits of these students were compared in the study.

The sample consisted of 900 adolescent students of which 300 were scheduled tribe, 300 were scheduled caste and 300 were from upper caste among the 300 in each group 150 were from remote rural areas and 150 were from urban and semi-urban areas. The age of these students ranged from 12 to 18 years and they were studying in 6th, 7th, 8th and 9th classes. They were all living in Udaipur district areas, Rajasthan.

The Higher Secondary Personality questionnaire (HSPQ) developed by Kapur and others (1985) was administered to the students. This test consisted of 14 personality traits ranged from A to Q_4. The results indicated that inhabitance (the places where they lived), had no influencing effect on all the personality traits. It had influence only on four traits. These traits are, B, less intelligent vs more intelligent, G, expedient vs conscientious, Q_2, group dependent vs self-sufficient and Q_3, uncontrolled vs controlled. This shows that inhabitance has influence in certain personality traits.

Conclusions

The adolescent period is a stormy one in which several types of problems emerge in all cultural societies. The adolescent boys and girls are highly sensitive to personal remarks and very much conscious of their self-esteem. They easily get emotional and frustrated. They also become aggressive and violent and go to the extent of facing any situation. The common unpleasant occurrences often take place among the adolescent boys and girls are, delinquency, antisocial activities like thefts, robberies, sex crimes, running away from homes and sometimes even committing suicide and dying. The mass media of communication every day report incidences like these.

There must be some changes in the rearing practices of the parents. Parents' love and affection towards their children should create a sense of reciprocation and respect towards the parents. Parents should feed their children with nutritious food and also take care of their health and also should meet their needs and demands.

They also must teach the sense of responsibility to their children. It is also important that children should follow disciplines in terms their cultural norms. Punishments sometimes are unavoidable for wrongdoers, but the reprimand should be acceptable by the children that what he/she has done is wrong and it deserves this punishment. The school authorities, particularly the teacher who handles the classes of the students should inculcate in them good manners and the human values and make them to realize the importance of duties and responsibilities that one has to perform for the welfare of the society. One of the important purposes of education is to cultivate the mind for right living and also to live free from harming others. Apart from the parents, the school teachers are partly responsible for moulding and shaping the conduct and character of the students.

But whatever efforts the parents and the teachers take to bring up these adolescent boys and girls, the adolescent boys and girls are highly influenced by the company of their peer groups. The peer group influence is found to be more powerful than the love and affection the parents shower on them. This is often observed in the behavioural patters of the adolescent students. Stanley Hall, the American psychologist has made very extensive study on the behaviour of the adolescent boys and girls. According to him, the adolescence is a storm and stress. Adolescence is representing a step in the development of the entire species of Homo Sapiens, a step characterized by conflict between impulses. Storm and stress therefore, are viewed as inherent continuing experiences throughout adolescence.

Incidents are often occurring in the society in which the behavioural patterns of the adolescence are revealed. They are all very unpleasant incidents. One very recent occurrence which shocked many parents is the disappearance of some eleven adolescent students studying in various schools in the city areas of Salem. These students were aged between 12 and 16 years. There were six girls and five boys. These students ran away from their homes on 4th January 2006 and on the next day another two girls also ran away. They all joined together and were moving from place to place without food for 36 hours. She parents made complaints to the Police and the Police were able to traceout, restore and handover them to their parents in 36 hours. The reason for running away from homes has been for fear of punishment by their parents for the poor performance in their half-yearly examinations (Fig 1). This incident was reported in all Newspapers (Daily Thanthi and The Hindu, 6.1.2006).

These students, sit appears, used to spend more hours everyday in viewing television programmes, neglecting their studies.

Another incident has taken place in Chennai City, in an affluent area. Three adolescent boys aged 16 and 17, studying in 9th and 10th standards, had committed the heinous crime of pouring acid in the mouth of an elderly lady aged 65, tied her hands and legs and robbed the jewels and other ornaments worth about 3 lakhs. She was alone at home, her husband was away and her two sons are in America. On Police complaint, these three boys were caught and on enquiry, it was known that they were stealing the jewels for money. This type activities among the adolescent boys are increasing in these days.

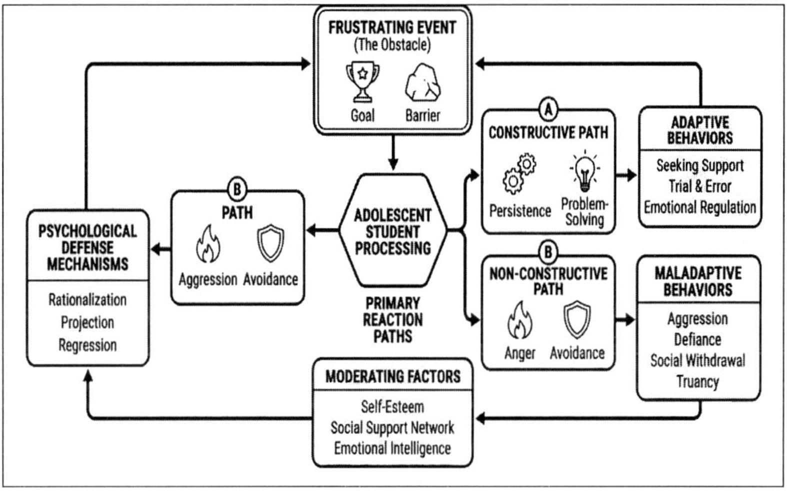

Figure 1: Adolescent Students' Reaction to Frustration

Adolescent boys and girls are very sensitive to personal remarks in these days. Psychologists are of the view that it all depends upon the child rearing practices of the parents. They show immediate reaction to the remarks or reprimands made by the parents for the mistakes they committed. The adolescent period is full of storm and stress. They are highly influenced by their peer groups. Parents' love and affection, care and nurture do not resolve their rebellious attitudes. They do not adjust to the situation. There are inherent conflicting impulses in adolescence which are continued throughout the adolescent period. The functions of these impulses are often found in the behaviour of the adolescent boys and girls. Incidents are occurring everyday and the newspapers report these unhappy events. Announcements appear in television screens with photographs about the sudden disappearance of the adolescent boys and girls from their homes. These six girls and five boys shown icy the picture-ran away from their homes. This is the result of reaction to the emotional frustration experienced by them at home for their failure in school achievements. The conflicting impulses in them were whether to accept the punishment and to continue their studies or to escape from it by running away from home. This was what they did.

Immediate medical attention saved the lady from death. The brutal activity of these three adolescent students wag pouring acid in the mouth of the innocent lady. This was done to prevent the lady from shouting. The Police investigation revealed that they have committed several thefts and robberies for making money for their expenditures. Among these three adolescent boys one acted as the leader of the gang and was directing others for all sorts of antisocial activities.

There were also other types of severe criminal incidences are occurred in coeducational college campuses. These are mainly sex scandals in which the adolescent boys were involved. The adolescent boys at the ages of 17 to 19 years are becoming highly sex starved and they are tempted to commit anything to fulfil their sex desires. Under the pretex of meeting the classmate, the girl, the adolescent boy in one of the cases, after meeting the girl several times, forced her to love him and when the girl refused to reciprocate, the boy, who was in an extreme to lusty state, became impulsive and went/ the state of murdering the girl. This type of incidences have occurred in one of the city college campus and one girls were killed in the college campus and one girls was killed in a higher secondary school campus.

It was during the periods of the second half of the year 2004 and in the first half of the year 2005. Every day one or two such cases are reported in mass media. It is viewed by some social scientists that these sex starved adolescent students and the youths take the sources from the motion pictures which are full of vulgar sex scenes. The hero of the play teases the heroine with all vulgar tactics till he wins the heart of the heroine. The adolescent boys and the youths take this as the model for their purpose and imitate the same on some girls. This is the behaviour pattern of the present day delinquent boys and youths.

In an impulsive emotional state the adolescent boys and girls do not realize the consequences of their behaviour. One very pitiable incidence has taken place on 8th January 2006 in the suburb of the city, Tambaram. An adolescent girl, aged 16, studying in plus one class has committed suicide and died. This was reported in Daily Tanthi on 9th January 2006. The reason stated was that her father did not take care of the family and did not help for her education. The girl became very much depressed and highly frustrated and she could not withstand the agony anymore. She might have thought that her death may solve one of the family problems. The mass media of communication is reporting every day some similar cases in these days.

We have discussed in the proceeding pages various behavioural problems of the adolescent period. Behind all these adolescent problems mere are psychological causes which the human beings fail to understand in their life situations. Particularly in the case of adolescent boys and girls the most prevalent problems are based upon adjustment of the individual in his/her life situations. When it fails to take place then the individual is subjected to many of the problems. The undesirable developments in, tribe adolescent period are the delinquency, antisocial behavioural patterns like theft, robbery, sex scandal, running away from home, aggression, violence, murder, isolation, depression and committing suicide and dying.

Becoming highly emotional and getting maladjusted is becoming the common occurrence among the adolescent boys and girls. This becomes the root cause of all the psychopathologies. Psychological treatment in time may resolve the maladjustment problems of the individuals.

References

Anjana Sharma., Ira Das and Sinha, S. P., Adolescents' Perception of Indian Women's Position in different areas, *Journal of Community Guidance and Research*, 1999, 16, 3, 271-274.

Asha, C.B., Adjustment and Creativity among Adolescents through nigh School years, *Journal of Community Guidance and Research*, 1985, 1, 39-50.

Cronbach, L.J., *Educational Psychology*, New York: Harcourt Brace and Company, 1956.

Eysenck, H.J., *Uses and Abuses of Psychology,* Penguin Books, 1953.

Feinberg, M.R., Relation of background experience to Social acceptance, *Journal of Abnormal and Social Psycholoy*, 1953, 48, 206-213.

Hota, N., School Achievement and Personality; A TAT Study, *Journal of Community Guidance and Research*, 1988, 8, 3, 59-68.

Ira Das, Intelligence and N-Achievement of Adolescent girls and their Attitudes towards the status of women, *Journal of Community Guidance and Research*, 2001, 18, 3, 269-273.

Kalpana Jain, and Chauhan, V. L., Effect of inhabitance on Personality traits of scheduled Tribe and Scheduled caste Adolescent in comparison with upper caste, *Journal of Community Guidance and Research*, 1990,9, 2, 49-54.

Kanwal Nalwa and Vidhu Mohan, Adolescents' Perception of Child-rearing Practices of the parents and Delinquency proneness, *Journal of Community Guidance and Research*, 2001, 18, 1, 1-18, and 1996, 13, 2, 191-206.

Kasinath, H.M. Relative efficiency of Piagetian conservation abilities and Academic Achievements in Science, *Journal of Community Guidance and Research*, 2002, 19, 2, 181-189.

Lazarus, R.S., *Patterns of Adjustment*, 3rd. ed. International Student Edition, Tokyo-MacGraw-Hill Ltd., 1976.

Mahmood Khan, and Tsehaie Jembaro, Influence of Family Socioeconomic Status on Educational and Occupational Aspirations of High and Low Achieving Adolescents, *Journal of Community Guidance and Research*, 2002, 19, 1, 113-118.

Mouly, G.J. *Psychology for Effective Teaching*, New York: Holt Rinehart and Winston, 1966.

Mukul Bhalla, and Pallavi Bhatnagar, Personal Problem solving The perception and Strategies of the Adolescent Girls, *Journal of Community Guidance and Research,* 1992, 9, 3, 269-283.

Nimai Charan Das and M. Rajamanickam, Adolescent students' Achievement in Science subjects in Secondary Schools: A Factor Analysis, journal of Community guidance and Research, 2002, 119 2, 181-189.

Promita joy Chadhury and Jayanti Basu, Parent-Child Relationship, School Achievement and Adjustment of Adolescent boys, *Journal of Community Guidance and Research,* 199, 15, 2, 215-226.

Rajamanickam, M. and Vasanthal, R., Adjustment Problems of Adolescent students in relation to their Achievements, *Journal of Community Guidance and Research*, 1993, 10, 2, 153-133.

Rajamanickam, M., and Mercy Arunmozhi, R. Adjustment Problems in relation to Psychosomatic disorders among Adolescent Girls, *Journal of Community Guidance and Research,* 1992, 9, 2, 151-179.

Ravi Sandhu, Adjustment Problems of High and Low Aspirant adolescent students, *Journal of Community Guidance and Research*, 1997, 14, 3, 241-251.

Sadhana Mittal, Self-Concept and Scholastic Achievements in girls of working and non-working mothers, *Journal of Community Guidance and Research*, 1997, 14, 1, 47-52.

Sarada Devi, M., and Kavitha Kiron, Family Backgrounds and Scholastic Achievements of Secondary School students, *Journal of Community Guidance and Research*, 2002, 19, 2, 167-172.

Shaffers, L.F., and Shoben. E.J. *The Psychology of Adjustment,* 2nd. ed., Boston: Houghton Mifflin, 1956.

Sreekumar, R., and George Mathew, V., The Root Personality Dimensions to intelligence and Quality of Social Interaction among adolescent students, *Journal of Community Guidance and Research*, 2003, 20, 1, 57-63.

Swatantra Jain, Personality traits of Adolescent girl students in relation to their parents' Acceptability, *Journal of community Guidance and Research*, 1992, 9 3, 213-221.

Swatantra Jain, Adjustment pattern of Discriminated girls of the 21st Century: An Empirical Study, *Journal of Community Guidance and Research*, 1995, 12, 3, 163-169.

Uma Devi I., and Mayuri, K. Personality Profile of Adolescent Delinquents, *Journal of Community guidance and Research*, 200, 18, 2, 157-171.

Vidhu Mohan, and Monica Bali, Perception of Feminine Work and its relation to fear of success in Adolescents with Army and Civilian Backgrounds, *Journal of Community Guidance and Research*, 1996, 13, 3, 265-280.

Vijayalaxmi A., Aminabhavi, Criminality and Adjustment Problems of High School Students, *Journal of Community Guidance and Research*, 199, 14, 2, 141-151.

CHAPTER 2

Adjustment Problems of Adolescent Students in Relation to their Achievements

M. Rajamanickam and R. Vasanthal

This is the result of the study conducted among the adolescent students in one of the districts of Tamil Nadu. The problem has been the adjustment problems of adolescent students in relation to their achievements in schools. The sample consisted of 300 students drawn randomly from ninth and tenth standards of four Higher Secondary Schools in Chidambaram area. The students' age ranged from 13 to 17 years. The Personal Information Questionnaire and the Bell's Adjustment Inventory were administered on the students in the respective schools on a fixed date. The annual examination marks of the students were taken as the achievement test scores. The scores of the individuals were obtained according to the procedure and they were treated statistically and analysed.

The study revealed certain interesting results. There is a positive association between the adolescent students' adjustment scores and their achievement scores. The study also revealed that the number of siblings had a determining effect upon the students' adjustments and school achievements. The lesser the number of siblings the better the adjustment the students had and the higher the achievement they made in schools. More number of siblings in the family adversely affected the adjustment and achievement of the students. Parents' higher educational levels had positive effects on students' adjustment problems and achievements. Parents' occupational level had some positive effect upon their children's adjustment and achievement, but it did not yield a reliable difference between the student groups.

Introduction

Adjustment is a state in which the needs of the individual on the one hand and the claims of the environment on the other are fully satisfied. Adjustment takes the form of variation of the environment and variation in the organism through the acquisition of responses appropriate to the situation. The variation in the organism may be biological. The adjustment process is a universal sequence that can be identified in the behaviour of organism from the lowest species up to man.

Adjustment, generally, means an effective adaptation to the environment, both external and internal, including conformity to group norms, mores, ideals, values and, so on (Abraham, 1968). According to Mouly (1966) adjustment is the process by means of which an individual seems to maintain physiological and psychological equilibrium and propels himself toward self-enhancement. It represents the quality of an individual's behaviour in relation to his interpersonal relations (Fradson, 1961). A well adjusted person, according to Cronbach (1954), is one who commits himself to socially desirable goals and uses his energies effectively in working towards them. He has a sense of security and feeling of adequacy which grow out of his feelings of belongingness, being desired and appreciated.

The word adjustment came into popular use in psychology during the 1930's and was given strong endorsement by Shaffer's classical book *The Psychology of Adjustment*, which appeared in 1936. Shaffer's treatment of adjustment in this book mainly emphasized the biological adaptation of the organism to its environment. This is a somewhat mechanistic approach to human behaviour on the lines of the behaviourists. John B. Watson and Fredrick Dashiel (1930) strongly influenced the thinking of psychologists during this time.

With the coming into prominence of gestalt psychology, psychoanalysis, and personalistic psychology, the term "adjustment" as used by Shaffer was subjected to considerable criticism particularly with reference to its emphasis upon the mechanical adaptation of human beings to the demands of the environment. Writers from these schools pointed out that man not only adapts to his environment, but through the use of his intelligence and his imagination changes his environment to meet his needs more effectively.

Lazarus (1976) briefly discussed forms of adjustment such as accommodation or assimilation and when man alluded to defence mechanisms, he was approaching adjustment as a process rather than as an end result that an individual successfully or unsuccessfully accomplishes. Chauhan et al. (1978) view that adjustment is an important psychological variable, which can be defined as an index of integration between needs and satisfaction, remains, related to achievement, social acceptance, age, sex, economic security and normal standards.

According to Eysenck et al. (1953) adjustment is dynamic rather than static in quality. Adjustment is a household word. We speak of people as being well adjusted or poorly adjusted. Well-adjusted people are regarded as successful in the art of living. The psychology of adjustment is, in fact based on the concern of many of us wish the quality of life.

Well-adjusted Person

Feinberg (1953) found that well-adjusted children like well-adjusted adults make good social adjustments and have harmonious relationships with the people with whom they are associated, whether in the home, at school, in business, or in play, because they accept themselves; they do not need to build up defences or project the blame for the discrepancy between what they are and what they would like to be, on others.

The degree to which a child adjusts to others is the indication of how well he is adjusted as a person. In describing the type of child who makes the best adjustment to others, Barrett and Leonard (1962) pointed out that he "genuinely appreciates and values others as he does himself." He is comfortable and open with himself. He is not guarded in a personal sense because he has nothing to hide. He does not discomfort himself to please others, nor does he use them as scapegoats for self-dissatisfaction.

According to Knutson (1963) mental health is the adjustment of human beings to the world and to each other with a maximum of effectiveness and happiness. It is the ability to maintain an even temper, an alert intelligence, socially considerate behaviour and a happy disposition.

A mentally healthy individual evaluates himself properly, and is aware of his own limitations. He easily accepts his faults and makes efforts to rid himself of them. According to Smith and Smith (1958) the well- adjusted person experiences conflicts and attacks his problems in a realistic manner.

A well-adjusted person experiences conflicts, but he is not unduly distressed by them. He attacks his problems in a realistic manner; he accepts it as the inevitable; he understands and accepts his own shortcomings and the shortcomings of those with whom he must deal. A mentally healthy or well-adjusted person, according to Atkinson et al. (1958), is a productive person. That is, he has a quality of spontaneity in work, and in social relations that we recognise as creative. A well-adjusted person has the zest for living: he does not have to drive himself to meet the demands of the day but enters into activities with enthusiasm.

The well-adjusted person is able to form satisfying relationships with other people. He is sensitive to their needs and feelings and does not make excessive demands for the gratification of his own needs, and is able to both give and receive affection. The well adjusted person has some awareness of his own motives and feelings. He does not try to achieve totally unrealistic goals and hence doesn't feel guilty when he fails. In addition to being aware of his own inpulses, the well-adjusted individual has a certain confidence that he can control and direct his own behaviour. He does not feel that he is a helpless victim of external forces.

Maladjusted Person

Eston Jackson Asher et al. (1953) found that when a person acts in a way that makes it more difficult to attain his fundamentals and ends, he is maladjusted. Maladjustment may be divided roughly into two classes. One is futile adjustments and the other one is thwarting adjustment.

In futile adjustments, the individual seeks to resolve a state of tension and disequilibrium, but instead of doing so he performs useless acts, which perhaps get him into more trouble. Like a person in quicksands, he sinks deeper with each effort to extricate himself. Thwarting adjustments, on the other hand, may resolve the original tension; however, without making for the full realisation of one's potentialities; by providing this relief they only make such development more difficult.

All kinds of mental illnesses may be cited as the maladjusted reactions. According to Coleman (1972), any state of contradiction to adjustment is called maladjustment. Fairweather (1964) reveals that the maladjusted individual fails to attain a state of adjustment with his circumstances and instead of trying to fact up to the situation, tries to run away from it.

People play a variety of roles every day in their lives. The more roles a person can perform adequately, the better satisfied his ego will be. If an individual's experience has not prepared him to play the roles of his assigned status, or if the environment is such that he is denied the normal status for which his experience has prepared him, and his fundamental needs are not met, then we say he is maladjusted.

Achievement

Every human being is interested to set up a standard for himself. The higher the standard the more efforts must be expended for attaining it. People differ with regard to their self-imposed standards. Some school students will be very much pleased and delighted to received an A or B grade indicating better than average mastery of academic subject matter. Same school students get frustrated for failing to get grade A, the mark of outstanding achievement. Any self imposed standards of achievement are largely products of socialisation. In life situations the students are exposed to many models including father, mother, teacher, playmate and they may observe standards of achievement. The setting up of personal standards is related to achievement striving. Achievement-oriented behaviours generally occurs in academic life, sports, arts. The student can show his competence in situations where there is a standard of excellence. Therefore achievement behaviour may be defined as any action directed to gaining approval where public standards of excellence are applicable. There are substantial differences in achievement among the school students.

Havighurst (1953) found that, success in mastering the developmental tasks set by the social group will bring the person, happiness, social recognition and success with new tasks which are dependent on the foundations laid earlier. Before the child enters school, for example, he is expected to learn to walk and talk and take care of his bodily needs. Before he reaches legal adulthood, he is expected to handle his affairs without help from adults and to be emotionally independent of his parents. If a person comes up to group expectations, he is regarded as a success. If not, he is judged a failure. The closer the group expectations and personal aspirations are to a person's capacities, the greater the likelihood that his achievement will be regarded as successful both by him and by the group.

The concept of achievement usually refers to the fact that the subject is not merely executing a task without assistance, but is trying to perform well with the aim of eliciting positive reinforcement for his demonstrated competence in the task. Scholastic achievement means achievement a student makes in school, namely, his marks in the examination which is the criterion for the achievement of a student.

Earlier Studies

Rao (1972), in a study on 328 male undergraduate students, found academic achievement significantly related to students, adjustment to the academic situation. In the year of 1975 a similar study was done by Bhagia. The sample of this study, 150 pupils of 9th class, found a marked positive relationship to exist between pupils' adjustment scores and scores on achievement. A study was done by Sharma, Janardha Prasad et al. (1974) of low achieving and high achieving students in schools at Rajasthan. They took the sample of XI class students from ten schools. In the first phase, the number of stars, rejects and isolates in each school were identified. Later, school records were pursued and interviews with students and teachers held. Results showed that the 'stars' in high achieving schools show higher achievement in scholastic and co-curricular pursuits, greater interest in literary, cultural and scientific activities. Peer group influence is more dominant and more conducive to academic achievement in high achieving schools. Social atmosphere in low achieving schools is less conducive to academic achievement.

An experimental study of the achievements in basic education was done by Bhatt (1961). He selected the sample of 180 children of eighth class at Baroda. Standardised achievement test form, personality ratings, social adjustment inventory; standardised physical education tests; and Minnesota Manual Dexterity Test were used. Results were as follows: (i) Highly significant difference was found between the achievement scores made by the two groups of a children in different school subjects, namely, language, social studies, and general science. The traditional school children were superior to basic school children in all these subjects, (ii) The basic school children were superior to the traditional school children and the difference was highly significant with respect to all the traits. (iii) The basic school children were superior to the traditional school children so far as the abilities such as speed ability, arm-strength, leg-strength, endurance and the accuracy were concerned. (iv) The basic school children were found to be superior to the traditional children in respect of social adjustment, manual dexterity, etc.

In a study of 328 male undergraduate students Rao (1972) found academic adjustment to be significantly related to neurotic difficulties. Subjects with high scores on neurotic difficulties were observed to be poorly adjusted to academic situation and performed unsatisfactorily.

Resnick (1951) undertook a study to investigate the relationship between marks and various factors of adjustment, such as school environment, socioeconomic status, aspects of mental health, etc. He used 350 high school students as his subjects. The relationship between grades and the scores on the psychometric instruments showed for the most part, that pupils earning high grades also made high mean soares, indicating a more satisfactory personal adjustment.

Family background characteristics and school adjustment problems was studied by Lorion et al. (1977). In two experiments using the sample of 267 primary school children referred to a school-based secondary prevention programme, subjects identified by teachers as having selected family characteristics were compared on teacher ratings of school maladjustment. The experiment first shows that subjects' pressures to achieve academic success coped with school demands in a significantly more shy, anxious, and immature fashion than subjects from homes lacking educational stimulation. The latter group experienced greater difficulty in mastering basic academic skills. Results of experiment two showed that subjects from rejecting parents had more serious acting out aggressive problems than did subjects from overprotective parents. The latter group, however, experienced anxiety and interpersonal discomfort.

A comparative study of the adolescent boys and girls in relation to their attitudes towards school adjustment and scholastic achievement was studied by Chandha and Chandra (1985). The study was to compare the adolescents in relation to their attitudes, adjustment and scholastic achievement on ninth and tenth standard students in the age range of 13 to 17 years. The sample included 40 boys and 40 girls. Rao's school attitude inventory, adjustment inventory and scholastic achievement through "school records" were used in this investigation. Results indicate that (i) attitudes towards school did not affect scholastic achievement of adolescent boys and girls, although there existed a positive relationship between attitude and scholastic achievement. (ii) There is no significant sex difference in the attitude towards school. (iii) Attitudes towards school affect the adjustment of an adolescent irrespective of the sex. (iv) Students who had a positive attitude towards their school were better adjusted. (v) Adjustment of an adolescent does effect scholastic achievement. (a) Better emotional and educational adjustment help to achieve more in the school (b) Social adjustment does not affect scholastic achievement. (vi). Adolescent boys are better adjusted than adolescent girls. Emotional and educational adjustment are better among boys. There is no difference between boys and girls in social adjustment. (vii) Adolescent boys have better scholastic achievement than the girls.

McCarmic (1967) viewed that achievement refers to the level of proficiency of individuals in some work activity or subject matter. Achievement is a concept frequently used in the school situations. Educational achievement tests are designed to measure an individual's quantity and quality of learning in specified subjects of study after a period of instruction. From the achievement tests, an individual's present position in a particular subject can be estimated.

Aptitute tests indicate what can be the individuals' future status; that is, they are prognostic in nature; they will enable him to chose a subject in turn with his potentialities. Achievement tests indicate their present status; they are diagnostic in nature and so they give him a chance to take remedial measures in the weak areas.

Eysenck (1953) in his book *Uses and Abuses of Psychology* pointed out the importance of non-intellectual factors in achievement. He states: "It has been found that the successful student is persistent, emotionally stable and has a level of aspiration not far too from reality. The unsuccessful student of similar intelligence lacks persistence, is unstable and his level of aspiration is unreasonably high or low."

Jamuars (1961) conducted an investigation in the Indian setting, attempted to observe the relationship between some personality variables and achievement. He tried to find out whether personal factors affected achievement independently of intelligence. The general conclusion was that achievement depended on personality adjustment of pupils.

Objectives of the Study

In the school situation, it is obvious that students may be dominant or submissive, and may be successful or fail in their school performances. There are students who might have limited their goals and feel uncomfortable in the company of other people. Some individuals tolerate some disturbances and others react immediately. All these are possible because of the variations in the personal qualities. There are certain personal qualities which enhance better adjustment and achievement and some lead to poor achievement.

Therefore the main objective of this study is to find out whether there is any relationship between students' adjustment problems and the level of school achievements.

The other objectives of this study are to know the influence of adjustment on achievement of the students, to find out whether the number of siblings, parents qualifications, occupational status of the parents, have any influence upon the students' adjustment problems and achievements.

In the earlier studies reviewed in the preceding pages these variables were not used in any of the studies. Therefore, an attempt has been made to test the influence of these said variables in the adjustment and achievement of the adolescent students studying in higher secondary schools.

The Problem

The students at the adolescent period are exposed to various kinds of rapid and drastic changes that are taking place around them. The scientific, industrial and technological advancement create the enormous need for technically trained men. The increase of population and unemployment problems and as a result of this the neck-to-neck competition and rivalry put the young minds in severe anxieties and uncertainties. Also on the other side there is an irrational creze for Western style of life. A third force that is fast intoxicating the minds and behaviours of young and old is the modern media, the motion picture and television. The modern youth does not find sufficient time even take care of himself. Developed nations learned to adjust to any change and adapt the style of life suitable to the time. But in India this is not occurring and also not easy for the youth. Parents and teachers face difficult problems in putting their children and the wards in correct positions. There are instances in schools that the school students attack teachers in the classroom for not allowing them for malpractices in examinations. What sort of adjustment have such students developed and what level of achievement can they make academically?

When there is lack of adjustment among the adolescent students both at home and school their educational achievement would be generally the jeopardised. The impact of adjustment problems is directly observed from concerned students' achievement in schools. Psychologists have long ago recognised that achievement is based upon adjustment and also both are interrelated. Though several other factors are operating in the achievement of the students in schools it is important to see that the student maintains his achievement in general. Individuals should generally develop the need to achieve. Individuals with high achievement motivation come up successfully in life and develop the ability to perform specific skills. But if the school student lacks the ability to make his standard achievement he is maladjusted and frustrated and takes his own decision about his future. Every day we see announcements on television about boys and girls deserting their homes. Sometimes the student who has failed to make his standard achievement in school commits suicide and dies. This is the result of directing his frustration against himself. Parents and teachers are helpless in such problem cases.

Further, the adolescents nowadays are too much attached to motion pictures and television programmes. The main themes in these media are vulgarity, violence and sex-perverted poor artistic imagination with rural backgrouds. The adolescents are very easily attracted by these themes and formulate their own way of life. It is only on witnessing these themes that adolescents and youth are attracted towards them and not as if they like them and want them. The television violence has caused disastrous consequences among the children in United States which resulted in modifying their programmes. It is too early for us to think of such healthy changes in our media. But the adolescent problems are increasing rapidly day by day affecting their achievement behaviour. Where does the adolescent student lack his ability to make his standard achievements? Studies of different types should be conducted and the causes be identified for working out strategies. This is a very humble study on this line which may throw some light on the problem.

In the present study the independent variables are students' adjustment, siblings, parents' qualification, and occupational status.

The independent variable is also known as stimulus variable. The dependent variable is achievement; the dependent variable is also known as response variable. The intervening variables are motivation, geographical areas, interest; distance between home and school and parents' treatment of their children. These variables were not taken into account in this study.

Hypothesis

Based upon this problem the following hypotheses have been formulated:

1. There is a positive association between adjustment and achievement of the students who are studying in schools. If the students are well adjusted then their achievement is higher.
2. If there are more siblings in the family then the students face more adjustment problems and hence their levels of achievements in schools are getting lower and lower.
3. Parents' educational qualifications have corresponding effect upon their children. The higher the educational qualifications the parents have the better adjustment their children have and the higher achievement they make in schools.
4. Occupational status of the parents has an influencing effect upon their children's adjustment problems and their school achievements. The children of white collar parents (better placed) are well adjusted and higher achievers than the children of blue collar parents (general, unskilled and industrial workers) in schools.

2. Methodology

The present study is an attempt to verify the hypotheses regarding the influence of certain independent variables on the adjustment problems and on the achievements of the school students. One of the aims of this study is to know the type of relationship between the students' adjustment problems and their achievements. The study is also concerned with the influence of the siblings parents, educational levels, and parents' occupation levels on adjustment problems and achievement in the students.

Sample: The population selected to test the hypotheses was the adolescent student group. The study was made on 300 students drawn from four different schools. By using one stage stratified random sampling procedure the 300 students were selected which constitute 25 percent of the total student population of the four schools. They are situated in Chidambaram Taluk, South Arcot district. One hundred and fifty students studying in ninth and 150 students in tenth standards alone were included in this investigation.

The age of the students ranged from 14 to 17 yeas. The monthly income of the students' parents as indicated by them ranged from Rs.500 / - to Rs.4000 /-.

Materials: The following test materials were used to collect data, in this investigation. 1. Personal Information Questionnaire. 2. Bell's Adjustment Inventory for School Students. 3. Achievement test.

1. *The Personal Information Questionnaire*: This was concerned with the individual's personal information such as class, age, sex, name of the school, place, parents' qualification, occupation, income, number of members in the family, brothers, sisters their birth order, etc.
2. *Adjustment Inventory for School Students*: This inventory was developed by Bell during 1962 to assess the adjustment problems of school students. It is a self-report inventory. This has six areas of adjustment but only four were used in this study. They are Home, Health, Social and Emotional. The inventory consists of 140 statements with 'yes' or 'no' answers. The high scores indicate maladjustment and low score-better adjustment. This has also one adult form.

   The Bell's Adjustment Inventory was empirically validated in a pilot study on 135 students. The reliability was estimated by split-half method, correlating the scores of odd-even items. The correlation coefficient was corrected by applying Sprearman-Brown formula to find out the reliability. The reliability coefficient was. 84 which is significant at. 01 level. The validity of this inventory was estimated by using the Intrinsic Validity method and the validity coefficient was. 92 which was significant at one per cent level
3. *Achievement Test:* The individual's examination marks in various subjects were taken as the scores of achievement tests. Among the various types of tests used in schools, achievement tests are the most common tests. They measure what and how much the pupils have learned as a result of

formal or informal instructions. They measure the present level of performance of the individuals in academic learning. Achievement test scores are used to judge the grade of a student based on his performance and also to infer his strength and weakness in study. Achievement tests are utilised frequently for evaluating courses of study, teaching methods, and other educational factors. The teachers-made achievement tests for various subjects were used in the current study and the examination marks in every subject were taken as the scores of achievement tests. The subjects included are Tamil, English, Science, Mathematics, History and Georgraphy.

Procedure: The first questionnaire consisted of personal information relating to the students' educational, social, economical and psychological backgrounds. It consisted of 25 questions. The two questionnaires, (1) Personal information (2) Students' adjustment's inventory were printed and bound into a booklet form. The questionnaire booklet in this stage was ready for administration except the achievement test. The marks obtained in the annual examination by the student in the teacher-made test in five subjects such as Tamil, English, Science, Maths, History and Geography were considered as their achievement test scores. Before the test was administered to the students in each of the four higher secondary schools, permission from the concerned headmaster of the schools was obtained. In order to conduct the test for the two sections of the ninth and tenth standards on the same day the headmaster has fixed the time in consultation with the concerned teachers of the sections.

The survey commenced on the fixed day. The students were given all the instructions with regard to the type of answers for each questionnaire they will have to give. Then the questionnaires were distributed to the randomly selected students according to the plan. They were told that there was no time limit and they can take their own time. They were told that they should give all the personal information asked for without omitting any of them. The students took about one hour to answer the questionnaires and as soon as they were answered they were collected by the investigator from the respondents.

The annual examination marks of these students awarded for the teacher-made test for the year 1989-90 were noted from the school records and these were treated as the achievement test scores of the students.

Results

Then the collected questionnaire, particularly the Bell's Adjustment Inventory, was scored according to the procedure as given in the manual of the test. The individuals' scores were obtained for the tests and they were given suitable statistical treatments. The important statistical treatments are correlation coefficient, the estimation of mean, standard deviation, standard error of the mean, analysis of variance and the critical ratio. All the statistical treatments were presented in tabular columns and the answers were analysed.

The hypotheses I that there is a positive association between the scores of adjustment inventory and achievement scores of the students has been verified in this study. It is found that there is a positive correlation (.67) between adjustment and achievement and it is significant at. 001 level which indicates that there is reliable relationship between students' achievements and their adjustment problems. This means that if the scores in the adjustment inventory were decreased then the scores on the achievement test were increased. This indicates that the students' adjustment level determines the achievement of the students. The result of this study established that the students' better adjustment and higher achievement in school go together. Therefore the hypotheses is accepted.

The hypothesis two is tested by comparing the adjustment scores with achievement scores of the three sibling groups: If there are more number of siblings in the family then the students face more adjustment problems and hence their levels of achievements in schools get lower and lower. The scores seem to support the hypothesis. The first group (sibling 1 to 3) has scored the lowest (44.70) with an SD of 13.14 in the adjustment inventory, but scored the highest (56.59) with an SD of 15.59 in the achievement test.

The second group (siblings 4-6) scored higher than the first group (56.97) with an SD of 16.26 in the adjustment inventory, but scored less than (3.07) the first group in the achievement test with an SD of 9.45. The third group which has the largest number of siblings (7-9) scored the highest (59.08) with an SD of 15.75 in the adjustment inventory and scored the lowest (41.08) in the achievement test (Table 2).

Table 1
Showing coefficient of correlation, t-value and the level of significance between the adjustment score and achievement scores of 300 students

S.No.	*Tests*	*Subjects*	*r*	*t-value*	*Level of Significance*
1.	Adjustment				
		300	.67	20.47	.001
2.	Achievement				

Table 2
Showing the distribution of mean scores, SD, SEM for three groups of students on adjustment and achievement tests

S.No.	*Sibling*	*Code*	*N*	*Type of scores*	*Adjustment scores*	*Achievement scores*
1	1 - 3	A	186	Mean	44.70	56.59
				SD	13.14	15.59
				SEM	0.97	1.15
2	4 - 6	B	89	Mean	56.97	43.07
				SD	16.26	9.45
				SEM	1.73	1.01
3	7 - 9	C	25	Mean	59.08	41.08
				SD	15.75	9.46
				SEM	3.22	1.93

The comparative analysis of the data, as given in Table 2, revealed that if the number of siblings are few the scores on the adjustment inventory are lower and the achievement scopes are higher. As and when the number of siblings increase the adjustment scores are increased and the achievement scores are decreased. It is because that in a family in which the number of siblings are many the children have more adjustment problems. As a result of this children in these families do not make better achievement in school performances. Instead, if the siblings are few then their adjustment problems are few and hence they make better achievement in schools. Therefore, we can conclude that the fewer the siblings least the problem and higher the achievement of the students in schools. The more the siblings more the adjustment problems and the lower the achievement.

The results at this stage seem to support the hypothesis. But this result is not sufficient to confirm the hypothesis reliably. Hence further treatment of the data is needed. The analysis of variance and the F-test indicate that the mean scores of the three groups show that they are not homogeneous. They are reliably different among themselves at. 001 level (Table 3). But the analysis of variance and the F test did not say how far each group is different from the other group. Therefore it becomes necessary to compute the critical ratio to find out the level of difference between the groups.

Table 3
Showing the analysis of variance for the scores of three sibling groups in Adjustment Inventory

Source of variation	*Sum of squares*	*df*	*Mean squares*	*F - ratio Sig.*	*Level of*
Between groups	11533.04	2			
			5766.52	27.69	.001
Within groups	618441.48	297			
Total	73374.52	299			

The mean differences between groups A and B (sibling 1-3 and 4-6) and between groups A and C (Siblings 1-3 and 7-9) are highly significant at. 001 Level. The mean score difference between groups B and C (siblings 4-8 and 7-9) is significant at. 02 level. The mean score difference between any two groups are reliably significant in adjustment problems. Therefore we can conclude that every group is different from every other group. The number of siblings determine the level of adjustment of the children in the family (Table 4).

Table 4
Showing the mean difference and critical ratios for three sibling groups in Adjustment Inventory

S.No.	*Sibling*	*Code*	*Mean*	*Mean*	*SEM*	*C.R.*	*Level of difference*
1	1 - 3	A	44.70				
				12.27	0.50	24.38	.001
	4 - 6	B	56.97				
2	1 - 3	A	44.70				
				14.38	0.84	17.18	.001
	7 - 9	C	59.08				
3	4 - 6	B	56.97				
				2.11	0.90	2.34	.02
	7 - 9	C	59.08				

The mean scores of the three sibling groups show much differences among themselves. But we do not know at what level these groups differ. Therefore to test the level of difference of the mean scores among the three sibling groups the analysis of variance and the F test were applied. The F-ratio (38.15) indicates that the three groups differ reliably and it is significant at. 001 level. Therefore we can conclude that the sibling groups differ among themselves reliably in their achievement test scores (Table 5).

Table 5
Showing the analysis of variance for three sibling groups of students on the achievement test

Source of variation	*Sum of square*	*df*	*Mean squares*	*F-ratio*	*Level of significance*
Between groups	14614.54	2	7307.27		
				39.15	.001
Within groups	55440.30	297	186.67		
Total	70054.84	299			

Since the analysis of variance and the F-test have established the difference among the three groups significantly the data were given further treatment of critical ratio to see whether these three groups really differ between them. The critical ratios for the mean scores show that groups A and B and A and C differ significantly at. 001 level. The groups B and C differ in their mean scores at. 01 level. Therefore the hypothesis has been accepted that the number of siblings in the family is having definite influence upon the siblings- school achievements. Each sibling group is different from the other and each may have its own problem in the school work. If the students come from families where there are few siblings they make better achievement in schools (Table 6).

Table 6
Showing critical ratios and level of significance for three sibling groups of students on the achievement test

S.No.	*Sibling*	*Code*	*Mean*	*Mean Difference*	*SEM*	*C.R.*	*Level of sig.*
1	1 - 3	A	56.97				
				13.9	0.44	31.89	.001
	4 - 6	B	43.07				
2	1 - 3	A	56.97				
				15.89	0.68	23.37	.001
	7 - 9	C	41.08				
3	4 - 6	B	43.07				
				1.99	0.69	2.86	.01
	7 - 9	C	41.08				

Table 7 shows scores of the students on the basis of their parents' educational qualifications on the adjustment inventory and on achievement test. The scores of the two tests are compared. The hypothesis is that if the parents' educational qualification is higher, then the students' adjustment is better and their school achievement is higher. This is tested in this study. A careful look at the Table gives to understand that the scores of the students in the adjustment inventory is gradually decreasing as and when the qualification of the parents increased. In the achievement test, the scores are gradually increasing as the qualifications of the parents are increased. The mean score for the secondary level is the highest (57.50) with an SD of 16.68, for the high school level it is 56.7 with an SD of 15.49. At the graduate level the mean is still lower (51.47) with and SD of 15.68, the score at the post-graduate level is still lower with an SD of 14.38. The score for the above P.G. level is the lowest (42.71) with an SD of 7.91. This shows that the educational qualification of the parents has some effect in the adjustment scores of the students. As and when the qualifications increase it seems that parental treatment of their children may vary and as a result of this their children may face less problems. Further, the SD scores provide an indication that the parents qualifications had also some influence on their children's responses to the adjustment inventory. As the qualifications increase the dispersion scores (SD) also go on the decreasing. This means that they have answered the items carefully much better than the less qualified parents.

Table 7

Showing the scores of flue groups of students on the Adjustment Inventory and Achievement test on the basis of their parents' qualifications

S.No.	*Parent's qualification*	*Code*	*N*	*Type of score*	*Adjustment score*	*Achievement score*
1.	Secondary level	A	146	Mean	57.50	42.40
			SD	16.68	9.75	
			SEM	1.39	0.81	
2.	High school level	B	95	Mean	56.75	44.31
			SD	15.49	11.59	
			SEM	1.59	1.1.9	
3.	Graduate level	C	30	Mean	51.47	47.83
			SD	15.68	14.67	
			SEM	2.91	2.72	
4.	Post-graduate level	D	15	Mean	47.40	53.13
			SD	14.38	14.52	
			SEM	3.84	3.88	
5.	Above P.G. level and	E	14	Mean	42.71	63.50
	additional			SD	7.91	13.17
	qualification			SEM	2.19	3.65

The achievement score is the lowest (42.40) with an SD of 9.75 for the first group of students whose parents have the qualification only at the secondary level. The score for the high school level is little lower than (54.31) the first group with an SD of 11.59 and for the graduate level it is 47.83 with an SD of 14.67. At the postgraduate level there is a steep increase (53.13) with an SD of 14.52. The score for above PG level is the highest (63.50) with an SD of 13.17. As and when the qualifications of the parents increase the achievement scores of their children also increase. But there is no consistency in the dispersion scores. There is more fluctuation in the achievement scores of the students. Some other variables, other than parents' qualification and the students' adjustment might have got influence in the achievement scores. At mean score level on both the tests the five student groups differ considerably (Table 7). At this stage it will not be possible to state the level of differences between groups even though the mean scores differ. The analysis of variance and the F-test may bring out the level of differences among the groups. It will also reveal whether these five groups are homogeneous or heterogeneous.

Table 8

Showing the analysis of variance and the F-ratio for the scores of five groups of students on the basis of their parents- qualifications on adjustment inventory

Source of variation	*Sum of squares*	*df*	*Mean squares*	*F - ratio*	*Level of sig.*
Between groups	4492.23	4	1123.05		
				4,43	.01
Within groups	74748.36	295	253.38		
Total	79240.59	299			

The analysis of variance and the F test bring out the level of difference among the five groups. The five groups differ reliably at. 01 level. The students are drawn randomly from the same population. But there are variances operating in the sample and bring out the differences.

The analysis of variance and the F test did not tell us the level of difference between groups. To know the difference between groups we have to compute the t test or the critical ratio. With five groups there may be $\frac{N(N-1)}{2} = \frac{5(5-1)}{2} = 10$ comparisons.

Since the F test revealed that the five student groups on the basis of their parents' qualification was significant reliably on the adjustment test the critical ratios were computed between groups (Table 9). The results show that the mean differences were reliably significant between the groups, secondary level and above P.G. level, high School level and above PG level at one per cent level and between secondary level and postgraduate level, between high school level and postgraduate level and between graduate level and above PG level at 5 per cent level. The mean score difference between other groups were not significant at any level. Therefore, the result seems to support the hypothesis partially.

The mean scores of the five groups on the achievement test on the basis of their parents' qualifications had considerable difference among them apparently. Are the differences real or dubious or are the five groups really hetrogeneous? This has been tested with analysis of variance and the F test. The F test shows that the five groups are reliably different among themselves: they are hetrogeneous in nature. These groups on the basis of their parents' qualifications are different from each other. But we must know at what level these groups differ from each other. A further treatment to the data may bring out the level of differences between them.

The mean score differences between groups and the respective critical ratios have been computed for assessing the level of differences between groups. It is observed in Table 11 that the secondary educational level of the parents differs from post-graduate level and above PG level at one per cent level. The high school level differs from above PG level at one per cent level. The graduate level varies from above P.G. level at one per cent level. But the high school level and post-graduate level and the post-graduate level and above PG level show a difference between them at 5 per cent level. But the secondary and high school levels, the secondary and graduate level, high school level and graduate level and the graduate level and post-graduate level do not show any reliable difference between them. In the case of six comparisons, the differences are reliable and significant. But in the case of four comparisons there is no significant difference between groups. Therefore, the hypothesis may be accepted partially.

Table 9

Showing the critical ratios for the mean differences between groups on the adjustment inventory on the basis of their parent's qualifications

S.No.	*Groups*	*Code*	*Mean*	*Mean*	*SEM difference*	*C.R. difference*	*Level of sig.*
1.	Secondary	A	57.50				
				0.75	2.1 I	0.36	NS
	High school	B	56.75				
2.	Secondary	A	57.50				
				6.03	3.18	1.89	NS
	Graduate	C	51.47				
3.	Secondary	A	57.50				
				10.01	3.96	2.55	.05
	Post-graduate	D	47.40				
4.	Secondary	A	57.50				

				14.79	2.52	5.86	.01
	Above PG	E	42.78				
5.	High school	B	56.75				
				5.28	3.27	1.61	NS
	Graduate	C	51.47				
6.	High school	B	56.75				
				9.35	4.04	2.32	.05
	Post-graduate	D	47.40				
7.	High School	B	56.75				
				14.04	2.62	5.31	.01
	Above PG	E	42.79				
8.	Graduate	C	51.47				
				4.07	4.69	0.87	NS
	Post-graduate	D	47.40				
9.	Graduate	C	51.47				
				8.76	3.56	2.46	.05
	Above PG	E	42.79				
10.	Post-graduate	D	47.40				
				4.69	4.27	1.09	NS
	Above PG	E	42.79				

The results show that there is not much difference between the secondary educational and the high school educational level. Similarly between high school level and graduate level and graduate level and post-graduate level there is not much difference in the mean scores. But the graduate-level, the post graduate level and above PG level show reliable difference with all other groups. This means that if the students' parents are graduate and above then the students' school achievement are considerably higher and these students differentiate themselves from other students whose parents' qualifications are less than graduation. Parents' educational qualifications have a definite impact upon their children's school achievements and they are also well adjusted compared to the children of less qualified parents.

Table 10

Analysis of variance and F test for the scores of five groups of students on the achievement test on the basis of their parents' qualifications

Source of tests sig.	*Sum of*	*df variation*	*Mean squares*	*F-ratio*	*Level of squares*
Between groups	7052.83	4	1763.21		
				13.44	.001
Within groups	38688.70	295	131.15		
Total	45741.53	299			

Table 11
Showing the mean difference and the critical ratios between five student groups in achievement test on the basis of parents' qualification levels

S.No.	*Groups*	*Code*	*Mean*	*Mean Diff.*	*SEM Diff.*	*C.R.*	*Level of sig.*
1.	Secondary level	A	42.40				
				1.91	1.44	1.33	NS
	High school level	B	44.31				
2.	Secondary level	A	42.40				
				5.43	2.79	1.94	NS
	Graduate level	C	47.83				
3.	Secondary level	A	42.40				
				10.73	3.83	2.79	.01
	Post-graduate level	D	53.13				
4.	Secondary level	A	42.40				
				21.10	3.61	5.84	.01
	Above PG level	E	63.50				
5.	High school level	B	44.31				
				3.52	2.93	1.20	NS
	Graduate level	C	47.83				
6.	High school level	B	44.31				
				8.82	3.93	2.24	.05
	PG level	D	53.13				
7.	High school level	B	44.31				
				19.90	3.72	5.17	.01
	Above PG level	E	63.50				
8.	Graduate level	C	47.83				
				5.30	4.61	1.15	NS
	PG level	D	53.13				
9.	Graduate level	C	47.83				
				15.67	4.42	3.54	.01
	Above PG level	E	63.50				
10.	PG level	D	53.13				
				10.37	5.14	2.02	.05
	Above PG level	E	63.50				

Patents' occupational status is also one of the factors having influence upon their children's adjustment problems and school achievements. The hypothesis based upon this is tested in this investigation and the results are given in Table 12. The mean scores among the first three occupational groups, i.e., unskilled, skilled and office assistants do not show much difference among themselves in adjustment inventory and achievement test. But the mean scores of other two groups, the children of teachers and professionals show some difference among themselves and with other three groups. We do not know whether these groups differ from other groups reliably. This is tested by computing the analysis of variance and F test for the scores of five groups and presented in Table 13.

Table 12
Showing the scores of the five groups of students on Adjustment Inventory and achievement test on the basis of their parents' occupational level

S.No.	*Occupational level*	*Code*	*N*	*Type*	*Adjustment of score*	*Achievement*
1.	Unskilled work	A	154	Mean	57.76	43.65
				SD	17.34	12.86
				SEM	1.40	1.04
2.	Skilled work	B	65	Mean	55.34	42.98
				SD	15.64	11.28
				SEM	1.96	1.41
3:	Office assistant	C	18	Mean	55.98	48.83
				SD	15.98	16.36
				SEM	3.88	13.90
4.	Teaching D	42	Mean	54.55	52.71	
				SD	16.35	13.21
				SEM	2.55	2.06
5.	Professional	E	21	Mean	49.50	59.81
				SD	16.73	16.31
				SEM	2.39	3.65

Table 13
Analysis of variance for the scores of five student groups in Adjustment Inventory on the basis of their parents' occupational level

Source of	*Sum of variation*	*df squares*	*Mean squaresSig.*	*F-ratio*	*Level of*
Between groups	1460.06	4		365.00	
			1.34	NS	
Within groups	80443.32	295		272.69	
Total	81903.38	299			

It is observed that the F-ratio is not significant at any level. This means that the mean scores of the five groups did not differ reliably among themselves. Parents' occupation as an independent variable did not have any impact upon their children's scores on adjustment inventory and achievement test. Since the F-ratio is not significant further treatment of the data is not necessary. The hypothesis, therefore, is rejected. The reason might have been that the sample is drawn from the same area and it is both rural and semi-urban area and the students' life is almost the same in ail respects. Hence the parents' occupation is not an effective variance.

Discussion

This study is an attempt to relate the level of adjustment of the adolescent students studying in ninth and tenth standards to their school performances. The examination marks were taken as their performance in schools. Though the sample was drawn from the same area the variables that caused a change in the scores are attributable to various sample areas. The study also relates the influence of siblings, parents' educational influence, parents' occupation to adjustment and achievement of the school students. The students in ninth and tenth standards are in the prime adolescent period and they are very sensitive to outside influences. Various forces, positive or negative, may be operating in their life aspects. All these may be expressed in some form in the adolescent students' adjustment problems and school achievements. There are very few or negligible studies in this area. Therefore the results of this study may throw some new light in this area.

The study revealed that there is a positive association between adjustment and achievement of the school students. The students who are well adjusted make higher achievements in school performances and the students who were not well adjusted make lesser achievements. It appears that students' adjustments and their achievements are interrelated since whatever variable affects adjustments also affects students' achievements in schools. This has been tested by the use of also other independent variables. The result of this study is in agreement with the result of the study conducted by Bhagia (1966). He conducted a study on 150 pupils of ninth standard and found that there was a positive relationship between adjustment scores and achievement scores. In Resnick's (1951) study also it was found that there was a relationship between better grades and personal adjustment. This study further confirmed the results of these studies.

The results of the study made by Chandha and Chandra (1985) seem to be in agreement with the results of this study. They found that the adolescents' adjustment had effect in actual achievement.

The students who had few number of siblings (brother and sisters) were found to be well adjusted and making better achievement and those who had more number of siblings lacked adjustment and failed to make the standard achievement. The reason might have been due to the divided attention of the parents, lack of care on every child equally. The greater the number of siblings in the family the more severe the problems the children face and the poorer the achievements they make in schools. The child who lives in a family where there are one or two siblings would certainly be well adjusted and free from problems of any sort and also maintain an excellent standard in school. If the children are free from problems then they make very good progress in their studies and the home is a happy home. The increase of siblings in any family would certainly be having more problems. The younger ones may receive more attention and care from the parents and this may cause resentment in the minds of other children. The eldest son or daughter may play the role of the father or mother which again may develop a grudge among other youngsters. All these may affect their adjustments in the family and will have corresponding effect in their school achievements.

If the parents are well educated they may realise their children's difficulties at home and at school and they may plan to bring up their children without creating any scope for problems. They may pay equal attention and care on every child. This sort of parental attitudes may reduce the chances for problems.

Instead, if the parents are not educated their treatment of the children would be different. They may compare one child with another and pass remarks. They may tease or punish one in the presence of another. This sort of parental approaches are quite common among uneducated parents. This may hurt the feelings of children and they develop some sort of hatred or disgust towards home and parents and lose their adjustments at home. They carry the same to school and this will have effect them in their studies and school achievements. The results of this study brings out varying achievement levels among the students on the basis of their parents' educational levels. This study ascertains that the higher qualification of the parents the better the adjustment of their children and the higher the achievement in their schools. Therefore it has been borne out by this study that students' adjustments and achievements are based upon their parents' educational level. There have been no studies of this type made earlier in this area.

Parents' occupational status is another independent variable that may have influence upon their children's adjustment problems and achievement. Children of well placed parents are supposed to make better adjustment and have higher achievement. There is no controversy on this matter in the common sense word. But this sort of result also depends upon the nature of population and sample. In this study it was observed that there were differences in the adjustment scores and achievement scores among the students on the basis of parents' occupations. But the differences among the five students' groups were not reliable and significant at any level. The main reason for this type of result is that the sample was drawn from the same geographical area. All schools are situated in rural areas and in semi-urban area. There are not much differences in the life-styles of the students who go to these schools. A fully urban sample compared with the rural sample may bring out reliable and significant difference among the students in this type of study on the basis of parents' occupations.

References

Abraham, P.A., An analytical study of some personality factors and academic achievement of secondary school pupils, Ph.D.Thesis, Trivandrum: Kerala University, 1968.

Alexander, C.N., Jr., Ordinal position and sociometric status, *Sociometry*, 1966, 29, 41-52.

Atkinson, J.W., et al., *Motives in fantasy, action and society*, Princetion, N.J., 1958.

Barrett and Lennard, G.T., The nature person, *Mental Hygine*, New York, 1962, 46, 98-102.

Bhagta, N.M., Study of problem of school -adjustment and developing an adjustment inventory, *Doctoral Dissertation in Education*, MSU, 1966.

Bhatt, G.P., An experimental study of the achievements in basic education, *Doctoral Dissertation in Education,* MSU, Baroda, 1861.

Chandha, N.K., and Sunanda Chandra, A comparative study of the adolescent boys and girls in relation to their attitudes towards school adjustment and scholastic achievement, *The Indian Journal of Community Guidance Service*, Vol. 2, No. 3, September, 1985.

Chauhan, S.S., et al., *Advanced Educational Psychology*, Vikas Publishing House Private Limited, Copyright Chauhan, 1978.

Coleman, J.C., *Abnormal Psychology and Modern Life* (Review edition) New, York; Scott Foresman, 1972.

Cronbach, L.J., *Educational Psychology,* New York: Harcourt, Brace and Company, 1954.

Eston Jackson Asher, et al., *Introduction to General Psychology*, D.C. Health sand Company Boston, United States of America, 1953.

Eysenck, H.J., *Uses and abuses at Psychology,* Penguin Book Ltd., 1953, p. 37 and p. 131.

Fairweather, G.W., *Social Psychology in Treating Mental Illness: An Experimental Approach*, New York; Wiley, 1964.

Feinberg, M.R., Relation of background experience to social acceptance, *Journal of Abnormal and Social Psychology*, 1953, 48, 206-214.

Fradson, A.N., *Educational Psychology; The Principles of Learning in Teaching*, New York: McGraw-Hill Book Company, 1961.

Havighurst, R.J., *Human Development and Education*, New York: Longmans, 1953.

Hugh, Bell, M., *Bell Adjustment Inventory Manual,* Pao Atto: Consulting Psychologists Press, 1962.

John B., Watson and Fredrick Dashiel, *Behaviourism,* Review Education, New York: W.W. Norton and Company, Inc., 1930.

Knutson, A.L., "New perspectives regarding positive mental health", *American Journal of Psychology,* 1963, Vol. 18, p. 300-301.

Lazarus, R.S., *Patterns of Adjustment,* Third edition, (International Student Edition), Tokyo, McGraw-Hill Kogakusha Ltd., 1976.

Lorion et al., Family background characteristics and school adjustment problems, *Journal of Community Psychology*, 1977 (Apr), Vol. 5(2), 142-148.

McCarmic, E.J., et al., *Industrial Psychology* (6th Edition), Englewood Cliffs N.J. Prentice-Hall, Inc., 1967.

Mouly, G.J., *Psychology for effective teaching,* New York, Holt, Rinchart and Winston, 1966.

Rao, N., A prognostic study of achievement in relation to academic adjustment, *Indian Psychological abstract,* Vol. 1 (5) September-October, 1972.

Resnick, J., "A study of some relationships between high school grades and certain aspects of adjustments", *Journal of Education Research,* 1951, Vol. 44, 321-340.

Shaffers, L.F., and Shoben, E.J., *The Psychology of Adjustment,* 2nd edition, Boston: Houghton Mifflin, 1956.

Sharma, Janardha Prasad et al., Study of low achieving and high achieving schools, *Rajasthan Board Journal of Education*, 1974, 10(3), 42-51.

Smith, K.V. and Smith, W.H., *The Behaviour of Man: Introduction to Psychology*, Holt, Rinehart and Winston, Inc., 1958.

CHAPTER 3

Adjustment Problems in Relation to Psychosomatic Disorders among Adolescent Girls

M. Rajamanickam and Mercy Arunmozhi

This is the result of the study of adjustment problems in relation to psychosomatic disorders among the adolescent girl students'. There are quite a number of studies on adjustment problems of the students studying in schools and colleges. But none of them relates adjustment problems to psychosomatic disorders. The sample of this study consisted of 300 adolescent girl students studying in higher secondary schools. The age of the students ranged from 15 to 19 years and they were all drawn from various socio-economic status and cultural groups. The Adjustment Inventory developed by Sinha and Singh, the Cornell Index Test and one Personal Information Questionnaire were used in this study.

The results brought to light certain important findings. There is a positive association between adjustment problems and psychosomatic disorders in the case of adolescent girls. The well-adjusted adolescent girls were emotionally stable and least prone to psychosomatic disorders and the maladjusted girls were emotionally unstable and more prone to psycho-somatic disorders. Girls from affluent families were well adjusted and had the least psychosomatic disorders, whereas the girls from impoverished families had more adjustment problems and psychosomatic disorders. Girls from forward communities were well adjusted and free from psychosomatic disorders while the girls from backward and scheduled caste communities had more adjustment problems and prone to more psychosomatic disorders.

Introduction

Adjustment is a continuous process of action in the life of a human being or an organism with a definite purpose of meeting the needs of the self, the needs of the environment and the needs of the culture or society. The ultimate end of the process of action of the adjustment is successful survival. The end result may be survival or extermination. A continuous close watch on the life of an organism or a human being may bring out many happy and unhappy events which are based upon the struggle for successful survival. Man is an interdependent creature, always expecting the help and the cooperation from other human beings and the culture or society in which he lives, for the fulfilment of his basic needs and also makes inevitable demands from them.

The concept 'adjustment' is used both in the common sense world and in the scientific world to indicate certain type of behaviour of an individual or a group. Though in the psychological world it refers to the behaviour of the individual it can be applied also to a group of people in a particular situation. It is an act of adjusting or adaptation for a particular purpose. It is the state of being adjusted. It is also the act of bringing something into conformity with the external requirement. In the psychological world it is stated that it is a process of establishing a satisfactory relationship between the individual and his environment. It is a process of constant successful interaction between the individual and his environment. During the course of interaction people learn to change their behaviour so as to get along with other people.

Adjustment is the combined influence of several forces in the adolescent's environment that operate to produce a well-adjusted or poorly-adjusted personality. It is emphasized that personality is the result of the interaction of hereditary factors and environmental forces. Though the concept 'adjustment' was in usage for a long time explaining certain processes referring to human behaviour, a systematic study came into existence only in the twentieth century. Only after that scientific studies on adjustment were started. Several authors in various fields of psychology and sociology attempted to make elaborate experimental studies. During the year 1906 Heymans and Wiersma (1971) developed a list of symptoms concerned with the problem of adjustment. This list was revised by Hoeh and Amsolen (1971) in the year 1913 and later by Wells (1971) in the year

1914. The word adjustment came into popular use in psychology during the 1930's and was given strong endorsement by Shaffer (1956) in his classical book *The Psychology of Adjustment*, which appeared in 1936. It mainly emphasized the biological adaptation of the organism to its environment. Later on 1961 Lazarus (1961) brought out his famous work, *Patterns of Adjustment*.

According to Lindgren (1965) the term adjustment means that the persons must accommodate themselves in order to meet certain demands of their environment. Therefore the study of adjustment has to do with how we make such accommodation and how successfully we meet the demands that are made on us. Shaffer said, "Adjustment is a process by which a living organism maintains a balance between its needs and the circumstances that influence the satisfaction of needs." These needs can be bio-genic, originating in society, personal or communal or arising from any other conceivable source.

On the other, hand, the circumstances influencing these needs can either be inside the individual or outside the individual. Factors within the individual that influence these needs are his physical and mental states, capacity, attitudes, interests, etc. Factors arising within the environment are usually geographic conditions, social conditions, political and cultural influences, and help in the fulfilment of needs while unfavourable influences hinder the satisfaction.

According to the view of Fredenberg (1971) adjustment involves transactions with the environment which may result in a change in one's behaviour, or a change in the environment or both. Each one of us experiences both internal as well as external needs. Adjustive behaviour may be viewed as concerned with three levels of adjustment, those meeting the psychological, the physiological and the sociological needs of the individual. Karen and Weitz (1955) state that the organism has certain needs or desires that must be fulfilled in order to adjust itself to the environment. As a result of this the organism changes, its behaviours in various ways for maintaining its behaviour in the environment. Thereby it fulfils its needs and wants and finds satisfaction. Wile discriminated the meanings of normality and abnormality in which he views that if we wish to indicate that an individual's behaviour departs from the normal, it is necessary to do more than merely label him as abnormal or maladjusted; we must use additional words such as unusual "atypical" "deviant" or "idiosyncratic", in order to convey our specific meaning about his behaviour.

In the adjustment of adults, their occupational or vocational adjustment plays an important role, the school or college environment casts its influence over the adjustment of the youngsters. How far a student is satisfied with his school building, its discipline, timetable, co-curricular activities, methods of teaching, class and schoolmates, teachers, and head of the institution, contribute significantly towards his total adjustment. Similarly, the occupational world of the adults dominates their mode of adjustment. The degree of satisfaction with the choice of occupation, working conditions, relationship with colleagues and boss, financial satisfaction and chances for promotion, decide one's adjustment to one's occupation and contributes significantly towards one's overall adjustment.

The chief characteristic of mental health is adjustment. A well-adjusted person knows his weaknesses. He tries to make capital out of his assets in some areas and by accepting his limitations in the other. The dislike for one's self is a typical symptom of maladjustment. An adjusted individual has respect for one's self as well as for others. His level of aspiration is neither too low nor too high in comparison to his own strengths and abilities. He does not try to reach for the stars and also does not repent over selecting an easier course for advancement. According to K.V.Smith and W.H.Smith (1958) the well-adjusted person experiences conflicts and attacks his problems in a realistic manner. A mentally well adjusted individual's organic, emotional and social needs are fully satisfied. He does not suffer from emotional craving and social isolation. He feels reasonably secure and maintains his self-esteem. He knows to appropriate the goodness in the objects, persons or activities. He does not try to search for weakness and faults. His observation is scientific rather than critical or punitive. He likes people, admires their qualities, and wins their affection. He can easily accommodate or adapt himself to the changed circumstances by making necessary changes in his behaviour. He holds a realistic vision and is not given to flights of fancy. He always plans, thinks and acts pragmatically.

Langner states that a mentally healthy individual is one who is himself satisfied, lives peacefully with his neighbours, makes healthy dozens of his children. As a student he likes his school mates, teachers and feels satisfied with his daily routine. When he enters a profession, he has a love for it and maintains his zeal and enthusiasm despite heavy odds. In the words of Sawrey and Telford (1971), the mature mind is constantly engaged in increasing his knowledge, behaves responsibly, expresses his thoughts, feelings and viewpoints.

According to Clavsen (1966) a mentally healthy individual maintains good adjustment with social situation, and is engaged in some project or the other intended to benefit society. According to Hilgard and et al. (1971) a mentally healthy person is a productive person. He has a philosophy which gives direction to his life while keeping in view the demands of the changed situations and circumstances.

Maladjustment

The failure of an individual to develop behavioural patterns necessary for personal and social structure is called maladjustment. According to Coleman (1966) any state that contradicts that of adjustment is called maladjustment. Faire-Weather (1966) reveals that the maladjusted individual fails to attain a state of adjustment with his circumstances and instead of trying to face up to the situation, tries to run away from it. Maladjusted individuals, in one way or another fail to learn the accepted methods for meeting the demands of their environment. These symptoms are the evidences of his maladjustive reactions.

Maladjustment is a deviant behaviour that goes beyond the limits of permissible behaviour established by the social norms, thus creating individual and social problems. When the behaviour of the individual includes emotional tension and disturbed behaviour, then the individual is frustrated, and hence his behaviour is a pattern of maladjustment.

The maladjusted person lacks in self-esteem and is so concerned with protecting his own security that he becomes extremely self-concerned. Hurlock (1978) says that there are certain patterns of behaviour that are characteristically associated with well-adjusted children and others with poorly-adjusted children. The maladjusted children show symptoms of anxiety and often complain about the surrounding environmental factors. Swanton (1930) and Mead (1928) argue that the maladjustments are due to personal and economic reasons. There are many factors which lead to maladjustment. In every society there are certain patterns of maladjustment. When one is unable to cope satisfactorily with adolescent stress and strains maladjustments and neuroses appear.

Maladjustment in Adolescence

Adolescence is a crucial age of storm and stresses. The varying physical and socio-psychological needs of this age have to be satisfied for the adjustment, moving between independence versus dependence, realism versus idealism, parental affection versus peer group norms, age temptations versus social taboos, etc. The adolescent must be made to satisfy himself / herself reasonably with his / her body development, somatic variations and organic and psychophyscial changes. He/ she must be helped in the proper exercising of his / her emotions and channelling the stream of his / her valuable energy.

According to Mangal (1984) adolescents are very sensitive and should therefore be treated and cared for adequately according to their needs and problems of their age. An attack on their situation may invite a host of problems. Their resentment, indifference and hostility should be helped to establish self-identity and meaningful standards of conduct to follow. Adolescents are then misunderstood, their problems are not cared for and their aspirations thwarted. It gives rise to conflicts, tensions and frustrations among the adolescents, and thus leading to abnormalities and mental disorders.

In the psychological study of adjustment we must look into two kinds of demands, one is internal which is primary arising out of biological make-up of the person. Certain conditions should be met for the individual's comfort and survival. One must be protected from dangers and must get sufficient food, water, warm and shelter. The other basic demand is external which arises from external physical or social environments. Of these the social demands are considered to be the most important for explaining the emotional life of human beings. The emotions are toned positively and negatively. The positively toned emotions are love, joy, thrill, excitement and the negatively toned emotions are fear, anger, anxiety, guilt, depression.

Adjustment appears to be essentially a matter of problem solving. The person must find out the characteristics of his environment and also how it can be dealt with in living. This learning begins at birth and continues throughout the life. In adjustive activity strong emotions, particularly the stress emotions such as fear, anger, anxiety, guilt and shame are also generated. This results when the environmental demands involve high stakes and entail frustration, threat and conflict. Therefore it may result in ineffective solution of the problem and production of stress and bodily disease. Lazarus (1961) states that stress is a bodily tension, which occurs when there are demands on the individual that tax or exceed his adjustive resources. The study of stress is very important in the health sciences because it can lead to bodily illness and maladjustment. It was observed that two-thirds of medical patients reveal symptoms that are psychological in origin. They are in fact stress linked.

The connection between psychological problem and bodily illness is called psychosmatic disorder. It may also be called stress disorders, diseases adaptation, and psycho-physiological disorders. This statement implies that a problem that begins psychologically may produce organic disturbances which may even end in permanent damage of the tissues. Psychosomatic illness refers to certain bodily disorders. To mention some of the most important are stomach ulcers, intestinal colitis (diarrhoea) hypertension (high blood pressure) and migraine headache.

There are also other forms of illness which psychological stress is capable of causing such as chronic indigestion, hives, allergies, susceptibility to infection, accident proneness and many others. Many thoughtful professionals think that all illnesses have psychosomatic overtones. They are of the view that most of the illnesses are not the results of attacks by viruses of micro-organisms or by conditions external to the body. Illnesses in part arise because the person's bodily resistance to it has been impaired by stress. It is also observed that emotional disturbances lie at the core of the causation of psychosomatic illness. The physiology of emotion will explain how particularly the negative emotions affect the body.

Stress has special importance in adjustment, because it implies a change from single problem solving to a situation having emotional overtones. A strong emotional situation often results in an irrational way of coping with adaptive problems. Stress increases potentials for maladjustment. Stress will impair the person's handling of life tasks. It produces bodily diseases. Stress emotions serve as distractions that interfere with productive thinking. A person's anxiety is an important stress emotion arising when a harm is anticipated. Life stress can result in maladjusted behaviour. Therefore a stress is an adjustive demand that requires coping behaviour on the part of an individual or group. It occurs when there are demands on the person which tax or exceed his adjustive resources. The idea is that chronic emotional status and their bodily reactions may result in change in certain organic and body functions. Many disorders have a psychosomatic basis in some people like stomach ulcer, high blood pressure, and asthma. Therefore emotional disturbance lies at the core of the causation of psychosomatic illness. Physical disorder is caused by or suitably influenced by the emotional state of the patient. Under stress some individuals develop bronchial spasms and some hypertension and still others migraine headaches. Therefore life stress is the underlying cause of all these disorders. Chronic emotional tension elicited by life stress can cause profound changes in the physiological functioning of the human body. These changes can play an turn important causal role in the psychosomatic disorders.

According to Liebert et. al. (1954) psychosomatic disorders are real physical illnesses that are either caused or markedly influenced by psychological factors. A variety of such difficulties are known to occur in childhood: asthma, rheumatoid arthritis, ulcertive colitis and peptic ulcers. Garner and Wenar (1959) found that youngsters with psychosomatic disorders have relationship with their mothers in which there is little personal closeness; rather mothers tend to be easily irritated and angered and the children themselves also are rated as high on anger.

Psychosomatic Disorder

The term psychosomatic is derived from the Greek words *psyche* and *soma. Psyche* in ancient times means soul or mind and more recently has come to mean behaviour. Some typically refers to the physical organism, the body. The term psychosomatic, therefore, indicates relationships between psychological processes or behaviour on the one hand and the somatic structures or bodily organs on the other.

During the middle of the nineteenth century psychologists had concentrated on the bodily functions. In the year 1950 Wolff (1950) had proposed a theory of psychosmatic disorders based on the physiological theory of emergency reaction. Alexander (1943), as one of the leading psychoanalysts, had worked in the field of psychosomatics. By 1943 Halliday (1943) had defined psychosomatics as a bodily disorder whose nature can be appreciated only when emotional disturbances, that is, psychological happenings, are investigated in addition to physical disturbances like somatic happenings.

Stalker (1950), during the year 1949, classified psychosomatic problems into three groups. The first group contained the functional disorders. The second, emotional factors even though the organic disease was present. The third, physical disease, has to do with the autonomic nervous system. Fenichel (1939) differentiated between two categories of functional disturbances. One of them is physical in nature and consists of physiological changes caused by the inappropriate use of the function in question. The other one is an expression of a fantasy in a body language and directly accessible to psychosoanalysis in the same way as a dream. In the same period, psychosomatic was also defined by Glover (1937) as the organic changes consequent on effective changes in the organic manifestation of dammed up instinct and physical consequences of unconscious attitudes or uncosciously determined behaviour patterns.

The twentieth century psychologists have concentrated more on the emotional tension status of individuals, which is a psychosomatic illness, the cause of which is primarily psychological. Different types of illnesses like ulcers, asthma, headaches, high blood pressure and skin eruptions are related to emotional stress. Modern psychologists stressed the importance of long-term emotional stress because this will influence an individual's physical health and mental efficiency. One of the earliest theories of emotion proposed that emotion is nothing but perception of the physiological changes.

Many psychologists have argued that emotions are the chief sources of disturbance and maladjustment. A mild level of emotional arousal tends to produce interest in the task at hand. When emotions become intense they usually result in some decrement in performance.

Reiser (1953) said that the word "Psychosomatic" has become so firmly established in common usage that it is not feasible to discard it. We prefer to speak of "psychosomatic approach" and "psychosomatic mechanisms" rather than of "psychosomatic illness" or "psychosomatic medicine". Psychophysiological disorders have been known as psychosomatic disorders which implies that the mind determines the disease or disorders of the body. It does not imply a dichotomy between mind and body.

Characteristics of Psychosomatic Disorders

Psychosomatic disorders show the disturbance of function together with damage in the organs of the body. In this they differ from mental disorders. In psychosomatic disorders emotional disturbances play an important role in precipitating the onset, and recurrence of symptoms. This distinguishes them from purely organic disorders. They are chronic disorders with a phasic course. They tend to be associated with other psychosomatic disorders. This may occur in the family or at different periods of life in one patient. They show a great difference in the incidence between sexes. Thus asthma is twice as common in boys as in girls, before puberty, and, it is less common in men than women. Duodenal ulcer is much more common in men and thyrotoseicosis is common in women. Psychosomatic disorders are classified on the basis of organ system affected and no part of the body is exempted. The American Psychological Association (1974) uses the term psychophysiologic disorders to synonymously psychosomatic disorders. The APA has classified them into 10 categories.

They are (1) psychosomatic skin disorders or neurodermatitis, strophic dermatitis, eczema and cases of acne and hives, (2) psychosomatic musculoskeletal disorders or backaches, muscle cramps, tension headaches and some cases of arthritis. (3) The respiratory disorders are bronchial asthma, hyperventilation syndromes, hiccoughs and recurring bronchitis. (4) The cardiovascular disorders are hypertension, paroxysmal tachycardia, vascular spasms, heart attacks and migraine headaches. (5) Heamic and lymphatic disorders are disturbances in the blood and lymphatic systems. (6) Psychosomatic gastrointestinal disorders are peptic ulcers, chronic gastritis and mucous colitis. (7) The genitourinary disorders are disturbances in menstruation and urination. (3) The endocrine disorders are hyperthyroidism, obesity and other endocrine disorders are those in which emotional factors play a causative role. (9) Chronic conjunctivitis are the disorders of organs of special sense. (10) The other types of disorders are disturbances in the nervous system in which emotional factors play a significant role, such as multiple sclerosis. All of these disorders are caused by stress. In essence, chronic emotional tension elicited by life stress perceived as threatening can cause profound changes in the physiological functioning of the human body; these changes, in turn, can play an important causal role in the various disorders we refer to as psychosomatic.

In general, the development of psychosomatic disorders appears to involve the following sequence of events, the arousal of negative emotions in response to stress situation, the degree of arousal depending not only on the nature of the stress situation, but also on the individual's perception of the situation and his stress tolerance; the failure of these emotions to be dealt with adequately either through appropriate expression or through a changed frame of reference or improved competence, with the result that the emotional arousal continues on the chronic basis and response stereotype, the damaging effects of chronic arousal becoming contracted in a specific organ system. There are three factors such as (a) biological, (b) psychological and (c) socio-cultural factors.

There were many research investigations and studies on adjustment problems of school students. Bansal's (1973) study was on adjustment differences among scheduled caste and high caste Hindu adolescent students. The sample consisted of 235 high caste Hindus and 195 scheduled caste Hindu students studying in tenth grade from five higher secondary schools. He used an intelligence test and B.P.T. Saxena Adjustment Inventory. The two community Hindu students showed difference in their adjustment problems in the areas of home, school, social and emotional. The high caste Hindu students were found to be better adjusted than the scheduled caste Hindu students.

A study was conducted at Annamalai University (1984) to explore the neuropsychiatric and psychosomatic problems of 100 students, of which 50 were athletes and 50 were non-atheletes. Cornell Index Test was used. The analysis of the results revealed that the atheletes, who were studying in various courses, were between the age of 18-19 and 22-23 years and they had neuropsychiatric and psychosomatic problems. Brar (1973) studied the adjustment problems of higher secondary students. The sample was 150 adolescents studying in ninth, tenth and eleventh classes. They were from urban and rural adivasis and non-adivasis. Mooney's Problem Checklist was used in this study. The results indicated that most of them had vocational problems. Adjustment problem was not so prominent among the girls. Social problem was acute among adivasis. There were studies like this and on adjustment problems. But studies relating to problems and psychosomatic disorders among adolescent girl students were not made.

Background of the Study

The nature of human beings in the primitive stage was hostile, aggressive and violent. Each one saw the other as his enemy and wanted to dominate him by some means or the other. The primitive man was in a constant state of fear and he was afraid of moving freely in his environment. This sense of fear and hostile attitude of others made man to come into an agreement for getting security for his life and property. This resulted in the organisation of social institutions and other security measures. The nodal organisations were based on the contract of each man's surrender of some of his rights and to get security for his life and property. These social organisations were the basis of correcting human behaviour and training him to be social and cordial with other human beings. The present state of human nature is the result of the functions of social institutions for thousand of years. With all that, man's problems are not solved and they are taking different roots.

Adjustment, though attained to some extent, the problem is not fully solved. It is seen right from the childhood days till man's death. The adjustment problem leads to some other problems and the problems become severe. This arouses the curiosity of the psychologists and many studies were made during the course of 50 years. Since the problem is in different forms at all ages the adolescent school students receive much attention in these days. It is often said that the period of adolescence is the period of "Storm and Stress". The adolescents may be easily influenced for any type of behaviour pattern.

In a school all students are taught by the same teacher, play in the same ground and participate in the same type of activities. But variations in their adjustments and achievements are taking place. Further the adolescents may have some problems at home or at school with peer groups. The nature of the adjustment problems may be also due to some kind of physical or physiological or psychosomatic problems. It is also observed that many adolescents were not able to do their work due to the consequences of the adjustment problems. Therefore this problem needs to be examined.

Many adjustment difficulties are caused by the system of bodily functions or physical difficulties and these disturbances are always reflected in mental concomitants, either directly or indirectly. Physical difficulties and disorders can be produced by emotional upheavals such as fear, rage, grief, worry, anxiety and frustrations. There is no doubt that the victim of emotional upsets may find difficulties in adjustments.

It has clearly been stated by medical and psychological scholars that emotional upheavals may aggravate or produce psychosomatic illnesses like stomach trouble, indigestion, metabolic disturbances leading to possible emaciation, heart diseases, insomnia, increased susceptibility to colds and dysentery. Many abnormalities or psychosomatic disorders have a psychogenic origin and it is important to note that these kinds of states may affect one's mental set-up and thereby create problems of adjustment.

The satisfactory adjustment and resolution of the individual's basic psychosomatic needs and urges are prime conditions for the attainment and preservation of mental health and sound physical health. The individual's failure to achieve inner harmony in himself, and to reconcile himself with the folkways and mores of society, will tend to produce in him personality modifications or distortions in varying degrees. This depends upon the nature and severity of the emotional stress. It is clear from the above statements that psychosomatic problems of any kind will affect the individual's normal life. When an individual has some problems he finds it difficult to adjust himself and with his environment. The present study is based upon this background.

Objectives of the Study

Adolescent period is a critical stage, during which the adolescents will have different kinds of problem. They may be physiological, social and psychological in nature. The psychological and physiological problems have one to one relationship. A student who has psychological problem also has some physiological problem, for example, the psychosomatic symptom. In the school situation students from different socioeconomic groups come together to pursue their education. The development of these problems are influenced by various factors. One of the main factors is their physical growth and development of adjustment problems. In this study (1) one main objective is to see the relationship between adjustment problems and psychosomatic disorders. The other objectives of this study are (2) to know the levels of adjustment problems and their corresponding effect upon psychosomatic disorders (3) to know the influence of other independent factors like the cultural factors and the socioeconomic status of the parents' upon the students' psychosomatic disorders.

The Problem

The present study is designed to assess the influence of adjustment problems of adolescent girl students on their psychosomatic problems. Psychosomatic symptom indicates relationships between psychological processes or behaviour on the one hand and somatic structures or bodily organs on the other—in other words, the influence of biological processes on the psychological reactions, that is on behaviour. Behaviour means all actions of the organism, includes internal and directly observable and unobservable responses.

The adolescent girls often complain that they have headache, stomach pain, giddiness, cold, etc. These are not without any cause. It may be rooted in their physiological changes, emotional stress and the development of adjustment problems at home, at school, playground with peer groups, etc. Everyone differs from others in bodily features. Therefore the differences in behaviour are directly dependent on differences in the anatomy and physiology of individuals. Whatever change occurs internally will be reflected in one's behaviour externally. Based on this, the study highlights that whenever there are problems in the system of physiology and psychological reactions there may be a problem of adjustment and psychosomatic disorders.

The constant severe emotional strains may lead to psychosomatic disorders that may be seen in one's outward behaviour of some kind. An individual who have somatic problems may feel that she has lost something and she no longer performs the task as she once did. Because of this her attitude become weaker and she develops a feeling of inadequacy or inferiority. The development of the feelings of inadequacy or inferiority prevents an individual from participating in all sorts of organisational activities. This separation and deviation from social involvement is a serious one which is normally faced by the girl student during the adolescent period. Particularly in situations like school, college, playground and other related fields these problem are likely to develop.

The adolescent girl students develop problems of various types because of the change in themselves and in their environment. Students from different cultural socioeconomic groups come into contact with one another in a common place where they may find it difficult to adjust to the situations. Their new contacts with place, persons and situations may lead to some kind of emotional stress and adjustment problems which in turn may develop into some kind of psychosomatic illnesses. Their differences in the interests, attitudes and the change of things all create problems. They come to the new environment with all sorts of imaginations and high hopes and when they fail to fulfil them, they are very much mentally disturbed and develop adjustment problems. Thus the chronic emotional stresses and adjustment problems make the school students prone to psychosomatic disorders.

It is reasonable to assume that the individual's emotional stress may have some bearing upon adjustment and psychosomatic illness. Those who have the psychosomatic problems may be lacking in their adjustment in home, school and with other persons and when the intensity increases the individual may have more adjustment problems and serious psychosomatic disorders. This study is an attempt to assess and discuss these problems.

Hypotheses

The following hypotheses are formulated for the study.

1. There is a positive association, between adolescent girl students' adjustment problems and a their psychosomatic disorders.
2. Students who are well adjusted are emotionally stable or have low emotional stress.
3. The well-adjusted adolescent girls are less prone to psychosomatic disorders than the maladjusted and moderately adjusted adolescent girls.
4. Students from affluent families are will adjusted, emotionally stable, and free from psychosomatic disorders.
5. Students' cultural background (communities) also have influence upon their psychosomatic problems: that is, students of forward communities are well adjusted and free from psychosomatic disorders whereas the students from

backward and scheduled caste communities are more prone to adjustment problems and psychosomatic disorders.

Method

Sample: The population chosen for this study is the school adolescent girls studying in eleventh and twelfth standards. It is felt that the adolescent period is the most suitable for studying this problem. The girls are between 15 and 19 years of age.. This is the age in which the girls develop all sorts of fantastic imagination, ambitions, aspirations and exhibit all sorts of emotional reactions. They also fall prey to all sorts of temptations. When their ambition and desires are not fulfilled they feel frustrated and develop various adjustment problems. Unlike boys they do not find any outlet for their problems by taking part outside activities. The emotional stress and their adjustment problems become chronic and they develop all sorts of psychosomatic disorders and show the symptoms. The more the emotional stress and adjustment problems they have the more they are prone to psychosomatic disorders or diseases. Therefore those who are studying in eleventh and twelfth standards are the best sample for this study. Further this problem was not studied earlier in this field. Therefore this study may bring out certain new results which may be of some use to the parents, teachers and the educationalists who formulate policies for secondary education.

The sample consisted of 300 school-going girls and they were selected randomly from six different schools in and around Chidambaram. It is a town situated in South Arcot district. There are eight higher secondary schools in this area and six schools were randomly selected for the study. The total number of students (boys and girls) studying in the schools were 3,200. The total number of girls were 1,200, our of which 25 per cent of the girls were selected at random, using the simple random sampling technique. The random selection was made from the list of girl students choosing one out of every four using the random table numbers. Thus there were 300 girl students from all six schools. The girls' age ranged from 15 to 19 years. These 300 girls were from eleventh and twelfth standards, 150 from each class.

Materials: The following test materials were used to collect data from the subjects:

Questionnaire 1 : Adjustment Inventory for school students.

Questionnaire 2 : Cornell Index

Questionnaire 3 : Personal Information questions.

Questionnaire 1: The adjustment inventory for the school students was developed by Sinha and Singh (1968) as a counselling inventory for the school students in the age group of the 13 to 18 years. This inventory was introduced to study the school students' personal problems in the areas of emotional, social and educational areas. The Inventory consisted of 60 items and it is self-administered. There is no time limit for answering it. The total score indicates the general adjustment level of the subject.

Questionnaire 2: The Cornell Index questionnaire was developed by Arthur Weider, Harold G.Wolff, Keeve Broadman, Bela Mittle-man and David Wechsler (1949). This test has been designed as an instrument to collect information on psychosomatic and neuropsychiatric symptoms for clinical interpretation that can be subjected to statistical evaluation to locate the individual on a scale of increasing neurotic and psychiatric disturbances.

This inventory has been used to find out the degree of psychiatric and psychosomatic illnesses among the higher secondary girl students belonging to various deprivation levels.

The Cornell Index form consists of 101 questions which can assess the problems into areas such as: (1) Defects in adjustment expressed as feelings of fear and inadequacy, (2) Pathological mood reactions especially depression, (3) Nervousness and anxiety, (4) Neuro-circulatory psychosomatic symptoms, (5) Pathological startle reactions, (6) Other psychosomatic symptoms, (7) Hypochondriasis and asthenia, (8) Gastrointestinal psychosomatic symptoms, (9) Excessive sensitivity and suspiciousness and (10) Troublesome psychopathy. There are two responses for each item such as 'Yes' and 'No'. The subjects should indicate whichever is suitable to them by making a check mark (4) on it. There is no time limit for answering it.

Questionnaire 3: The personal information questionnaire consisted of 30 questions. They were all related to the individual's personal, family, social, demographical and socio-economic status information. It also included the individuals interests in extracurricular activities, family size, siblings, etc.

Reliability and Validity of the Test Materials: All the three questionnaires were first cyclostyled into 50 copies, and were given to

50 girl students in five schools at the rate of 10 in each school to see how successfully they could answer the questions. On scrutinising the answers it was found that some of the girls in both the classes (11th and 12th standards) found it difficult to understand the correct meaning of the questions in English. Therefore all the questionnaires were translated into Tamil and scrutinised with the help of a language specialist. Then the questionnaires were printed into 300 copies and a pilot survey was conducted by administering them on 300 girl students of six higher secondary schools. The printed questionnaires were distributed among 50 students in each school. Of the 300 questionnaires 270 were returned. They were scrutinised and tabulated.

The split-half method and the Spearman-Brown formula were used to find out the reliability of the two tests. The correlation coefficient between scores of the odd-even items for the Adjustment Inventory was found to be 0.68 and it was corrected with Spearman-Brown formula. The reliability was found to be 0.82 and it was significant at 0.01 level. The reliability of the Cornell Index test was 0.79 and it was significant at 0.01 level. The intrinsic validity of the Adjustment Inventory was 0.91 and for the Cornell Index test 0.88 and both were significant at 0.01 level. In the case of questionnaire-3 certain words were reworded and rewritten.

Procedure: The test materials were found to be very satisfactory with their reliabilities and validities. They were printed in Tamil language into 300 copies and bound into booklet forms. Then the selected higher secondary schools headmasters/headmistresses were met and permission to conduct the survey was sought and the lists of girl students in eleveth and twelfth standard were also obtained. Then using the random table numbers 10 per cent of the students were selected from the whole list of students. Then the students of eleveth and twelfth standard who were selected from each school for the investigation were informed to be present on the fixed day at the fixed time. Then with help of the class teacher the questionnaires were distributed to the students with a short instruction and they were asked to complete all the three questionnaires one by one without omitting any of the item. As there was no time limit they were told to take their own time. They took on an average 90 minutes. The questionnaires were collected as soon as they were completed and verified. The same procedure were followed in all the six schools.

Scoring: The questionnaires were then scrutinised and tabulated and scored according to the procedure devised by the authors of the tests. In the case of Adjustment Inventory there were three areas, like emotional, social and educational. A high score in the emotional area indicates unstable, and a low score emotionally stable. In the social area a high score is indicative of being submissive and retiring and a low score, aggressive and active. A high score in the educational area indicates poor adjustment with curriculum programmes and a low score means interested in school programmes. The total score in all the three areas is taken as the general adjustment level of the individual.

In the case of Cornell Index the 'Yes' and 'No' answers marked by the subject were compared with the key. An agreement with the key is given one mark, otherwise no mark. The individual score is the total mark for all the items. A high score indicates more psychosomatic disorders in the particular area and a low score less psychosomatic disorders. The individuals' scores were obtained for both the tests and the scores were treated statistically. Some of the treatments were correlation coefficient, analysis of variance, the mean scores, standard deviations, standard error of the mean differences and critical ratios. The results were analysed through these treatments.

Results

The age of the students studying in higher secondary schools range from 15 years to 19 years according to this investigation. They study in higher secondary schools only for two years and therefore their age normally should be 15 and 16 years but their age goes up to 19 years. They all come under the category of adolescents. This is the period in which the boys and girls develop problems of various types. Generally and mostly they face adjustment problems at home, at school, at playground. If the conditions are not cogenial and agreeable to them they may become highly emotional, irritative, hostile and quarrelsome. As a result of it they are maladjusted leading to the development of psychosomatic problems. To what extent are this sort of psychological processes taking place in the case of adolescent girls studying in higher secondary schools? While testing with suitable test it is observed that there is a positive association between the scores of adjustment Inventory and the scores of Cornell Index test, and it is significant at 0.01 level. This means that the adolescent girls who have adjustment problems (emotional, social and educational) have also psychosomatic problems (Table 1). Therefore the hypothesis is accepted.

Table 1
Showing the correlation coefficient between the scores of Adjustment Inventory and Cornell Index test

	Tests	*No. of subjects*	*Correlation*	*Test of significance*	*Level of significance*
1.	Adjustment Inventory				
		300	0.42	7.58	0.01
2.	Cornell Index Test				

The adolescent girls' adjustment levels may vary on the basis of its intensity or severity. Adverse effects may be caused if the level of maladjustment is increased. The hypothesis is that if the girls are well adjusted then their emotional state is low and the psychosomatic problems are also low. This is tested by arranging the adjustment scores from the lowest to the highest. The top 25 per cent of the cases are considered as the upper group, the bottom 25 per cent the lower group and the middle 50 per cent as the middle group. The mean scores for all the three groups were worked out with S.D. and S.E.M. These groups, with corresponding scores in emotional scale and in Cornell Index test, also were treated in the same manner. Thus there are three groups, the upper group, the well-adjusted (scored low), the lower group maladjusted (scored high) and the middle group moderately adjusted (scored in between) (Table 2).

It is clear that the well-adjusted group scored low in the emotional scale (5.13) and also in the Cornell Index test (25.29) which shows that this group is emotionally stable and has the least psychosomatic problems.

The second group, moderately adjusted, scored (6.91) just above the first group indicating its moderated emotional instability and the moderate psychosomatic problems (33.52).

The third group, which is maladjusted, scored high in the adjustment inventory, scored the highest in the emotional scale (7.75) and in the Cornell Index test (39.31). This means that the girls of this group have severe adjustment problems and are emotionally very unstable and they have severe psychosomatic problems. Thus more adjustment problems, emotional instability and severe psychosomatic problems go together. The psychosomatic problems were consequences of the girls' maladjustment and emotional strain. Therefore the hypothesis is accepted.

The students who are highly maladjusted seem to be highly emotional and develop more psychosomatic disorders than the students who are well adjusted and stable emotionally. This is one of the important findings of this study.

Table 2

Showing the distribution of mean scores, SD and SEM for three groups of girl students on the level of adjustment, emotional stability and psychosomatic disorders

Sl.	*Groups*	*Code*	*N*	*Type of scores*	*Emotional scores*	*Psychoso- No matic*
1.	Well adjusted	A	75	Mean	5.13	25.29
				SD	3.23	12.60
				SEM	0.38	1.47
2	Moderately adjusted	B	150	Mean	6.91	33.32
				SD	4.01	13.32
				SEM	0.33	1.10
3.	Maladjusted	C	75	Mean	7.75	39.31
				SD	3.17	15.73
				SEM	0.37	1.83

The three adolescent groups—upper, middle group, and the lower group—showed much differences in their adjustment problems. The upper group which scored the lowest in .the adjustment inventory is the well adjusted group, the group that scored the highest is the maladjusted group and the middle group the moderately adjusted group. All these groups showed marked differences in their scores in the emotional scale and in the Cornell Index test. Whether the differences are real or spurious, was tested with an analysis of variance (Table 3). It is found that these three groups vary significantly among themselves at 0.01 level and really differ from each other in their scores on Cornell Index test.

Table 3 Showing the analysis of variance for the three groups of students on the Cornell Index test who vary on the adjustment levels

Source of variation	*Sum of squares*	*df*	*Mean square*	*F.Ratio*	*Level of sign.*
Among groups	7,410.58	2	3,705.19		
				19.42	0.01
Within groups	57,049.47	297	190.80		
Total	64,460.05	1299			

Since the analysis of variance has established that the three groups differ among them at significant level on the Cornell Index test it is also important to see how far these groups differ from each other by working out the critical ratios. Table 4 shows that the critical ratio between groups A and B, A and C, and B and C are significant at. 01 level. This means that the adolescent girl students who were maladjusted have scored high on the Cornell Index test indicating that they are more prone to psychosomatic disorders.

Table 4

Showing the critical ratios and the level of significance for the three groups on Cornell Index Test

Sl.	*Groups*	*Code*	*Mean scores*	*Mean difference*	*S.E. of Mean*	*C.R.*	*LevelNo. of sign*
1.	Well adjusted	A	25.29				
				8.03	1.82	4.42	.01
	Moderately adjusted	B	33.32				
2.	Well adjusted	A	25.29				
				14.02	2.33	6.02	.01
	Maladjusted	C	39.31				
3.	Moderately adjusted	B	33.32				
				5.99	3.13	2.94	.01
	Maladjusted	c	39.31				

The well adjusted adolescent girls were the least inclined to psychosomatic disorders and the moderately adjusted fall in between the two groups in the level of psychosomatic disorders. This is borne out by this enquiry. Therefore the hypothesis is accepted. The hypothesis is that if the students are from affluent families then they are well adjusted and free from psychosomatic disorders as tested in this study. Families' economic position is not without any effect upon the children's life. The poor income of the parents may cause maladjustments which may also lead to the development of psychosomatic disorders.

Table 5 shows the scores of the adolescent girl students who were drawn from various income groups. It is found that the highest score (34.44) on the Cornell Index test was obtained by the lowest income group girls. This group also scored (20.11) high on the Adjustment Inventory. This means that the girl students who come from the lowest income group had more adjustment problems and also psychosomatic disorders than the other groups.

The scores of Cornell Index test maintained a systematic order from the highest to the lowest (34.44 to 24.78) in accordance with the income order, i.e., from the lowest to the highest income. Though the adjustment scores of the four income groups did not maintain a decreasing order systematically the Cornell Index test scores maintain the order and support the hypothesis. The adjustment scores on the basis of income did not show much difference among the four income groups. The scores are in a zigzag manner. Therefore, the adjustment scores of the girls students are not in line with the income of their parents.

Table 5

Showing the distribution of Mean, SD, SEMs for different income groups on the Adjustment Inventory and Cornell Index test

Sl.No.	*Income*	*Code*	*N*	*Adjustment*			*Cornell Index*		
				Mean	*SD*	*SEM*	*Mean*	*SD*	*SEM*
1.	Below Rs.500	A	110	20.11	6.85	0.66	34.44	14.24	1.36
2.	Rs. 500 to 1,000	B	117	18.26	6.07	0.56	32.37	12.28	1.14
3.	Rs. 1,001 to 2,000	C	49	19.00	6.51	0.94	27.78	11.64	1.68
4.	Rs. 2,001 and above	D	23	19.78	6.06	1.26	24.78	10.38	2.21

The adolescent girl students who were drawn from four income groups have scored with considerable variation on the Cornell Index test indicating the presence of different levels of psychosomatic problems. The analysis of variance was applied to the scores to find out how far the groups differ among them in Cornell Index test. It is found that the groups differ (F - 7.30) at. 01 level which shows that the groups really differ in psychomatic problems (Table 6). Since the four income groups were found to be heterogeneous on the Cornell Index test it has further tried to see how far they differ from each other.

Table 6

Showing the analysis of variance for different income groups on the Cornell Index test.

Source of	*Sum of variation*	*df squares*	*Mean*	*FR.50 square*	*Level of sign.*
Between groups	3,697.62	3	1232.54		
				7.30	.01
Within groups	49,967.46	296	168.81		
Total		53665.08	299		

Table 7 shows the results of the test. It is found that groups A and C, A and D, B and D differ at 0.01 level and groups B and D differ from each other at. 05 levels. Groups A and B, C and D did not show much difference between them. The two low income groups have small difference between them. This means that the two high income groups go together and the two lowest income groups go together having a small difference between them on the basis of income. Therefore it may be stated that the girl students who come from high income groups are free from psychosomatic problems and the girl students who come from the lowest income groups are prone to more psychosomatic problems. Therefore the results further support the hypothesis (Table 7).

Table 7

Showing the critical ratios and the levels of significances for the difference income groups on the Cornell Index test

Sl.No.	*Group*	*Code*	*Mean*	*S.E of difference*	*C.R. mean difference*	*Level*
1.	Below Rs. 500	A				
			2.07	1.77	1.18	N.S.
	Rs. 501. to 1,000	B				
2.	Below Rs. 500	A				
			6.66	2.15	3.09	.01
	Rs. 1,001 to 2,000	C				
3.	Below Rs. 500	A				
			9.66	2.55	3. 79	.01
	Rs. 2,000 and above	D				
4.	501 to 1,000	B				
			4.59	2.01	2.28	.05
	Rs. 1,001 to 2,000	C				
5.	50 to 1000	B				
			7.59	2.44	3.11	.01
	Rs. 2,001 and above	D				
6.	1001 to 2000	C				
			3.00	2.76	1.09	N.S.
	Rs. 2,000 and above	D				

One of the important hypotheses verified in this study is that students' cultural backgrounds (communities) are found to have an influence upon their adjustment and psychosomatic problems. That is, the students of forward communities are well adjusted and free from psychosomatic problems whereas the students of backward and scheduled caste communities are prone to more adjustment and psychosomatic problems.

The adolescent girl students at the higher secondary schools are drawn from different cultural groups, and the cultural groups belong to varied socioeconomic status. In this study the three cultural groups included are the forward community, backward community and the scheduled caste community. These three cultural groups have certain advantages and disadvantages. The forward community people generally belong to the highest socioeconomic status and they are economically in better positions, whereas the scheduled caste people belong to the lower socioeconomic status and economically poor. The socioeconomic status of the backward community people is moderate. The girls who were born and brought up in such cultural backgrounds were tested with Adjustment Inventory and Cornell Index test and the scores are given in Table 8.

Table 8
Showing the distribution of mean scores, SD, SEM of the three cultural group girl students on the Adjustment Inventory and Cornell Index test

Sl.No	*Community*	*Code*	*N*	*Adjustment*			*Cornell Index*		
				Mean	*SD*	*SEM*	*Mean*	*SD*	*SEM*
1.	Forward community	A	42	17.88	6.91	1.06	26.10	11.40	2.09
2.	Backward community	B	144	19.15	6.41	0.54	32.25	14.19	1.19
3.	Scheduled community	C	114	21.11	6.29	0.60	35.48	14.62	1.38

As presumed, the scores of the forward community students were low in both the tests, 17.88 in Adjustment Inventory and 26.10 in Cornell Index indicating the least problems in both the areas. But the scheduled caste students scored the highest (21.11) and (35.48) in both the tests. They have more adjustment problems and psychosomatic problems. The backward community students scored moderately indicating that they have problems but not so severe. The test results show that the cultural backgrounds have definite influence upon the adolescent girl students' day-to-day affairs. Therefore the hypothesis is accepted.

All the three cultural groups differ in the adjustment and psychosomatic problems. To what extent the three groups differ among themselves was tested with the analysis of variance. The F-ratio 6.70 is significant at. 01 level (Table 9). Therefore the three cultural groups vary in their problems significantly. The test of analysis of variance has revealed that the three cultural groups were heterogeneous in nature with regard to the psychosomatic problems as revealed by the Cornell Index test. Therefore it is further tried to see the extensity of the difference between the groups by working out the critical ratios.

Table 9
Showing the analysis of variance of the scores of three cultural group students on Cornell Index test

Source of variation	*Sum of squares*	*df*	*Mean square*	*F-Ratio*	*Level of sign.*
Between groups	2,741.83	2	1,370.92		
				6.70	.01
Within groups.	60,835.08	297	204.83		
Total		63,576.91	299		

Table 10 shows the critical ratios between the groups. It is found that groups A and B, A and C differ significantly at. 01 level. But the groups 13 and C did not show significant difference. The difference is greater between the forward community and backward community and between the forward community and the scheduled caste community. The forward community students who were enjoying certain advantages socially and economically differentiate themselves from the other two groups, particularly from the scheduled caste community students who were socially disadvantaged and economically impoverished and because of this scheduled caste community girls were more prone to adjustment and psychosomatic disorders.

Table 10
Showing the critical ratios and the level of significance of the scores of three cultural group students on Cornell Index test.

Sl.No		*Group*	*Code*	*Mean difference*	*S.E. of Mean difference*	*C.R. Level of sign.*
1.	Forward community	A				
			6.16	2.38	2.59	.01
	Backward community	B				
2.	Forward community scheduled caste community	C	9.40	3.59	4.80	.01
3.	Backward community scheduled caste community	8	4.23	1.91	1.89	N.S.

Attempt also has been made in this study to find out the specific psychosomatic illness mostly suffered by the adolescent girl students and the number of cases in each. It is observed that out of 300 girls 70 reported that they were often suffering from fever, 57 reported of headache, 47 stomach pain, 38 cold, 20 chest pain, 16 stomach ulcer, 14 tooth pain and cough, 13 fits and 11 eye defects. Out of 300 adolescent girls 232 reported that they were often suffering from fever headache, stomach pain, cold and chest pain. It can be seen that 77.3 per cent of the girls were often suffering from these five psychosomatic illnesses (Table 11).

Table 11

Showing the number of cases and the percentages of the girl students and the type of psychosomatic and other illnesses suffered by them.

S.No.	*Illness suffered.*	*No. of girls.*	*Percentage.*	*Mean score in CMI test*
1.	Headache	57	19.00	38.47
2.	Stomach pain	47	15.67	33.79
3.	Fever	70	23.33	32.38
4.	Cold	38	12.67	31.63
5.	Stomach ulcer	16	5.33	27.38
6.	Tooth pain	14	4.67	29.79
7.	Cough	14	4.67	31.29
8.	Chest pain	20	6.67	32.95
9.	Fits	13	4.33	30.69
10.	Eye defect	11	3.67	29.36

It is also observed that the girls who were exposed to various illnesses also scored high on the Cornell Index test showing that they have more psychosomatic problems. They have scored high on headache (38.47), stomach pain (33.79), fever (32.38), cold (31.63), cough (31.29), chest pain (32.29), fits (30.69). This shows that the adolescent girl students in rural and semi-urban areas were often prone to these types of psychosomatic illnesses. A separate study must be designed to find out the root cause of this and the levels of seriousness of the psychosomatic illnesses.

Discussion

The higher secondary education is an intermediate stage in between the high school education and the college education. The students who go to the higher secondary schools are normally between 15 and 17 years of age. In this investigation the age of the students ranged from 15 to 19 years. This shows that some of the students either might have started their school life late by two or three years or might have failed in two or four classes once. The higher secondary school period is the period of prime adolescence and often subjected to the emergence of problems. Particularly the girls who are studying in higher secondary schools, often express all types of feelings and emotions, show different levels of reactions to situations and develop different kinds of problems. They also complain of some kind of pains and illness and parents have anxieties as to how to deal with them. The adolescent girl students often face adjustment problems and also become emotional. These may contribute to several types of psychosomatic illnesses.

Therefore this is an attempt to study the adjustment problems in relation to psychosomatic disorders among the adolescent girls studying in higher secondary schools in semi-urban and certain rural areas. The hypothesis that there is positive association between adjustment problems and psychosomatic disorders is verified and it is found to be significant at. 01 level. Those adolescent girls who have adjustment problems have also developed psychosomatic disorders. Those who had no problems were free from psychosomatic disorders.

The maladjusted girl students or those girls who had more adjustment problems were also found to be emotionally upset. Such frequent instances might become the cause of psychosomatic illnesses. The hypothesis based on this was accepted as the results were highly significant. Among the three groups (well adjusted, moderately adjusted and maladjusted) the well-adjusted girls were found to be emotionally stable and were with least psychosomatic disorders, whereas the maladjusted girls had more emotional stress and severe psychosomatic disorders. The moderately adjusted group had some emotional upsets and moderate psychosomatic problems.

Therefore it may be stated that in the case of adolescent girl students more adjustment problems, more emotional instability or stress and severe psychosomatic disorders go together. The psychosomatic disorders may be stated as the consequence of the adolescent girls' maladjustment and severe emotional stress. It is also interesting to see that these three groups differ from each other significantly at various levels of psychosomatic disorders (Tables 2 and 4). This is one of the important results borne out by this enquiry.

In one of the studies conducted at Annamalai University (1984) it was observed that the students who participate in games and sports, when emotionally maladjusted developed psychosomatic disorders. The economic status or the financial positions of the families were not without any effect in the adjustment problems and psychosomatic disorders of the adolescent girls. The study revealed that girls from affluent families were better adjusted and had the least psychosomatic disorders than those girls who came from impoverished families. This study also has highlighted that the lower the income the higher the psychosomatic disorders were and the higher income the lower the problems and this result was found to be significant at 0.01 level (Table 5). Generally the adolescent students are highly sensitive and critical to life events. Girls from poor families go to schools with great difficulties and in the midst many domestic problems. They will have to do all the household works, take care of the younger ones, take care of themselves, go to the schools, which are far away from home, in time and also do their homework. Because of these they cannot do better in schools as they are always in a tense state and easily susceptible to psychosomatic illnesses. But this is not the case with the girls who come from affluent families. Therefore they can do better in school work as they keep themselves emotionally stable and free from psychosomatic illnesses.

The cultural factors also play important role in determining the level of problems in the life of girls. The community hierarchy maintains the same order in all aspects of life. The forward community is enjoying a social status and also economic advantages over the other two communities. The economic and social status have certain psychological consequences also. This is revealed in the adjustment problems of the cultural groups. Among the three the forward, backward and the scheduled caste communities the last two are economically and socially backward. It is observed in this study that they are also psychologically backward. The scheduled caste community students scored the highest on both the Adjustment Inventory (21.11) and on Cornell Index test (35.48) showing that they have more adjustment problems as well as more psychosomatic illnesses. They differ from the other two groups significantly. The forward community students scored the lowest in both the tests (17.88 and 26.10) indicating that they have the adjustment and psychosomatic problems the least. The backward community girls fall in between the two.

The reason for the forward community girls to have the problems the least, may be that they are economically and socially well placed and they enjoy certain status in the society, whereas the scheduled caste community people will have to depend upon others for their work and living. Also the girls of this community might have developed worries and anxieties because of their economic and social deprivations. This must be the cause for the development of more adjustment problems and psychosomatic disorders. The backward community also has some advantage over the scheduled caste community. Most of them also may have some inherited property and they are in a better financial position and therefore they are not so much prone to psychosomatic disorders seriously. A somewhat similar study was conducted by Bansal (1973) involving high caste and scheduled caste adolescent students' adjustment problems. He found that the high caste Hindu students were better adjusted than the scheduled caste community students. The results of Bansal's study are quite similar to the results of the present study with regard to adjustment problems.

The adolescent girl students often complain of illness of some kind. Most of them were found to be psychosomatic illnesses (Table 11). In this study it was found that 232 adolescent girl students out of 300 have reported that they were often suffering from feaver (70), headache (57), stomach pain (47), cold (38), chest pain (20). They were also suffering from stomach ulcer (16), tooth pain (14), cough (14) fits (13) and eye defects (11). It can be seen that 77.3 per cent of the girls were often suffering from the first five psychosomatic illnesses. These results show that adolescent girls from semi-urban and rural areas were often prone to psychosomatic illnesses.

The adolescent period in the case of girls is more problematic than the boys for the parents and others. Incidents are occurring every day that the adolescent girls run away from homes on some pretext. The cause was not actually understood by the parents. At the later adolescent period even though sex and the love affair may be very virulent and may result in elopements, the girls never realise what their real problems are.

This is a systematic study on semi-urban and rural adolescent school girls who were between 15 and 19 years of age, reveal that they all have some kind of psychosomatic illnesses. It is very essential that the adolescent girls from the age of 15 to 19 should be given personal counselling by the school psychologists as the girls at this level are highly imaginative and often have daydreams about sex and about their future life.

Conclusions

The following are the conclusions of the present. study and some of them are new results and not found in any of the earlier studies.

1. There is a positive association between adjustment problems and psychosomatic disorders in the case of adolescent girl students.
2. The well-adjusted adolescent girls students are emotionally stable and the least prone to psychosomatic disorders. The maladjusted girl students are emotionally unstable and more prone to psychosomatic disorders.
3. Parents' economic status has a definite impact upon the adolescent girls' problems. The higher the income the better the adjustment and the least psychosomatic disorders; the lower the income the more adjustment problems and more psychosomatic disorders.
4. The adolescent girl students from the forward community are well adjusted and have least psychosomatic disorders whereas the girls from the scheduled caste community have more adjustment and psychosomatic problems.
5. Most of the adolescent girls were suffering from some kind of psychosomatic illnesses. The more prevalent illnesses were fever, headache, stomach pain, cold, chest pain and stomach ulcer.

References

Alexander, F., Fundamental Concepts of Psychosomatic Research, Psychogenesis, Conversion, Specifiaty, *Psychosoms. Med:* 1943, 5, 205-210.

Bansal, J.P., A Study of the Adjustment Differences among the Scheduled Caste and High Caste Hindu adolescents, *Educational and Psychological Research Journal,* 1973 Vol. 1 (1), 39-41.

Brar J.S., The Adjustment Problems Faced by the Higher Secondary School Students, *Journal of Educational Research and Extention,* 1973, Vol. 9 (4), 202-208.

Clausen, J.A., Metron, R.K., and Nirbert, R.A., *Contemporary Social Problems,* New York, HarCourt, 1966.

Coleman, J.C., *Abnormal Psychology and Modern Life,* New York: Scott Foresman Inc., 1966.

Coleman, J.C. and Broen, W.E., *Abnormal Psychology and Modern Life,* Bombay: D.B. Taraporevala Sons & Co. Private Ltd., 1974.

Faire - Weather, G.W., *Social Psychology in Treating Mental Illness: An Experimental Approach,* New York: Wiley, 1964.

Fenichel, O., Problems of Psychoanalytic technique, parts, *Psychoanal Qusrt,* 1939, 8, 1-4.

Fredenberg, F.A., *The Psychology of Personality Adjustment,* California: Gunninage Publishing Co., 1971, 151-152.

Garner, A.M. and Wenar, G., *The mother-child interaction in psychosomatic disorders,* Urbana: University of illinois Press, 1959.

Glover, E., Penichel, O., Strachey, J., Bergler, E. Nunberg, E., and Bibring, E., Symposium on the theory of the therapeutic results of psychoanalysis, *Int. J. Psychoanal,* 1937.

Halliday, J.L. Concepts of a psychosomatic affection, *Lancet,* 1943, 6, 205-210.

Heymans, Wiersma and Good-Stein, L.D., *Personality Assessment,* New York: John Wiley and Sons Inc., 1971.

Hilgard, R.E., Atkinson, R.C. and Atkinson, R.L. *Introduction to Psychology,* New York: Harcourt Brace Javannovich Inc., 1971.

Hoch, Amsolen and Goodstein, L.D., *Personality Assessment*, New York: John Wiley and Sons Inc., 1971.

Hurlock, E.B., *Child Development,* Tokyo: McGraw-Hill, Kogakhusha Ltd., 1978.

Karen H.W. and Weitz, J., *An Introduction to Psychology*, New York: John Wiley and Sons Inc., 1955.

Langner, T.S., *Normative Behaviour and Emotional Adjustment.*

Lazarus, R.S., *Patterns of Adjustment,* New York: McGraw-Hill Book Company, 1961.

Liebert, R.M. Poulos, R.W. and Stranss, G.D., *Developmental Psychology*, Englewood Cliffs, New Jersey: Prentice Hall, Inc., 1954.

Lindgren, H.C. and Marie, J., Emotional problem off over and under achieving children in a Brazilian elementary school, *Journal of Genetic Psychology*, 1965.

Mangal, S.K., *Abnormal Psychology*, New Delhi: Sterling Publishers Private Ltd., 1984.

Mead, M., *Coming of age insoma*, New York: Marrow, 1928.

Reiser, M.P., Emotional stress and the precipitation of congestive heart failure, *Psychosom. Med.,* 1953, 15, 38-60.

Samraj, P. and Rajamanickam, M. Neuropsychiatric and Psychosomatic symptoms in athletes and non-athletes, *Indian Journal of Community Guidance Service*, 1984, Vo1.12, 55-63.

Sawrey, J.M., and Telford, C.W., *Psychology of Adjustment*, 3rd Edn. Boston: Alllyn & Bacon, 1971.

Shaffer, L.E., and Shoben, B.I., *The Personality of Adjustment*, London: Constable and Co., 1956.

Sinha, A.K.P. and Singh, R.P., Adjustment inventory for school students, *Indian Psychological Review,* 1968, Vol. 5 (1), 46-47.

Smith K.V., and Smith, W.H., *The Behaviour of Man: Introduction to Psychology,* Holt: Rineheart and Winston, Inc., 1958.

Stalker, E., The psychosomatic diseases: a hypothetical formulation, *J. Ment. Sci.* 1950, 06: 355-368.

Swanton, J.R., An Indian Social Experiment and Some of Its Lessons, *Scientist,* 1930, Vol. 41, 368-376.

Weider A., Wolff, H.G., Broadman, K., Mittleman. B., Wechsler, D. *Cornell Index Inventory*, New York: The Psychological Corporation, 1949.

Wells, In Lanyon, R.I. and Good Stein, L.D., *Personality of Assessment,* New York: John Wiley and Sons, Inc., 1971.

Wile, IRA. S. *American Journal of Orthopsychiatry,* 10, 216-228.

Wolff, H.G., *Life Situations, Emotions and Bodily Disease Feelings and Emotions,* Remert, New York: McGraw-Hill, 1950.

CHAPTER 4

Adjustment Problems of High and Low Aspirant Adolescents

Ravi Sandhu

The purpose of the present study was to assess whether there was any positive association between the adolescents' level of aspiration and their adjustment problems, and also to find out the difference in adjustment problems of the high and low aspirant boys and girls and also to see whether the adjustment problems of boys and girls had any difference. The sample of the study consisted of 150 male and female students studying in twelfth standard of the selected schools of Agra city. Adjustment Inventory for college students and Aspiration Measure were used for collecting data. Results indicated that there was no relationship between adjustment problems and the aspiration of the boys and girls. There was no difference in the adjustment of high aspirant boys and high aspirant girls. There was also no difference between boys and girls in the adjustment of low aspirants.

Introduction

Adjustment refers to the smooth relationship between the individual and the environment and interacting in a harmonious way with the world in which he or she lives. Every individual has certain need and desires which may be externally imposed or internally aspired. These needs and desires have to be fulfilled if a person wants to lead a satisfactory life. As Lindergren and Marie (1965) have said adjustment means the person must accommodate himself in order to meet certain demands of the environment.

Adjustment means an effective adaptation to the environment, both external and internal which also includes conformity to group norms, mores, ideals values and so on (Abraham 1968). Thus adjustment is a process which goes on all the time and by which an individual tries to maintain physiological and psychological equilibrium and motivates himself towards the goal of self-enhancement.

A state of good adjustment is one in which the needs of a person and the demands of the environment are adequately satisfied. These needs and demands vary from person to person and in the same person from situation to situation. A school-going student is confronted with demands of success in school from at least four sources, i.e., home, school, society and self. These demands and expectations from the four sources may or may not be identical. Every child will make an effort to fulfil the demands of all four sources. The nature of adjustment made by the child will depend to a great degree on how for he has been successful in fulfilling the demands and expectations imposed on him. The three environmental demands may vary and the child has to learn, in his process of adjustment, to acquire appropriate responses for each situation. The lesser the difference between the demands and achievements the better the adjustment. If becomes the goal of the adolescent to fulfil the demands and thus he begins to aspire. In this competitive world an adolescent aspires for many things. He aspires for better marks, he aspires for admission to a course of his choice, he aspires for an affluent vocation. In fact there is a never-ending list of aspirations of an adolescent and thereby begins his struggle for adjustment.

Aspiration is an ego involved goal that a person sets for himself. The more ego involved in his aspirations the more they relate to areas of behaviour and simultaneously effect his adjustment.

In the day-to-day life situation, we as human beings tend to aspire for higher and higher status. Thus with the change in aspiration, whether they are imposed by the person himself or imposed by the society, the adjustment of the person will be affected. The type of adjustment he is going to make will affect to a greater extent the goal seeking behaviour. Thus it may be assumed that aspiration level which is an independent variable is likely to influence the adjustment of the boys and girls

Based on these problems the following null hypotheses have been formulated and tested in this study:

1. There is no significant positive association between the aspiration level and the adjustment of the school students

2. There is no significant difference between the boys and girls of high aspirants in their adjustment in the areas of home, health, social, emotional, and educational aspects.
3. There is no significant difference between the boys and girls of love aspirant in their adjustment in the areas of home, health, social, emotional and educational aspects.

Method

Sample: The sample consisted of 150 boys and girls studying in the intermediate colleges of Agra city, randomly drawn from the selected Institutions. The institutions were selected by lottery technique: It was a multistage random sambling technique purposely planned and drawn for this study.

Since all the boys and girls were studying in twelfth standard the educational level, age, environmental factors, and the socioeconomic status were all kept constant.

Material: The following two test materials were used for the collection of data.

1. *Adjustment Inventory for College Students (AICS):* This was constructed by Sinha and Singh (1971). This was used to identify the adjustment level of the boys and girls in different areas (Health, Home, Social, Emotional, Educational). The test contains 120 items, Maximum score obtained is 120 and lowest is zero. A high score is indicative of more maladjustment and a low score shows better adjustment.
2. *Level of Aspiration Scale:* This was prepared and revised by Shah and Bhargava (1987). This was used to measure the level of aspiration of students. This test has performance sheets which are used by the subjects. The level of aspiration is measured in terms of goal discrepancy score. The extent and difference between actual score on the previous trial and goal set up in the next trial is known as goal discrepancy. The total performance sheets are eleven. The duration for performing each trial is fixed. The level of aspiration is measured in terms of goal discrepancy. The highest score obtained is +5 and the lowest –5.

Procedure: After the random selection of institutions, the elements of the sample were also selected randomly. The investigator contacted the students in their respective classes and administered the tests, giving a break of 15 minutes between the two tests to avoid monotony.

The level of aspiration was administered to the students first. The high and low aspirants were identified by applying quartile Q1 and Q3. The nature of scoring is such that a high score indicates a high aspiration and a low score indicates a low aspiration. Students whose level of aspiration score fell above the computed Q3 value were considered high aspirants and those whose level of aspiration score fell below the computed Q1 value were the low aspirants for the present study.

Results and Discussion

The first hypothesis of the study was that there is no significant positive association between adjustment and aspiration of high aspirant boys and girls and low aspirant boys and girls. To test this hypothesis the scores of adjustment and aspiration were correlated. Table - 1 shows the correlation values and indicates that there is no significant association between aspiration and adjustment as the obtained correlation values are not statistically significant (0.14).

Table 1
Showing the correlation coefficient between the scores of adjustment Inventory and the scores of level of aspiration scale

	Variables	*N*	*r*	*Significance*
1)	Level of Aspiration	150	.14	N.S
2)	Adjustment			

From the table it is clear that the coefficient of correlation. 14 between the two variables is indicative of very poor association between the two. Similar results have been obtained by Bajaj (1979), who found that the level of aspiration was not significantly related with adjustment. Similarly, Shaffer and Shoben (1956) said, "Adjustment is a process by which living organism maintains a balance between its need and the circumstances that influence the satisfaction of need." On the other hand, the circumstances influencing these needs can either be inside the individual or outside the individual. Factors within the individual are his physical, mental states, aptitude, attitude, interest etc., which emphasize the desire to improve or to rise above one's present status. The environmental factors, such as social reward, reinforcement from parents and competition with sibling increases his/her desire to become more ambitious.

It is also a parents' desire that their children should have some high goals and aspirations by knowing their demands and, desires, set certain goals, which may or may not be within his/ her reach. That is why, the impact of these goals does not affect their adjustment in the society, because their need of adjustment in the society is stronger than the one to achieve some goals Here adjustment becomes the primary need and to aspirate is their secondary need for them. They want to conform to standards which have been set by the society for them. So it seems easier for them to make adjustment in their surrounding rather than the attainment of same goals they had aspired.

Thus the first hypothesis of the study, that there is no significant relationship between the level of aspiration and adjustment of high aspirant boys and girls and low aspirant boys and girls, is accepted.

The second hypothesis states that there is no significant difference in the adjustment of high aspirant boys and girls in the areas of home health, social, emotional and educational adjustment. To test the hypothesis two Q1 and Q3 were computed, and the students, whose aspiration scores fell below the computed Q1 value, were considered as low aspirants and those whose aspiration scores were above the computed Q3 value were considered as high aspirants. Students, whose level of aspiration scores were above Q1 and below Q3 were not considered for testing hypothesis two and three.

Table 2

Showing the t values of adjustment level of high aspirant boys and girls

	Adjustment	*High Aspirant Boys*		*High Aspirant Girls*		*t Value*
		Mean	*SD*	*Mean*	*SD*	
a)	Home	4.1	2,22	4.83	2.21	1.02
b)	Health	3.025	2.32	4.44	1.92	2.02
c)	Social	8.2	2.67	7.44	1,36	1.13
d)	Emotional	11.55	4.54	13.94	4.04	1.71
e)	Educational	6.5	2.83	7 33	2.16	1.02

Table 2 reveals that the 't' values of adjustment in home, health, social, emotional and educational areas are 1.02, 2.02, 1.13, 1.71, and 1.02 respectively and all these values are insignificant. This leads to the inference that there is no significant difference in the adjustment of high aspirant boys and girls in any area of adjustment studied. That is to say, that the adjustment level as well as sex variables together also do not affect the adjustment level in areas of home, health, social, emotional and educational. The scores show that adjustment of adolescents in the area of home was found moderate. This shows that high aspirant boys and girls both have the same type of adjustment at home. It can be said that this is due to the changing lifestyle, values and attitudes of parents as well as of adolescents. In the modern time both the sexes are treated equally and are provided the same opportunities and facilities at home as well as outside the home. Girls of today are not neglected and ignored at home and in society. Both are equally motivated by their parents to achieve certain goals. Similar changes are also evident in the attitude of boys. Now they share the responsibilities of home which was earlier left for only the girls. Hence it can said that this is perhaps the reason that there is no significant difference of high aspirant boys and girls in the adjustment at home.

Both boys and girls shows moderate adjustment in the area of education showing no significant differences. In our present education system, the abilities of an individual are of profound importance and opportunities are provided to those who are deserving. In the present hypothesis both boys and girls were high aspirants, that is, there was a strong desire in both the sexes to achieve their goal. Both groups face probably equal number and nature of educational problems as well as success and failure. They perhaps even solve their problem in a like manner. There are very few environmental differences due to the homogeneity of the sample. Also, an important variable is that their aspiration was controlled, which has a profound influence on the interrelated facts. They faced a similar nature and a similar degree of frustrations and satisfaction, which has probably resulted in no difference in adjustment in the area of education. The aspiration level can affect one's goals as well as the amount of hard work that one wants to put to achieve these goals. This group, as stated earlier, had a similar aspiration level, therefore the nature of adjustment was also similar for reasons stated above.

The social adjustment of high aspirant boys and girls is also not significantly different. Now in such a changing period of time the girls and boys both are exposed to a greater stimulating environment of the society. Girls do not live quietly in the four walls of the house.

Both sexes participate in social and cultural functions. There is no area in the society where the girls are not giving their contributions. Both of them have to face similar types of problems although the nature of the problems may be slightly different due to sex differences. These differences are not grave and are treated by people in authority almost on an equal footing. A similar level of pressure is exercised on them to achieve the standards.

Results show that emotional adjustment of adolescents is not significantly different, since in this group both are high aspirant and both boys and girls are striving to attain their goals. Hence, to achieve their goals, they have to make emotional balance to adjust in the society. Both sexes experience varying degrees of anxiety concerning his/her level of aspiration. Each child is affected emotionally by the level of his aspiration and thereby his success and failure, in attainment of these goals. Society now places almost identical demands on them as far as their emotional expression and emotional control are concerned. A girl too now wants to show the society that she is emotionally mature and can deal with emotions calmly without letting the whole world know about her emotional state.

Since both the sexes were high aspirants it is likely that many of the situations which lead to emotionality would be alike. The demands of the society will of course be alike as stated earlier. Cohen (1954) has stated that goal setting is not related to a feeling of adequacy but related to one's feeling of acceptance. That is to say, goal setting behaviour will be affected by his/her readiness to achieve the goal or by accepting the goal, that the aspirations are not affected by the emotional inadequacy, which again accounts for the reason of the present result.

Adjustment of high aspirant boys and girls in the area of health adjustment is also not significantly different. The marked physical and emotional growth of adolescents results in strains that frequently precipitate stress and anxiety, as reflected in physiological, psychological and social behaviour. The nutrition of the adolescents is affected by these and other growth characteristics during this period. The result may be overweight or underweight. Studies of nutrition indicate that older boys and girls have poor food habits and the least satisfactory nutritional status. Both boys as well as girls, in order to maintain a good figure, undergo a rigid diet and thus fail to get the desired nutrients for maintaining optimum health.

Thus, it is felt that health adjustment is affected to a greater degree by other factors, such as a desire to look attractive and appealing and it is found almost in equal intensity in both sexes. Thus the second hypothesis that there is no significant difference in the adjustment of high aspirant boys and girls is accepted.

The third hypothesis states that there is no significant difference in the adjustment of low aspirant boys and low aspirant girls in the areas of home, health, social, emotion and education. To test this hypothesis mean, the standard deviation and 't' values were calculated which are evident from Table 3.

Table 3
Showing the 't' values of adjustment level of low aspirant boys and girl

Adjustment	*Low aspirant boys*		*Low aspirant girls*		*'t'*
areas	*Mean*	*SD*	*Mean*	*SD*	*Value*
Home	4.25	2.69	5.22	3.52	.95
Health	4.03	1.71	5.22	2.93	1.5
Social	7.2	2.28	7.5	2.27	.41
Emotional	10.8	3.21	15.0	5.97	2.67*
Educational	4.9	2.49	7.44	2.92	2.88**

** Significant at. 01 level. * Significant at. 05 level.

The results shows that there is a significant differences in boys and girls only in two areas of adjustment. The obtained 't' values are 2.67 and 2.88 for emotional and educational adjustment and are significant at. 05 &. 01 level respectively. In the remaining areas of adjustment, that is, adjustment at home, health and society, the low aspirant boys and girls did not differ significantly, indicating that the boys and girls having low level of aspiration did not differ in their adjustment.

This indicates that both aspiration level and sex variables affect only two areas of adjustment, that is, adjustment in emotional and educational areas and the remaining three areas of adjustment are not effected by sex and aspiration level.

The adjustment of low aspirant boys and girls in the area of education is significantly different. In the present study boys and girls are both low aspirant. Hence, we can say that both do not have high goals, desires, aims and ambitions. However, the scores indicate that both are making moderate to good adjustment in the area of emotion.

If we speak in the Indian context, it may be said that low aspirant girls do not have high goals and ambitions and their ultimate goal is not to build their career but to get the academic qualification, so as to be called literate. They accept their academic position whatever they obtain and do not bother about their performance in the education area.

Boys also fall in the same situation but the superior adjustment of boys as compared to that of girls is perhaps due to the fact that boys rely more heavily and are affected to a greater extent by their level of aspiration than girls. That is to say, that the level of aspiration is perhaps a stronger driving force in boys than in girls. This is the most important reason in the view of the investigator but other factors cannot be overruled

The adjustment of low aspiration boys and girls in the area of emotion is significantly different. There is a tendency of the individuals that when they fail to achieve some goal, they become disappointed and discouraged. When a person faces constant failures, it is likely to affect the self concept of the person. Hence, it is of great importance, how low aspiration effects the emotional adjustment of boys and girls separately. Although both sexes are likely to face emotional problem of equal number and intensity, yet due to their masculine and feminine characteristics, each of them reacts in his/her own sex-appropriate way. Girls generally are sensitive and submissive in nature and therefore become more introvert, submissive and tolerant. They feel more stress and anxiety but have a great tolerance for the same. Boys react to all these situations in their own way. They express their deep feelings of anxiety, frustration and mental tensions by covert or overt forms of behaviour such as brooding, moodiness, restlessness, aggression, distraction, hostility and antisocial behaviour. Therefore, it can be said that there is a significant difference in the emotional adjustment of low aspirant boys and girls.

Adjustment of low aspirant boys and girls in the area of home, social are not significantly different. Frank (1935) studied that low aspirants are generally from the poor family background, low socioeconomic status, poor parental education and occupation and were the victims of unrealistic aspirations.

Gould (1938), Sears (1940), Halt (1946) studied that by such phenomena of personality, the child may take a defensive attitude, blaming others for his failure or blaming their poor health or lack of training, may become discouraged, give up their goals and maybe substitute daydreams of success for attempts to achieve real success. Similarly Gruen (1945), Halt (1946), and Taylor (1952) found that this uncertainty causes the child to be unsure of himself. All these factors will affect the social and home adjustment of both sexes similarly. Ultimately they will be more submissive in their attitude towards others. All of these contribute to poor self-concept with poor adjustment and unhappiness on the child's part.

The effect of all these adverse conditions will be the same on the individual, whether it may be girl or boy. Hence both of them feel insecure, lack inspirations and receive low appreciation from parents as well as society. Therefore due to a similar impact, the two groups did not show significant difference in the social and home adjustment.

Adjustment of low aspirant boy and girls in the area of health is not significantly different. Hereby, it can be said that whether the aspiration is low or high it does not make any difference on the part of adolescents. Perhaps there are other more important factors which affect health adjustment rather than aspiration and sex.

Thus the third hypothesis that there is no significant difference in the adjustment of low aspirant boys and girls is accepted with reference to there areas of adjustment (home, health and social) and rejected with reference to two areas of adjustment (emotional and educational).

Conclusion

Results indicate that there is no relationship between adjustment and aspiration of boys and girls. There is no difference in the adjustment of high aspirant and low aspirant boys and girls.

References

Abraham, P.A., An analytic and academic achievement of secondary school pupils PhD. Thesis Trivandrum; Kerala University, 1968.

Beyey, L., A study of test anxiety adjustment, level of aspiration in relation to scholastic attainment M. Ed. Dissertation Agra University, 1979.

Cohere, L D., Level of Aspiration, behaviour and feeling of adequacy and self acceptance. *Journal of Abnormal and Social Psychology,* 1954 49, 84-86

Frank, J. D., Some psychological determinants of level of Aspiration, *America Journal of Psychology,* (1935).

Gould, R., Factors Underlying Expressed Live of Aspiration, *Journal of Psychology,* 1938 6, 265-279.

Holt, R., R Level of Aspiration, Ambition or Defence, *Journal of Experimental Psychology,* 1946 36, 398-410.

Lindergren, M.C. and Marie, J., Emotional problems of over and under achieving children in Brazilian Elementary School, *Journal of Genetic Psychology*, 1965.

Sears, P.S., Level of Aspiration in Academically Successful and Unsuccessful Children, *Journal of Abnormal Social Psychology* 1940, 39, 498-536

Shaffer, L. F. and Shoben B. J., *The Psychology of Adjustment,* 2nd Edition, Boston, Houghton Mifflins, (1956).

Shah, M A. and Bhargava, M., *Level of Aspiration Measure,* National Psychological Corporation Agra, 1983

Sinha, A.K. and Singh, R. P., *Adjustment Inventory for College Students*, National Psychological Corporation, Agra (1992).

Taylor, C. and Comb, A.W., Self acceptance and adjustment, *Journal of Consult Psychology 1952*, 16, 89-91.

CHAPTER 5

Adjustment and Creativity among Adolescents through High School Years

C.B. Asha

The present study investigates the relationship between adjustment and creativity among adolescent girls. The Tests of Creative Thinking Abilities and Adjustment Inventories were administered on 510 boys and 590 girls from 24 secondary schools. The results show that creativity facilitates good adjustment.

Adjustment, generally means an effective adaptation to the environment, both external and internal, including conformity to group norms, mores, ideals, values and so on (Abraham, 1968). According to Mouly (1968) adjustment is the process by means of which the individual seems to maintain physiological and psychological equilibrium and propel himself toward self-enhancement. It represents the quality of an individual's behaviour in relation to his interpersonal relations (Fradson, 1961). A well adjusted person, according to Chronbach (1954), is one who commits himself to socially desirable goals and uses his energies effectively in working towards them. He has a sense of security and feeling of adequacy which grow out of his feelings of belonging, being desired and appreciated.

A careful perusal of the available literature suggests that creative children cannot be expected to attain this level of adjustment so long as their creative potentialities are not properly recognised, approved, appreciated or encouraged. A large number of studies reveal that because creative children differ from the general population and creativity is fostered only under certain conditions and circumstances, they encounter numerous problems of adjustment (Greencare, 1958; Holland, 1961; Torrance, 1961, 1962, 1963 and 1971; Mac Kinnon, 1961, 1962 and 1963; Garwood, 1964; Garfield, Cohen and Roth,

1969; Schaefer, 1969; Singer and Rummo, 1973). The factors that operate to produce problems for them may be personal, familial, educational or social. Most of these factors are also found to have their origin in the relationship of the creative children with their associates —parents, teachers, sibblings, classmates and friends, in the nature of the organisations to which they belong, in the kind of supervision they have, etc.

A few earlier attempts (Laycock 1933; Roc, 1946; etc.) to relate creativity and adjustment, however, have yielded contradictory results. These researchers have reported that superior children make superior adjustment. The view that creativity is a sign of optimal adjustment is supported by the works of Rogers (1954), Anastasi (1958), Kirk (1962), Bloom (1963), and Wallach and Kogan (1965). Findings reported by Gupta (1975), Singh (1977), Sinha and Sharma (1978), Asha (1978, 1980 and 1984) and Singh (1980) also tend to link creativity with good adjustment.

The present study to some extent is an attempt to replicate the previous research reported, but with a new frame of reference.

Method

Sample

The sample consists of 1,100 secondary school students from 24 schools in the Trivandrum Educational District in Kerala, India. These 24 schools are selected from a total number of 77 secondary schools in the district, giving proportional representations to (1) rural and urban schools, (2) boys, girls and coeducational schools and (3) government and private schools. The sample selected consists of 510 boys and 590 girls. The ages of the students range from 14 through 16 years.

Procedure

Malayalam adaptation of the Wallah and Kogan Tests of Creative Thinking Abilities (1975) were utilised in obtaining creativity indices of the subjects. TCTA consisted of five sub-tests of which three are verbal (Instances, Alternate uses and Similarities) and two are non-verbal (Pattern-Meanings and Line-Meanings) in nature.

In order to obtain measures of adjustment subjects were given (1) Two Scales of An Adjustment Inventory viz., Home Adjustment and Social Adjustment (Rajalakshmi, 1968) (2) School Adjustment

Inventory (Abraham, 1968) and (3) Personal Adjustment Inventory (Asha, 1978). The Personal Adjustment Inventory consists of two parts A and B, Part A, emphasising adjustment concerning situational aspects and Part B, emphasising adjustment to personality characteristics.

The tests and inventories were administered to the students during regular class sessions.

Scoring

All the items in the five sub-tests of the TCTA were scored both for 'number' and 'uniqueness' of responses. The number scores refer to the total number of responses given by a subject for each stimulus material in each subtest. A subject's total score for a particular subtest consists of the sum of responses to all the items comprising that subtest. In the present study 'uniqueness' was defined as the response to a given item that is offered by not more than one per cent of the subjects in the whole sample. A subject's total score for uniquess for a particular subtest consists of the sum of his/her unique responses to all the items comprising that subtest.

Adjustment inventories were scored with keys prepared for each scale. Here a high score indicates unsatisfactory adjustment whereas a low score shows satisfactory adjustment.

Results and Discussion

The samples of boys and girls were classified into three groups, viz., highly creative, moderately creative and less creative. This was done by dividing the score distribution (total creativity) at the first and third quartiles. Thus, the subject who fell above Q3 constituted the highly creative group, those who fell below Q constituted the less creative group and those who fell between Ql and Q3 constituted the moderately creative group.

Table 1
Number of Subjects in Each Group

Creativity group	*Boys*	*Girls*	*Total*
Highly creative	226	28	254
Moderately creative	208	325	533
Less creative	76	237	313
Total	510	590	1100

This classification of the sample is given in Table 1. The scores obtained by the three groups on each of the different areas of adjustment were subjected to two-way analysis of variance with a view to study possible interactions if any.

The results given in Table 2 show significant F-ratios for sex in all but school adjustment. Significant effect for creativity is obtained in home adjustment only. The interaction effects are found not significant in all the cases.

The results show that highly creative, moderately creative and less creative groups of boys are more or less homogeneous with respect to social adjustment, school adjustment, adjustment to situational aspects and adjustment to personality characteristics. A similar trend is observed in the case of girls also. In home adjustment, the three groups of boys seem to differ among themselves. The highly creative group of boys show better home adjustment than their moderately creative and less creative peers. However no significant difference among the three groups of girls is observed.

In home and social adjustment and adjustment to personality characteristics significant differences are observed between moderately creative and less creative groups of girls. In the first two cases girls seem to be better adjusted whereas in adjustment concerning personality characteristics boys seem to be better adjusted.

Even though the results do not give a clear picture of the relationship between creativity and adjustment, they suggest that creative children are generally on the better rather than the poorer side with regard to their adjustment to home and society and also with regard to their school situations, or situations in general confronted by them in home, society, etc. These findings agree with the suggestions of Kubic (1961) that creativeness will increase with better mental health and vice versa. It is also possible that some of the maladjustments observed by researchers are actually personality variances as suggested by Schubert and Biondi (1977) and not the adjustment-maladjustment continuum.

In the present investigation, the performance of boys in TCTA is found to be superior to the performance of girls. This finding is supported by Prakash (1966), Raina (1966) and Dharmahgadan (1976), Wallach and Kogan (1965) find very few instances of sex difference in the matter of creativity. And these differences they observe are always in favour of boys.

The results of the studies conducted in India regarding ability tests are in line with the present findings. In tests of intelligence both verbal and non-verbal investigators like Pillai (1954), George and Mathew (1967a, 1967b), Abraham (1968), George (1968), Menon (1972) and Thampurati (1969) report superiority of Kerala boys over Kerala girls.

Table 2

Analysis of various of scores on different areas of adjustment of three groups of boys and girls

Areas	*Source*	*DF*	*MSS*	*Ratio*
Home	Sex	1	1115.73	45.55*
adjustment	Creativity	2	163.27	6.67*
	Interaction	2	21.25	0.87
	Error	1094	24.29	
Social	Sex	1	411.32	19.45*
adjustment	Creativity	2	2.09	9.09
	Interaction	2	14.91	0.71
	Error	1094	21.13	
School	Sex	1	12.07	0.39
adjustment	Creativity	2	20.21	0.66
	Interaction	2	1.17	0.04
	Error		10.94	30.36
Adjustment	Sex	1	241.79	12.74*
concerning	Creativity	2	0.23	0.01
situational	Interaction	2	4.25	0.22
aspects	Error	1094	18.98	
Adjustment	Sex	1	616.17	31.45*
concerning personality	Creativity	2	55.67	2.84
characteristics	Interaction	2	11.99	0.61
	Error	1094		

*p less than 0.01.

Contrary to the present findings are the studies reported by Terrance in 1961, 1963, 1964 and 1965 and Ogletree in 1971. Terrance in his studies observes sex difference mostly in favour of girls. A cross-cultural study of the creative thinking ability of public and private school pupils of England, Scotland and Germany, using Terrance Tests, finds that girls are superior to boys in all creative measures in England and Germany. In the case of pupils of Scotland, boys seem to obtain higher figural scores than girls, even though their scores do not yield significant sex differences.

Table 3
Means, SDs and critical ratios of adjustment scores of highly creative, moderately creative and less creative groups of boys and girls

Area of adjustment	*Sex*	*Groups*	*N*	*Mean*	*SD*	*Groups compared*	*Critical ratio*
		1. HC	226	15.60	4.70	1 and 2	2.79*
		2. MC	208	16.83	4.45	1 and 3	3.09*
	Boys					2 and 3	1.08
		3. LC	76	17.49	4.59	4 and 5	0.19
						4 and 6	0.56
Home							
		4. HC	28	14.50	5.79	5 and 6	1.93
		5. MC	325	14.29	4.31	1 and 4	0.96
	Girls					2 and 5	6.05
		6. LC	237	15.14	5.00	3 and 6	3.79
		1. HC	226	13.11	4.44		
	Boys	2. MC	208	12.98	4.57		
		3. LC	76	12.43	4.78		
Social		4. HC	28	13..82	5.32	1 and 4	0.68
	Girls	5. MC	325	14..27	4.54	2 and 5	3.23*
		6. LC	237	34..37	4.63	3 and 6	3.06*
		1. HC	226	15..36	4.25		
	Boys	2. MC	208	15..29	4.72		
		3. LC	776	15.56	4.32		
Situational							
		4. HC	28	14.32	5.04	1 and 4	3.25*
	Girls	5. MC	325	14,36	4.24	2 and 5	2.33**
		6. LC	237	14.18	4.15	3 and 6	2.50**
		1. HC	226	13.44	4.60		
	Boys	2. MC	208	14.19	4.78		
Personality		3. LC	76	14.80	3.59		
				4. HC	28	12,07	4.57
	1 aid 4	1.49					
	Girls	5. MC	325	12.65	4.24	2 and S	3.78*
		6. LC	237	12.54	4.35	3 and 6	4.61

*Indicates the one per cent level of significance.

**Indicates the five per cent level of significance.

HC - Highly creative; MC - Moderately creative; LC - Less creative.

Recent findings by Terrance (1972) and Halpin *et al* (1973), that there is no sex difference in performance of creativity tests, also run counter to the findings of the present investigation. Mearing (1967), in her study of the school children of the Isle of skye, also sees no significant sex difference in performance of creativity tests. However, in two instances she finds some sex difference and these two are in favour of boys.

Superiority of boys over girls in creativity tests may be attributed to cultural factors. In Indian society girls are expected to be modest and submissive with a view to train them. A number of restrictions are imposed upon these girls. Rules and regulations very often prevent them from getting exposed to a varied environment, unlike in the case of boys. The result is that girls may be more anxious at the time of test taking. Because of this they may fail to perform well in many tests. Moreover, in their attempt to be modest they even try to inhibit the most wild and creative responses (Dharmangadan, 1976).

References

Abraham, P.A., An analytical study of some personality factors and academic achievement of secondary school pupils. *Ph.D.Thesis,* Trivandrum: Kerala University, 1968.

Anastasi, A., *Differential Psychology. Individual and group differences in behaviour.* The Macmillan Company, 1958.

Asha C.B., An empirical study of the adjustment problems of creative children in secondary schools, Ph.D. Thesis 1978, Trivandrum.

........., Health adjustment and creativity of the secondary school children, *Psychological Studies 1980*, 25, 122-125.

Asha C. B., Emotional adjustment and creativity: A study among secondary school children, *Journal of Institute of Educational Research.* 1984, 3, 16-20.

Bloom, B. S., Report on creativity research by the examiners office of the University of. Chicago. In C.W. Taylor and F. Brron (Eds): *Scientific Creativity: its recognition and development,* New York: John Wiley and Sons, 1963.

Chronbach, L. J., *Educational Psychology,* New York: Har Court, Brace and Company, 1954

Dharmangadan, B., Creativity in school children: An analytical study, Ph.D. Thesis, 1976, Trivandrum, Kerala University.

Fradson, A. N., *Educational Psychology: the Principles of learning in teaching.* New York: McGraw-Hill Book Company, 1961.

Garfield S. J., Cohen, H. A., and Roth, R.M., Creativity and mental health, *Journal of Educational Research,* 1969, 63, 147-149.

Garwood, D. S., Personality factors related to creativity in young scientists, *Journal of Abnormal and Social Psychology,* 1964, 68, 413-419.

George, E. I., and Mathew V.G., *General Mental Ability Test. Verbal Form A.* Trivandrum: University of Kerala, 1967

George, E.I. and Mathew V.B., *General Mental Ability Test, Non-verbal,* Trivandrum: University of Kerala, 1967.

Greenaere P., Childhood of the artist: Psychoanalytic study, *Child,* 1957 12-47, 1957.

Gupta R.P., Second order personality factors as functions of sex and creativity among young adults. Ph.D. Thesis, Agra University, in Govind Tiwari and Roma Pal (Eds). Status of Indian Researches in Creativity, Agra: Agra Psychological Research Cell, 1983.

Halpin G., and Torrance E.P., Effects of sex, race and age on creative thinking abilities of blind children, *Perceptual Motor Skills,* 1972, 37, 389-390.

Aollan J.L., Creativity and academic performance among tarbulent adolescents, *Journal of Educational Psychology,* 1961, 52, 136-147.

Kirk, S.A., *Educating exceptional children,* Bombay: Oxford and IBH Publishing Co., 1962.

19.Kubie, L.S., *Neurotic distortion of the creative process,* New York: Noonday Press, 1961.

Laycock, S.R., Adjustments of superior and inferior school children, *Journal of Social Psychology,* 1933, 4, 353-366.

Mac kinnon, D.W., The personality correlates of creativity: A study of American Architects. In Nielsen, G. S. (Ed): *Proceedings of the XIV International Congress of Applied Psychology.* Coppenhagen: Munksgard, 1962.

........."The nature and nurture of creative talent," *American Psychologist,* 1962, 17, 487-495.

Personality correlates of creativity, A paper presented at the second conference on productive thinking, National Educational Association; Washington: D.C.: May 2 - 4 cited in Gowan et al: 1963, *Creativity its educational implications,* New York: John Wiley and Sons, 1967.

Menon, S.K., A comparative study of personality characteristics of over-achievers and under-achievers of high ability, Ph.D. Thesis, 1972, Trivandrum: University of Kerala.

Mouly G.J., *Psychology for effective teaching,* New York: Holt, Rinehart and Winston, 1966.

Pillai P.G., Preparation of a standardised test of general Mental Ability, Ph.D., Thesis Banaras: Banaras Hindu University, 1964.

Prakash, A.G., Understanding the fourth grade slump, A Study of the creative thinking abilities of Indian Children, Masters research paper, University of Minnesota, 1966.

Raina M.K., A study of sex differences in creativity, Research Paper, Regional College of Education, Ajmir, 1966.

Rajalakshmi V.M., A comparative study of the repeaters and non-repeaters in secondary schools in Kerala, Ph. D, Thesis, Trivandrum: University of Kerala, 1973.

Roe, A., Artists and their work, *Journal of Personality,* 1946, 15, 1-40.

Rogers, C.R., Toward a theory of creativity etc. A review of general Sememantics, 11, 249-260, In *Journal of Child Psychology and Psychiatry*: 1967, 8, 153-164.

Schaefer, C.F., Self concept of creative adolescents, *Journal of Psychology,* 1968, 72, 273-274, In Govind Tiwari and Roma Pal (Eds.), *Status of Indian researches in creativity,* Agra: Agra Psychological Research Cell.

Schubert D.S. P., and Biondi A.M., Creativity and mental health: Part III Creativity and adjustment, *The Journal of Creative Behaviour,* 1977, 2, No. 3, Third Quarter.

Singer, D.L., and Rummo, J., Ideational creativity and behavioural style in Kindergarten age children, *Developmental Psychology,* 1973, 8, 154-161.

Singh R.P., Education for creativity, *Indian Psychological Review,* 1977, 14, 67-68.

Singh, D., *Scientific creativity and personality,* Agra: National Psychological Corporations, 1980.

Singh N.C.P., and Sharma M., Creativity and adjustment, In Govind Tiwari and Roma Pal (Eds.) *Status of Indian Researches in Creativity,* Agra: Agra Psychological Research Cell, 1978.

Thampurati, N.S., The effect of timing on predictability of Ravens' Test Scores, M. Ed. Thesis, Trivandrum: University of Kerala, 1969.

Torrance, E.P., Problems of highly creative children, *Gifted Child Quarterly,* Educational Digest, 1961, 27, 40-42.

........., *Guiding Creative Talent,* Englewood Cliffs, N. J: Prentice-Hall, 1962.

, *Education and Creative Potential,* Minneapolis: University of Minnesota Press, 1963.

........., Identity: the gifted child's major problem, *Gifted Child Quarterly,* 1971, 15, 147-155.

Wallach, M.A., and Kogan N., *Modes of thinking in young children: A study of the creativity - Intelligence distinction.* New York: Holt, Rinehart and Winston, 1965.

CHAPTER 6

Criminality and Adjustment Problems of High School Students

Vijayalaxmi A. Aminabhavi

The aim of the present study is to assess the level of criminality of high school students in relation to their adjustment problems. The sample consisted of 80 students, of which 40 were boys and 40 were girls, studying in ninth and tenth standards in Dharwad city. The Bell's Adjustment Inventory and the Criminality Scale were administered to the students. The investigator personally met the students in the classroom situation, administered the test and collected the data The results show that adjustment problems had the influencing effect on the criminal tendencies of the high school students The gender of the students and the birth order also had the determining effect on student's criminality.

Introduction

Criminal behaviour pattern has been classified as antisocial behaviour in the society. Generally the antisocial behaviour like delinquency, theft, violence, homicide and other similar behaviour are found to be prevailing more among the persons maladjusted in society. Especially, how an individual becomes a delinquent and develops criminal tendencies in him is a phenomenon for the psychologists to investigate, as several psycho-social factors have been found to have influence on the criminal and antisocial behaviour of the individuals and also considered as one of the personality factors.

The review of literature in this field with regard to the development of criminal and antisocial behaviour reveal various causes for the development of such behaviour. Pati (1966) has observed in his studies that most of the delinquents were found to be neurotics, psychotics and psychopathics. The study made by Singh (1967) revealed that the criminals scored significantly higher than the non-criminals on the neuroticism scale. Similar results were obtained by Chandra Shivanandam (1990) in a study among the female criminals and girl delinquents. Nagarathnamma and Vijayalakshmi (1995) have observed in their study that persons with severe mental disorder (schizophrenia) commit all sorts of crimes from mild to heinous crimes. Kishore Verma and Shah (1970) observed that crime was significantly higher among male mental patients. Verma and Jha (1966) reported that the ratio between male and female was 10:1 in their criminality. Stattin and Maggausson (1984) found that the boys who had high aggressive behaviour in their early life committed more violent crimes in their later life than the girls. Pedersen Willey (1994) observed that perception of low care by fathers contributed strongly to the development of anxiety and depression, while low care by mothers strongly contributed to delinquency.

The study of Lowry Richard et al (1995) revealed that the individual factors such as developmental, family and peer group influences and the broader societal factors also contributed to violence. Suklofske and Eysenck (1980) found significant differences between delinquents and badly behaved boys in the degree of antisocial behaviour. The well-behaved boys differed significantly from badly-behaved boys and delinquents The well-behaved boys differed from the delinquents also on psychoticism scale. Marri (1994) observed that 94 per cent of the subjects had mental disorder prior to committing suicide. Interpersonal separations and conflicts were the most common precipitating psychosocial stressors in the month before suicide. Mukharjee and Kundu (1961) have observed in their study that the largest proportion of criminals were neither first born nor last born, but the middle issues among the siblings. The same type of results were observed by Muthayya and Baskaran (1964) that delinquents were occupying the middle birth order more in number. The review of the literature in this area shows that there were no studies of criminal behaviour relating to the psychosocial factors among the high school students. Therefore, the recent study was undertaken with the view to assessing the levels of criminality of high school students in relation to their various levels of adjustment problems.

Problem: Are the criminal tendencies having any relationship with varying levels of adjustment problems of high school students? Are the high school boys differing from the girls in their criminal tendencies?

Is there any relationship between criminal tendencies and birth order of the high school students?

Based upon these problems the following hypotheses are formulated.

Hypothesis

1. There is a positive association between high school students' adjustment problems and their criminal tendencies.
2. The criminal tendencies of the high school students increase if their adjustment problem are increased in home, health, social and emotional areas.
3. High school boys have more criminal tendencies than high school girls.
4. The middle born high school students are more criminal minded than the first and the last born.

Method

Sample: The sample of the present study consisted of 80 students, of which 40 were boys and 40 were girls. They were the students of ninth and tenth standards, studying in K.B. Boards School, Dharwad, Karnataka State. The age of the boys and girls ranged from 14 to 16 years. All of them were from middle socioeconomic status group.

Materials: Two test materials and an information schedule were used in this study to collect data. The two instruments are (1) The Criminality Scale and (2) The Bell's Adjustment Inventory.

1. *The Criminality Scale*: This scale was designed and developed by Professor Krishnan as a part of his Mysore Personality Inventory to measure the criminal tendencies of the subjects. This scale consists of 28 items in the form of statements. The respondents have to answer the items in terms of 'True' or 'False' responses. The high score in this scale indicates high criminal tendencies and the low score low criminal tendencies.
2. *The Bell's Adjustment Inventory:* This is a well-known instrument, designed and developed by Bell to measure the adjustment problems of the students in various areas. This inventory has two forms the student's form and the adult's form. The student's form was used in this study. It consisted of 140 items with two response categories, 'Yes' and 'No'. This

inventory measures adjustment problems of an individual in four different areas such as Home, Health, Social and Emotional. The high score in this inventory indicates poor adjustment and the low score indicates better adjustment.

3. *Information Schedule:* This schedule was prepared and used to collect demographic information such as age, sex, order of birth, parental education, occupation and income. The test materials were revalidated and the reliability and validity of these materials were tested and they were found to be highly significant.

Procedure: The test materials were printed and bound into booklet form and were administered to 80 high school students as planned in the classroom situation. Brief instructions were given to the students as how to answer the items. The test materials were collected as soon as the students had answered all the tests.

Method of Scoring: The collected teat materials were scrutinised to see if they were correctly answered. Then the responses provided by the students were scored according to the procedure with the help of a scoring key and the individual snores were obtained.

Further, in the entire sample the top 25 per cent of scores in Adjustment Inventory were taken as top group and middle 50 per cent as middle group and lowest 25 per cent as low group, Thus the obtained three groups were considered as well adjusted, moderately adjusted and poorly adjusted. The criminality scores corresponding to these three groups were taken for further statistical analyses.

Results

The obtained individual scores were treated statistically and presented in tables. The scores were classified according to the needs to verify the hypotheses and presented in the respective tables. Some of the treatments are the coefficient correlation, the means, SDs, SEM, SEM diff, and 't' test.

Table 1
Showing the coefficient of correlation between the scores of adjustment inventory and the criminality scale (N-80).

Variables	*N*	*r*	*t*	*Level of significance*
Adjustment Criminality	80	0.77	10.48	0.001

The data reveal a positive association between the scores of adjustment and the scores of criminality of the students. The obtained correlation coefficient 0.77 is highly significant at 0.001 level, which means that there is a positive relation between adjustment and criminality among the school students. As the scores in adjustment inventory increased the scores in criminality also were increased correspondingly. The students' poor adjustment and their criminal tendencies go together in this study. Therefore, hypothesis one is accepted.

Table 2
Showing the scores of the students on criminality scale and the difference between the groups in criminal tendencies

Groups	*N*	*Mean*	*S.D*	*SEM*	*Mean diff*	*SEM diff*	*t*	*Level of sig.*
A.. Well Adj.	20	35.25	8.03	1.79	AB. 10.00	2.13	4 69	0.001
B. Moderate Adj.	40	45.25	7.24	1.14	AC. 23.50	2.37	9.92	0.001
C. Poorly Adj.	20	58.75	9.78	2.19	BC. 13.50	1.92	7 03	0 001

The data, as presented in Table 2, show that the poorly adjusted students scored (58.75) higher than the moderately adjusted (45.25) and well adjusted (35.25) students, which means that the poorly adjusted students had more criminal tendencies and the well adjusted had the lowest criminal tendencies while the middle group had moderate criminal tendencies. The differences among these groups were also highly significant at 0.001 level. Every group is different from every other group on the basis of their level of adjustment. The results show the lower the adjustment the higher the criminal tendencies are among the high school students. Therefore, hypothesis two is accepted.

The results in Table 3 reveal that the students who were poorly adjusted at home have scored (56.30) higher than those who were moderately adjusted at home (45.87) and the well adjusted at home (35 10) on the criminality scale. The differences among these groups on the criminality scale also vary very much high to the extent of yielding the differences at 0.001 level between any two groups.

Table 3
Showing the scores of the students on the criminality test and the level of differences on the basis of home adjustment

Groups	*N*	*Mean*	*S.D*	*SEM*	*Mean Diff*	*SEM Diff*	*t*	*Level of Sig,*
A. Well Adj.	20	35.10	8.85	1.98	AB	10.77 2.39	4.51	0.001
B. Moderate. Adj.	40	45.87	8.51	1.34	AC	21.20 2.99	7.09	0.001
C. Poorly Adj.	20	56.30	10.00	2.25	BC	10.432.62	3.98	0.001

The home adjustment has considerable effect upon the high school students' criminal tendencies. The more they are maladjusted the more criminal tendencies they have. Thus this result also supports hypothesis two and therefore it is accepted.

Table 4
Showing the scores of the students on the criminality scale on the basis of health adjustment

Groups	*N*	*Mean*	*S.D*	*SEM*	*Mean diff*	*SEM diff*	*t*	*Level of sig.*
A. Well Adj.	20	37.00	9.60	0.48	AB 8.12	2.50	3.25	0.01
B. Moderate. Adj.	40	45.12	8.13	1.28	AC 20.75	2.98	6.96	0.001
C. Poorly Adj.	20	57.75	9.21	2.06	BC 12.63	2.43	5.19	0.001

A perusal of the data in Table 4, shows that the students who had poor health adjustment scored (57.75) significantly higher on the criminality scale than the students who were well adjusted (37.00) and the moderately adjusted (45.12) in health problem. The differences among the groups on the criminal tendencies are highly significant. Therefore, it is evident that the higher the health adjustment problem among the students the higher the criminal tendencies prevailing among them. The results support hypothesis two.

Table 5 Showing the scores of high school students on the criminality scale based upon the social adjustment scores

Groups	*N*	*Mean*	*S.D*	*SEM*	*Mean Diff*	*SEM Diff*	*t*	*Level of Sig,*
A. Well Adj.	20	35.25	10.26	2.29	AB 12.00	2.74	4.38	0.001
B. Moderate Adj.	40	47.25	9.47	1.49	AC 18.75	3.29	5.69	0.001
C. Poorly Adj,	20	54.00	10.55	2.36	BC 6.75	2.79	2.42	0.05

The data in Table 5 indicate that students with poor social adjustment scored (54.00) higher on criminality scale than the students who were well in social adjustment (35.25) and those who were moderate in social adjustment (47.25). There is considerable amount of difference among these groups in their criminal tendencies The differences among these are highly significant at 0.001 and 0.05 levels, indicating that socially maladjusted students vary in their criminal tendencies. Therefore, it can be concluded that social maladjustment is a contributing factor to the high school students' criminal tendencies. The results support hypothesis two.

The data reveal that the students with poor emotional adjustment have scored high (56.75) on the criminality test than the students well adjusted (38.00) and moderately adjusted (45.50). These three groups show considerable amount of differences among themselves in their criminal tendencies. The results show that emotional maladjustment has a definite influence in the criminal tendencies of high school students. Therefore, hypothesis two is accepted.

Table 6
Showing the scores of the students on criminality scale on the basis of Emotional adjustment

Groups	*N*	*Mean*	*S.D*	*SEM*	*Mean diff*		*SEM diff*	*t*	*Level of sig.*
A. Well Adj.	20	38.00	9.64	2.16	AB	7.50	2.62	2 87	0.01
B. Moderate Adj.	40	45.50	9.41	1.49	AC	18.75	3.02	6.21	0.001
C. Poorly Adj.	20	56.75	9.49	2.12	BC	11.25	2.59	4.34	0.001

Table 7
Showing the scores of the high school boys and girls on the criminality scale and the difference between them

Groups	*N*	*Mean*	*S.D*	*SEM*	*Mean diff*	*SEM diff*	*t*	*Level of sig*
Boys	40	49.63	10.12	1.59				
					6.63	2.45	2.71	001
Girls	40	43.00	11.72	1.85				

It is observed that the boys scored (49.63) higher than the girls (43.00) on the criminality scale indicating that the boys have more criminal tendencies than the girls. It is evident that both the boys and girls have criminal tendencies, but the boys have little more than the girls. But the difference between them is significant at 0.01 level. Therefore hypothesis three is accepted.

Table 8
Showing the scores of high school students on criminality scale on the basis of order of birth

Groups	*N*	*Mean*	*S.D*	*SEM*	*Mean Diff*	*SEM Diff*	*t*	*Level of Sig,*
A. First Born	28	42.75	10.15	1.92	AB 8.42	3.40	2 48	0.05
B, Middle Born	23	52.17	13.46	2.81	AC 1.77	2.02	0.88	N.S.
C. Last Born	29	45.52	11,41	2.12	BC 6.65	2 88	2.31	0.05

We can understand from the results that the middle born scored high (52.17), the last born scored (45.52) second and the first born scored (42.751 third, indicating that the middle born have more criminal tendencies than the last born and the first born. While the first born and the last born do not have much difference in their scores, the middle born and the first born and the middle born and the last born show much difference in their criminality at 0.05 level. Therefore, the middle born is definitely more criminal minded than the first born and the last born. Therefore, hypothesis four is accepted.

DISCUSSION

There is a definite relationship between adjustment problems and the criminal tendencies among the high school students as revealed by this study. This may be attributed to the fact that persons with poor adjustment to life develop the feeling of frustration in life. Such psychological state stimulates the person more for destructive attitude than for constructiveness. Hence such individuals are often driven to antisocial and criminal activities.

Another observation from the results of this study that we can make is the close relationship between home adjustment and the criminal tendencies. These results are in agreement with the earlier findings of Pedersen Willey (1994). The boy or girl who gets sufficient care and affection from the parents and other family members would be better adjusted at home. The children who lack care and affection naturally indulge in criminal and antisocial activities. They resort to criminal and antisocial behaviour in order to find out an outlet for their psychological problem of frustration. These children develop the feeling that they are neglected by their parents. They feel that they have become destitutes in this world.

The findings of the study show close relationship between health adjustment and criminality which may be attributed to the fact of existence of a sound mind in a sound body. The inability to keep a person on work more effectively makes him develop the feeling of helplessness which in turn leads him to aggressive and antisocial behaviour patterns.

The finding that the student's social maladjustment being closely related to criminality reminds us of the importance, necessity of healthy interpersonal actions for a happy life. The impairment in social adjustment turns the mind to militant behaviour as a sort of defence mechanism.

Emotions do play a major role in one's life. Emotions are releasing ways of pent up tensions. If such ways are blocked through poor adjustment, certainly it finds its expression in antisocial behaviour. Along with biological differences, the discrimination in child rearing practices concern boys and girls; further, the differential sociocultural attitude towards boys and girls may lead to higher criminality among boys.

The last finding of this study that the middle born has higher criminality than other siblings may be due to the developed competitive nature in these children. The middle born struggles hard constantly to surpass the elder and younger ones who enjoy all facilities and encouragement given by parents. Middle siblings try to draw the attention of their parents by developing destructive tendency, if proper opportunities, guidance and support are not given to them.

All these findings seem to imply the need for facilitating the development of healthy personality.

Conclusions

1. Poorly adjusted high school students have significantly higher criminality than well-adjusted and moderately-adjusted students. And also moderately-adjusted students have significantly higher criminality than well-adjusted students.
2. High school students with poor adjustment at home show significantly higher criminality than those with well adjustment and moderate adjustment at home. And also the students with moderate home adjustment have significantly higher criminality than the students with well home adjustment.
3. High school students with poor health adjustment have significantly higher criminality than the students with well and moderate health adjustment. And also students with

moderate health adjustment have significantly higher criminality than those with well health adjustment.

4. High school students with poor social adjustment have significantly higher criminality than those with well and moderate social adjustment And also students with moderate social adjustment have significantly higher criminality than those with well-adjusted social adjustment.
5. High school students with poor emotional adjustment have significantly higher criminality than those with well and moderate emotional adjustment. And also students with moderate emotional adjustment have significantly higher criminality than emotionally well-adjusted students.
6. High school boys have significantly higher criminal tendencies than high school girls.
7. Middle born of the high school students have significantly higher criminal tendencies than the first and last born.

References

Chandra Shivanandam, Personal Adjustment Problems of Women Criminals and Girl Delinquents, *Journal of Indian Academy of Applied Psychology*, 1990, 16 (1), 29-34.

Kishore, B. Verma, H. C. and Shah, D. K., An Analysis of 380 Criminal Mental Patients, *Indian Journal of Psychiatry*, 1970, 18 (1&2), 117-124.

Lowry Richard, Sleet David, Duncan Carlton, Powell Ken, et al. Adolescents at Risk for Violence, *Educational Psychology Review*, 1995, 7(1), 7-39.

Marttunen Marri, Psychological Maladjustment, Mental Disorders and Stressful Life Events Precede Adolescent Suicide, *Psychological Abstracts*, 1995, Vol. 82, Sept. No. 33438

Mukharjee, K. and Kundu, S., A Study of Birth Order and Family Positions of the Criminals, *Indian Journal of Psychology* 1961, 36(3), 127-132.

Nagarathnamma, B. and Vijayalakshmi, R., Study of Mental Illness and Criminal Behaviour. *Journal of Community Guidance and Research*, 1995, 12(2), 97-105.

Pati, G. Personality Pathology of Delinquents. *Psychological Studies*, 1996. 11(1), 35-41.

Pedersen Willey. Parental Relations, Mental Health and Delinquency in Adolescents, *Psychological Abstracts*, 1995, Vol. 82, May, No. 17937.

Saklofske and Eysenck, Personality and Antisocial Behaviour in Delinquent and Non-Delinquent Boys, *Psychological Reports*, 1980, 47, 1255-1261.

Singh, V. P. Extroversion-Neuroticism: Their Distribution in Criminals, *Indian Journal of Applied Psychology*, 1967, 4(1), 24-27.

Stattin, H. and Maguausson, D., The Role of Early Aggressive Behaviour for the Frequency, the Seriousness and the Types: of Later Criminal Offences, *Psychological Abstracts,* 1987, Vol. 74, No. 4418.

Verma, L,. P. and Jha, B. K., Characteristics of Murderers in Mental Disorder, *American Journal of Psychiatry,* 1966, 122(11).

Note: This paper was presented at the XXIV Criminological Congress held at Bangalore from 9 to 11 February 1996.

CHAPTER 7

Adjustment Pattern of Discriminated Girls of the Twenty-first Century: An Empirical Study

Swatantra Jain

This study is the final form of an intensive and a longitudinal study of the author on "the effect of discrimination psyche". The sample of this study consisted of 300 adolescent girls from Karnal, Kurukshetra and Yamunanagar districts of Haryana State. A Questionnaire devised by the author was administered on the samples. The Questionnaire has 12 areas referring to various aspects of discrimination. The high and low discriminated girls were identified and they were further classified into two categories as acceptance and non-acceptance. There were 50 highly discriminated girls. Among them 30 were acceptors and 20 were non-acceptors. All the 20 non-acceptance comprised 12 passive (PRs) and 8 active revolters (ARs). Then they took the Bell's Adjustment Inventory which measured the adjustment problems in five areas, viz., Home, Health, Social, Emotional and General field. Results revealed that the passive revolters were poorer in health and emotional areas while active revolters were poorer in home, social and general areas. However, the difference was not significant in the emotional area.

Introduction

Human behaviour, according to Kurt Lewin (1951), is a function of one's life space. But Roger (1961) says that it is the stimuli situation as experienced by the individual in question. The experiencing of the stimuli situation gradually gives birth to a self-concept. A girl child develops a positive concept about herself if she perceives and experiences a climate of acceptance and warmth, if she feels that she is considered a full- fledged human being like other members of the family. The converse is also true, i.e., she develops a negative concept, if she perceives that she is not loved and accepted in her own capacity, that she is not considered like other members, that she is discriminated against other siblings or she is a burden to her own parents. In such circumstances, she feels insecure, anxiety ridden, maladjusted and unhappy (Jain, 1992, 1993, 1994).

It is more so in the case of the girl child who does not get her due share of love, respect recognition, medical care and other facilities even from her own parents. In most of the Indian families, she is given much less in every respect in comparison to her male siblings and made to work much more, subjected to different standards of reward and punishment, disciplined harshly and treated many a time much less than a human being in her own family. This discrimination is done across all cultures, castes and communities and also in the families belonging to low as well as middle and high socioeconomic status, with the only difference in the nature and degree of discrimination from being very rough and crude in low and lower middle socioeconomic status families to subtle and very subtle in middle, upper middle and higher socio economic status families.

Due to differential conditioning and pattern of reinforcements right from their infancy, the girls are made to believe that they are born to lead different kind of lives, that their male folk are superior and supreme. This is done, so that they may not only accept the discrimination happily but also perpetuate it through generations and the process goes on unchecked. In spite of it, there are girls who are sensitive to this discrimination against them. They perceive it and experience it as great unjust and inhumane. So they react to this discrimination against them by their parents. The reaction is not confined to their parents alone. They don't tolerate this injustice by their in-laws when married, and their employers/boses if and when in jobs.

The manifestations can be many. The surrendering and sacrificing ones drink the cup of this injustice by accepting this discrimination as part and parcel of the gift of this birth at the hands of God, while non-surrendering and more sensitive girls don't accept it easily. They protest covertly or overtly. Their protest can be against the parents or the favoured siblings or even against God which is manifested in their wish or attempt to commit suicide or withdraw from active life leading to severe depression. All these manifestations adversely affect their mental health and their adjustment with their own selves, family and society.

The person who is submissive, docile, obedient, humble and polite in his behaviour or response or outlook is, generally, appreciated by others. It is specially the case with girls in contemporary Indian society.

On the other hand, the one who is assertive, revolutionary, overreactive and challenging is not welcome. Now the girls whose docile and submissive behaviour pattern is reinforced positively by others would be a happier lot than those revolters who are negatively reinforced and discouraged and hence, who are less welcome due to their assertive and dominating nature, especially in middle class conservative families. The parents, the friends, the relatives, the neighbours all would find fault with the latter category, i.e., the revolutionary. And if, unfortunately, there are two sisters in the same family with just the opposite nature, life will be a hell for the one who is revolutionary and reactive. She would always be compared by her elders with her docile sister, taunted and jeered at. This constant comparison would add salt to her wounded psyche. So, this differential handling by parents and other significant members of the family is likely to create different adjustment patterns. Some would show better adjustment in home and society, others would be more at peace with themselves. What exactly would be the difference was studied empirically.

The present study is the final part of an intensive longitudinal study which was undertaken by the author to study:

a) The nature and extent of discrimination as perceived in 12 different areas of family life,

b) Differential effect of discrimination on the general personality traits of low and high discriminated girls,

e) Effect of acceptance and non-acceptance of this discrimination as a, part of their lot, and

d) Effect of differential way of revolt on (i) the mental health and (ii) adjustment of the girls who revolt passively and those who act aggressively.

Hypothesis: Based upon this problem the hypothesis formulated is that: "There, is difference between the adjustment pattern of the girls who revolt passively and those who revolt actively to the discriminatory attitudes of their parents."

Methodology

Initial sample: A self-devised questionnaire to study the nature and extent of discrimination as perceived in 12 different areas of family life was administered to 300 adolescent girls from Karnal, Kurukshetra and Yamunanagar districts of Haryana. The twelve areas are: (1) General attitude of acceptance and welcome, (2) Food and nutrition, (3) Health-care including parental sensitiveness to child's moods and problems, (4) Education and exposure to various sources of knowledge, (5) Opportunities given for the development of various potentialities, (6) Sports and recreation, (7) Utilisation of leisure time, (8) Assignment of household chores, work-load and work expectations, (9) Decision making, (10) Extent of economic independence, (11) Recognition and encouragement, (12) Importance given in religious ceremonies.

Screening of high and low discriminated girls: High and low discriminated girls were screened out on the basis of Mean ± ½ SD. The highly discriminated girls (50) were further classified into two categories.

a) *Acceptors:* Those who had accepted this discrimination as part and parcel of their lives, as was apparent from their responses to the last question.

   "How do you feel when you perceive your parents discriminating against you?"

   Sixty per cent of the high discriminated group (i.e. 30) answered that they had accepted it as part of their lot; and

b) *Non-acceptors:* Forty per cent of the high discriminated girls (20) turned out as non-acceptors who would react to the discriminatory attitude and behaviour of their parents overtly or covertly (on the basis of their response to above question):

Screening of the final Target sample: Above 20 nonacceptance (NA's) were further classified into 12 passive revolters (ERs) and eight active revolters (ARs) who were outspoken in their reaction.

All the above stated 20 non-acceptors comprised 12 passive and 8 active revolters. Then they took the injustice test. They just condemn themselves, curse their lot and have grievances against God. They don't show any ill will against their parents or brothers. Hence, they are welcome to their parents. On the other hand the active revolters don't show any patience, they revolt and put resistance to any set or attitude of discrimination against them. Sometimes they even challenge the supremacy of their brothers and authority of their parents. They demand equality. Their resistance, arguments, discussion, challenge and open rebellion are not welcomed by their parents. Hence they are mostly disliked by their parents. A sort of tussle always gees on between the parent and the daughter. For example, many girls out of these ARs reported that they demand and insist on equality of treatment, which they never get.

This constant tussle and their rebellious spirit is not liked by their parents and kith and kins. Hence, they are poorer in adjustment with their family members and with society in general. Their poor adjustment with family and their friend circle affect their overall adjustment and so they are poorer in general adjustment too. A passive revolter's (PRs) poorer adjustment in the areas of health and emotions is justified on the basis that the persons who are not able to give an outlet to their emotions, i.e., anger, who can't have the guts to say 'no' to their parents, if they perceive them to be doing some injustice, would never be at peace with their own selves. They will remain unhappy with their lot, depressed and worrysome persons. Hence, they are likely to be poorer in adjustment in these areas in comparison to their counterparts who show resistance.

The above results make it obvious that perceived discrimination, whether reacted actively or passively, affect the victims adjustment in some area or the other. The need is wholesome adjustment, happiness and complete satisfaction. The present results indicating poorer adjustment of active revolters bring home the fact that the girls who perceive their parents discriminating against them, and react covertly or overtly, axe the ones who are little more conscious, more awakened and aware towards their right. They seem to be asking for their rights from the society in general and parents in particular and hence the following questions: Whether they should be vocal in asking their rights and are all sorts of odds and maladjustment in every sphere of life, or Bells Adjustment inventory which measures adjustment problems in five erase, viz. Home, Health, Social, Emotional and General.

Results and Discussion

The scores obtained in all the five areas of adjustment from both the groups were given suitable statistical treatment and are presented in Table 1. The higher the score, the poorer is the adjustment.

It is apparent from Table 1 that the adjustment scores of the active revolters (ARs) are significantly different from the adjustment scores of passive revolters in almost all the five areas of adjustment. The passive revolters (PRs) have scored lower in the areas of home (9.15 Vs 15.10), social (12.50 Vs 18:40) and general areas (55.40 Vs 58.64). The t-ratios indicate that they (the PRs) are significantly better than the active revolters (ARs) in the areas of home and social at one per cent level and in general at five per cent level.

Table 1

Showing the scores of active and passive revolters in the five adjustment areas of Bell's Adjustment Inventory

Area	*Mean*		*SD*		*SED*	*t-ratio*	*Sig. level*
	Active	*Passive*	*Active*	*Passive*			
Home	15.10	9.15	3.35	5.22	2.07	2.87	.01
Health	8.20	11.88	4.62	3.65	1.82	2.02	.05
Social	18.40	12.50	4.75	4.25	2.01	2.95	.01
Emotional16.25	22.85	5.16	5.09	2.23	2.96	.01	
General	58.64	55.40	3.36	3.24	1.48	2.19	.05

The active revolters (ARs) have scored lower on the dimension of health (8.20 Vs 11.88) and emotional (16.25 Vs 2.85). The t-ratios indicate that they are significantly better than the passive revolters in these two areas. However, the t ratio failed to reach significant level by a very small margin (P. < 10).

The superiority of passive revolters in the areas of home, social and general is justified because passive revolters are the ones who perceive some injustice (discrimination) but don't react to it actively. They don't put any resistance in the face of any

ii) Should they suppress their awakened spirit of equality? Are they poorer in personality, adjustment and behaviour to their counterparts who perceive the discrimination and accept it as part of their lot?

If the above dilemma is seen with reference to the modern concept of criminality according to Gandhiji, that 'tolerating injustice is as big a crime as doing it', then these non-acceptors and active revolters are doing a lip-service for half the population but for their own selves they are inviting the wrath of society at each and every step.

The challenge before the society in general in the twenty-first century is twofold.

i) How to react to these awakened and sensitive souls? Should it help and encourage these girls by reinforcing them or discourage them by showing its disapproval?

ii) If the society's reaction is positive towards this social revolution, how to shoulder the responsibility of re-educating the menfolk, parents and other significant members of society to get them mentally prepared for this change? And it has to try to bring about a change in the conditioning pattern of boys and their attitude towards females through the electronic media, and other sources.

References

Jain, S., Personality traits of adolescent girl students in relation to their parental acceptance, *Journal of Community Guidance and Research,* 1992, 9(3). 213-221.

.... Has parental acceptance something to do with criminality? *National Conference on Psychology*, Bangalore (June 1993).

.... Effect of family relationship on "Child's Mental Health", Transactions of XXX IAAP Conference of Psycho, Jodhpur, India, 1993.

.... Child needs something else also. Abstract No. 17, National Conference of Psychology, Bangalore, June, 1994.

Lewin, K., *Field theory in social science,* New York: Harper, 1951.

Rogers, C. R., *On becoming a person: A therapist view of psychotherapy,* Boston: Houghton, Mifflin, 1961.

CHAPTER 8

Parent-Child Relationship, School Achievement and Adjustment of Adolescent Boys

Paromita Roychaudhury and Jayanti Basu

Parent-child relationship is recognised as a highly significant determinant of children's personality and performance. Here, the impact of this relationship on the school achievement and adjustment of adolescent boys is investigated. Since intelligence is a recognised factor in school success as well as in social competence, its effects have been considered and controlled. The sample consisted of 105 boys of 14 to 15 years of age. The parent-child relationship scale by Rao, the Adjustment Inventory for school students by Sinha, and the Culturefair test by Cattell and Cattell were administered. Achievement scores were taken from school records. The correlation coefficient values obtained after partialling out the effect of intelligence indicated that the pattern of mothering, significantly influenced school adjustment. Both mothering and fathering styles were associated with academic success. Particularly, rejection and neglect from parents were found to be highly detrimental.

Introduction

The available literature concerning the impact of the adolescent's family life on his or her developmental adequacy and functional effectiveness unequivocally highlights the significant contribution of the parents. The general finding is that the parents provide the required environmental facilitation so that the adolescent is able to meet the typical developmental needs of the period, acquire gradual autonomy, achieve sufficient level of interpersonal and intrapersonal adjustment and blossom into a competent, caring, self-reliant adult with a positive self-image. It has been repeatedly observed that in the history of adolescents with behaviour problem, incidents of parental hostility rejection and neglect are more frequent than acceptance, love and trust (Bachman, 1970; Scott and Scott, 1991). Apart from this direct effect on emotional tone, self-concept and socialisation, some secondary influences are also likely to be reflected in their performance and achievement behaviour (Reynolds, 1989; Bronfenbrenner, 1989).

In the present study, we intend to observe the impact of parenting on the adolescent boys' school performance. The school is, undoubtedly, the most significant social context in the life of a child as almost one-third of a day is spent here. The school is not only an organisation to teach cognitive skills and to impart information, it is also a social system in which the child learns the rules of morality, social conventions, attitudes and modes of relating to each other. Thus, for an adolescent, the school life signifies both adjustment and achievement, entailing the emotional as well as the cognitive aspects of life.

Therefore, in our study we would use both the concepts of school achievement as well as school adjustment as our dependent variables to observe the adolescent boy in the context of his school. A survey of earlier studies in this regard indicate that, indeed, the achievement and adjustment in school are determined, to some extent, by environmental facilitation, particularly by the parenting pattern, although the exact extent and mechanism of this influence is not clearcut (Douvan and Adelson, 1966; Anderson et al., 1994; Ryan et al. 1994). The extent of relationship in various studies have been found to vary between low to moderately high. From a meta analysis of 47 such studies Rothbaum and Weisz (1994) attempted to account for this discrepancy. They concluded that the parental impact on school behaviour is not a homogeneous affair, but closely interwined with a number of demographical and cognitive factors. Lack of awareness and control of these variables have led to misleading findings in many of the studies conducted in this respect.

Keeping the above fact in mind we would try to isolate the specific contribution of a few positive and negative dimensions of parenting on school achievement and school adjustment of adolescent boys, when the effect of intelligence, one of the singularly influencing cognitive factors, has been partialled out.

The following hypothesis for the study were formulated:

1. There is a significant relationship between each of the parenting dimensions and school achievement of the adolescent boys.
2. There is a significant relationship between each of the parenting dimensions and every domain of school adjustment of the adolescent boys.

Method

Samples: The sample consisted of all the 105 boys studying in Class VIII of two government schools of Calcutta. Their age ranged between 13 and 14 years. The general standard of the two schools were comparable.

Selection of Variables: The independent variables in the study were five parenting dimensions, namely, Love, Protection. Demandingness, Neglect and Rejection. They were assessed for both the parents.

The dependent variables were twofold. The first was the achievement in examinations and the other was adjustment in school. Adjustment is, however, a multifaceted term and in the context of a school three domains were highlighted. These were emotional adjustment, social adjustment and educational adjustment, referring to one's self-image in the context of the school, in relation with peers and teachers, and orientation to curricular and extracurricular demands respectively. The control variable was intelligence defined as the general ability of obstruction.

Tools used: The following scales were used in this study.

1. The Parent-Child Relationship Scale or the PCRS by Rao (1989) was administered to assess the five dimensions of parenting experienced by the child from their parents. This is a 100-item scale assessing 10 dimensions of parenting. The child responds on a 5-point response category separately for the father and the mother. A high score on each scale implies high loading on that dimension. In the present study the five dimensions specified for our purpose only were taken.
2. The Adjustment Inventory for school students or the AISS by Sinha (1984) was used to assess the three aspects of school adjustment, namely, emotional adjustment, social adjustment and educational adjustment. This is a 60-item scale with a

Yes/ No response format. A high score in each domain indicates greater maladjustment in that area.

3. The Culture-Fair Test for assessing 'g' (Scale-2) by Cattell and Cattell (1960) was used as a measure of general intelligence. A high score implies greater intelligence.
4. Achievement was assessed in terms of the average of three consecutive major school examinations as obtained from school records.
5. An information schedule was used to obtain general information about the respondent's personal and familial conditions.

Administration: The subjects were approached through the school authorities. The achievement scores were collected from school records. All other scales were administered in small groups following a predetermined schedule and distributed over two days.

Scoring and Statistical Treatment: Each scale was scored according to the manual. Subsequently the scores were subjected to statistical treatment. Descriptive statistics involved computation of Mean and Standard Deviation for each variable. Then the Pearson's Correlation Coefficients (r) were computed among all the variables. Then the effect of intelligence was partialled out and the correlation coefficients between the parenting dimensions and achievement as well as between the parenting dimensions and adjustment were computed.

Results

The means and standard deviations of all the variables are presented in Table 1 which reveals that the mean score for 'Loving' was slightly higher for mothers (35.02) than the fathers (33.65), mean 'Protection' score was also higher for the mothers (35.71) than the fathers (32.72), indicating more positive parenting by the mothers. But the mothers were also slightly more 'demanding' (28.50) than the father (27.99), the mothers were more 'Neglecting' (23.30) than the fathers (22.91), as well as more 'Rejecting' (23.81) than the fathers (22.17). Thus it can be said that they were more involved with their children. The mean values also indicate that both the parents scored higher on the 'Love' and 'Protection' dimensions than on the other three, that is, more or less positive parenting was available from our sample. Table 1 further reveals that the subjects demonstrated maximum maladjustment in the social domain (4.59), that is, in their relation with the peers and the teachers, than in the emotional (2.43) or educational (2.70) spheres. The mean achievement score was found to be 494.71 out of 800, and the mean intelligence score was 25.85.

Table 1

Showing the means and standard deviations of the 5 dimensions of parenting for the father and the mother, the 3 domains of adjustment, school achievement and intelligence

	Parenting Dimensions				
	Love	*Protection*	*Demand*	*Neglect*	*Rejection*
Father					
Mean	33.65	32.72	27.99	22.91	22.17
SD	8.97	8.13	6.20	6.01	5.46
Mother					
Mean	35.02	35.71	28.50	23.30	23.81
SD	8.39	8.82	6.31	7.15	6.73

	Maladjustment Domains			*School Achievement*	*Intelligence*
	Emotional	*Social*	*Educational*		
Mean	2.43	4.59	2.70	494.71	25.85
SD	1.84	2.15	2.12	92.83	6.32

Table 2

Showing the Pearson's product moment correlation coefficients (r) between intelligence and parenting dimensions, adjustment domains and achievement

	Parenting Dimensions				
	Love	*Protection*	*Demand*	*Neglect*	*Rejection*
(Father)	.004	.02	–.008	–. 004	.14
(Mother)	.008	–.002	.002	.04	–. 001

Maladjustments			
Emotional	*Social*	*Educational*	*Academic Achievement*
.20 *	.20 *	.005	.54 **

* P <. 05 ** P <. 01

Table 2 reveals the relationship of intelligence, the control variable, with each of the parenting dimensions and school achievement and adjustment. It is observed that the Pearson's product moment correlation coefficient values were significant for emotional maladjustment (r =. 20, p <. 05), social maladjustment (r =. 20, p <.05) but not for educational maladjustment (r =. 005, p >. 05). Intelligence was highly related to achievement (r =. 54, p <. 01). But it was not significantly associated with any of the parenting dimensions of the father or mother.

Subsequently correlation co-efficients between the parenting dimensions (separately for the father and mother) and for the school adjustment and achievement were computed This was done twice, initially without taking into consideration the role of intelligence and then, a second time after partialling out the effect of intelligence. The results are presented in Table 3.

Table 3
Showing the Pearson's product moment correlation coefficients (r) between the parenting dimensions sod the spheres of maladjustment and achievement before and after partialling oat the effect of intelligence

	Maladjustments							
Parenting	*Emotional*		*Social*		*Educational*		*Achievement*	
(Father)	*Before Before*		*After After*	*Before*	*After*	*Before*		*After*
Love	–. 05	–.05	.07	.07	.01	.01	.13	.15
Protection	.05	.05	.06	.06	.03	.03	.14	.15
Demand	.12	.12	–.07	–.07	.02	.02	.10	.12
Neglect	.11	.11	.06	.06	.09	.09	–.17	. 20**
Rejection	.13	.12	.02	.02	.04	.04	–.14	–.26**
(Mother)								
Love	–.07	–.07	.18	.18	–.06	–.06	.08	.09
Protection	.07	.07	.19*	.19*	–.08	–.05	–.49**	–.58**
Demand	.23*	.23*	–.05	–.05	.06	.08	–.38**	–.45**
Neglect	.26*	.26**	–.14	–.14	.04	.01	–.18*	–.24**
Rejection	.21*	.21*	.14	.14	.12	.012	–.17	–.20*

*P<. 05 **P<.01

It is clear from Table 3, that as far as the fathering dimensions were concerned, none of the relationships with school adjustment variables was significant. But mothering was significantly associated with emotional and social maladjustment. In case of emotional maladjustment greater demand, neglect and rejection on the part of the mother resulted in increased emotional disturbance, the correlation coefficients being. 23,. 26 and. 21 respectively. As far as 'Protection' and 'Love' were concerned the 'r's were. 07 and -07 only. For social maladjustment the correlation with protection of mother yielded significant result, 'r' being. 19, p <. 05. No other mothering dimension had any significant relation with social maladjustment. Educational maladjustment on the other hand was relatively unaffected by any mothering dimension.

Table 3 further reveals that partialling out the effect of intelligence did not significantly alter the 'r' values. It implies that the impact of parenting on adjustment was not moderated by the intellectual level of the adolescent boys.

From Table 3 it is also observed that academic achievement was negatively and significantly related to three of the mothering dimensions, namely, 'protection' ($r = -.49$, $p < .01$), 'demandingness' ($r = -.38$, $p < .01$) and 'neglect' ($r = -.18$, $p < .05$). The 'r' between mother's 'rejection' and achievement was $-.17$, which, though not statistically significant, pointed at the same direction. 'Love' was not significantly associated with achievement ($r = .08$, $p > .20$). But fathering in any dimension was not significantly associated with achievement, at least when the effect of intelligence was not controlled.

When however the effect of intelligence was partialled out the correlation coefficient values between all the parenting dimensions and achievement increased. From Table 3 it is apparent that mother's 'Rejection' was, after partialling out the effect of intelligence, significantly and negatively associated with achievement ($r = -.20$, $p < .05$). Two of the fathering dimensions had also acquired significance; when the intelligence had been controlled, his 'rejection' was found to be negatively contributing to the son's achievement ($r = -.26$, $p < .05$), similarly with regard to neglect ($r = -.20$, $p < .05$).

These inferences are implied that the effects of parenting on academic achievement in adolescent boys were moderated by the intellectual level of the students.

Discussion

The present results have to be understood in the context of the specific, developmental needs of the adolescents. All the interpersonal experiences, including the care and authority of the parents, are interpreted in relation to the adolescent boy's demand for increasing autonomy and self-competence, as well as his need of a secured and loving backdrop of parental care.

Our findings indicate that the mothering pattern is immensely important in this respect. This does not deviate from the general expectation regarding the impact of mothers; indeed, Bachman (1970) suggested that the single best indicator of adolescent adjustment is the relation between the mother and the child. This is supported by other researchers as well (Cressey & Ward, 1969; Gold, 1970).

But why did the fathers exert relatively inconsequential influence on their son's adjustment, particularly, since recent research reports are increasingly demonstrating the impact of fathering on adjustment and achievement (Hill, 1967; Medinnus, 1965). A probable explanation may be found in the sociocultural features of our country. While in the west, the parents share, at least to some extent, the offspring's developmental responsibilities, the role definitions in our country are much more rigid. Here, mothers are more often held responsible for children's upbringing and behaviour, and the fathers are relatively distant onlookers (Mitra, 1985). This functional absence of the fathers from their child's intrapsychic life, coupled with the natural mother-son affective bond probably prompts the insignificant social impact of paternal behaviour. Indeed the empirical verification of this perceived distance between the father and the son is supported by a study in the Indian context by Bhushan (1993), who observed that male adolescents felt more restrained with their fathers than with their mothers.

Achievement, on the other hand, is a more masculine quality, and the male children are likely to identify, at least to some extent, with their fathers as far as success is concerned. Starrels (1994) observed that fathers of adolescent boys concentrate more on the instrumental aspects of their sons, and achievement is, undoubtedly, instrumental in connotation (Spence & Helmreich, 1978). Hence paternal impact was prominent in case of the son's achievement.

It was also interesting to note that negative parenting was more important, by casting detrimental influence, since rejection, demand and neglect from mothers resulted in disturbed emotional adjustment. Similar findings have been obtained by Mackinnon et. al (1994). Similarly, school success was affected by parental rejection, demand and neglect as well as by maternal over protection. The detrimental effect of rejection and neglect on academic self-esteem and competence have been demonstrated by Mussen et al. (1963) and that of over-protection by Killer (1972). But the positive dimension of love did not significantly facilitate these factors. Indeed, excessive love and protection was found to increase social inefficiency in school (Table 3).

It may be assumed that what an adolescent boy, trying earnestly to grow into an effective adult, needs is not an over-pour of expressive love but just a stable loving and accepting background for enacting his independent overtures. Excess of love may breed submissive and retiring social coping style as well as a dependency on a careful mother figure.

Finally, the enhancement of the negative correlation value in case of school achievement, when the effect of intelligence is being partialled out, implies that in real life, the negative outcomes of faulty parent-child relationship may be somewhat buffered by high level of intelligence; but in case of boys with overage or low cognitive ability, inadequacy of parenting may be disastrous, specially for academic success.

Conclusion

From the above results it can be concluded that parenting had significant association with school adjustment and school achievement. The relation however was not equally significant for all parenting dimensions, nor for all adjustment spheres. Thus, our hypotheses were only partially supported.

As far as emotional and social adjustment was concerned, mothering was more important than fathering. Educational adjustment was unrelated to any kind of parenting. School achievement was most significantly associated with the parenting dimensions. It was further concluded that positive parenting contributed less to adjustment and achievement than negative parenting, which significantly hampered normal and healthy development of the emotional, interpersonal and academic faculties.

Finally, a significant relevance of the study resides in its revelation that intelligence plays a moderating role between parenting style and academic success. It implies that the effect of parenting is by no means a straightforward influence, but his perceived and utilised differentiality depending upon the cognitive status of the children. Further, in-depth studies are required to unfold the mechanism behind this moderating effect of intelligence to a greater extent.

References

Anderson, C. A. Hinshaw, S. R. & Simmel, C., Mother child interactions in ADHD and comparison boy: relationship with overt and covert externalising behaviour, *Journal of Abnormal Child Psychology,* 1994, 22 (2), 247-265.

Armentrout, J. A. & Burger, G. K., Children's reports of parental child rearing behaviour at 5 grade levels, *Developmental Psychology,* 1972 7, 44-48.

Bachman, J. G., *Youth in transition (Vol. 2) The impact of family background and intelligence on 10th, grade boys,* Ann Arbor: Institute for Social Research. University of Michigan, 1970.

Baidwin, A. L., Socialisation and parent-child relationship. *Child Development,* 1948, 19, 127-136.

Bhushan, R. A. A study of family communication: Parents and their adolescent children, *Journal of Personality and Clinical Studies* 1993, 19 (1&2), 79-85.

Biller, H. B., The mother-child relationship and father absent boys' personality development in U. Bronfenbrenner (Ed), *Influences on Human Development,* Hinsdale III: Dryden Press, 1972, 306-319.

Bronfenbrenner, Ecological Systems Theory, *Annals of Child Development,* 1989, 6, 187-249.

Cattell, R. B. & Cattell K.S., *Culture Fair Intelligence Test Scale 2, Illinois,* IPAT, 1960.

Cressy, D. R. & Ward, D., A. *Delinquency, Crime & Social Presence,* New York: Harper & Row, 1969.

Douvan, E. & Adelson, J., *The Adolescent Experience,* New York, Wiley, 1966.

Gold. M., *Delinquent behaviour in an American city,* Californian Brooks/ Cole, 1990.

Hill. J. P., Similarity and accordance between parents and sons in attitudes towards Mathematics, *Child Development,* 1967, 38, 777-791.

Mackinnon, L. C., Volling, B. L., Lamb, M. E., Deahman, K. et al. A cross contextual analysis of boys' social competence from family to school, *Developmental Psychology,* 1994, 30 (3), 325-333.

Medinnus, G. R., The relation between interparent agreement and several child measures, *Journal of Genetic Psychology,* 1965, 102, 130-144.

Mitra, S. K., Indian personality: A perspective, *Samiksa,* 1985, 37, (2), 31-55.

Mussen. P. H., Young, H. B., Gaddini, R. and Morante, L., The influence of father-son relationship on adolescent personality and attitudes, *Journal of Social Psychology,* 1963, 4, 3-16.

Rao, Manual for the Parent-Child Relationship Scale (PCRS), Agra, *National Psychological Corporation,* 1989.

Reynolds, A. J., A structural model of first grade outcomes for an urban, low socio-economic status minority population, *Journal of Educational Psychology,* 1989, 81, 594-603.

Rothbaum, F. B. Weisz, J. R., Parental caregiving and child externalising behaviour in non-clinical samples: A Meta-analysis, *Psychological Bulletin*, 1994, 116, (1), 55-74.

Ryan, R. M., Slitler. J. D. & Lynch, J. H., Representations of relationships to teachers, parents and friends as predictors of academic motivation and self-esteem. Sp. Issue. Middle grades schooling and early adolescent development, *Journal of Early Adolescence,* 1994 14, (2), 226-249.

Scott, W. A., Scott, R. & McCobe, M. Family relationships and children's personality: A cross-cultural, cross-source comparison, *British Journal of Social Psychology,* 1991 30, (I) 1-20.

Sinha, A. K. P., *Manual for Adjustment Inventory for School Students* (AISS) Agra, National Psychological Corporation, 1984.

Spence, J. T., & Helmreioh, R., On assessing androgyny, *Sex roles,* 1978, 5, 721-738.

Starrels, M. E., Gender difference in parent child relations, *Journal of Family Issues,* 1994, 15, (1), 148-165.

PART II
INTELLIGENCE, ACADEMIC ACHIEVEMENTS AND SKILLS

The human individual right from the time of birth till the maturity stage is undergoing various processes of development. The person's physical growth and development can be clearly observed but not the other developments like the mental, emotional, social and other developments. These developments can be observed only in the behaviour of the individual. The hereditary factor have the influencing effects in the mental and social developments mainly. But, however the role of the environment also has equal importance in all the developmental processes. To the process of mental development, parents and teachers provide suitable stimuli and other opportunities to the child and to the adolescent. The level of the development of intelligence and problem-solving skills are revealed only in the behaviour of the individual. In the case of adolescents the academic achievement in schools is the test of the level of intelligence.

The adolescents always aspire for high achievements and also may work hard to achieve their aims. Towards this the family background of the students always function as the feeding source. The socioeconomic status of the family, the educational standard and the occupational status of the parents are the highly influencing factors for the school achievements of the adolescent boys and girls. By the encouragement of the parents and teachers the adolescents develop their creative skills and other talents.

CHAPTER 9

Intelligence and N-Achievement of Adolesent Girls and Their Attitudes towards the Status of Women

Ira Das

It is the study of the effect of intelligence and n-achievement of adolescent girls upon their attitude towards the status of women. The sample consisted of 400 adolescent girls drawn from rural and urban areas of Agra and nearby districts. Their age ranged from 13 years to 16 years. Bhatia's Battery of Performance tests of Intelligence, McClelland's N-Achievement test and a scale of attitude towards the status of women, developed and validated by the investigator were used to collect data. The investigator personally met the subjects in a group situation and the tests were administrated. The tests were scored according to the procedure and the individual scores here obtained. The data were statistically treated. Results indicate that girls with high intelligence have more positive attitude than the girls of low in intelligence. There was significant interaction effect between intelligence and n-achievement. High intelligent girls with low n-achievement had a high positive attitude towards women.

Introduction

Attitude starts developing from the childhood stage onwards and therefore even a young Indian girl develops a feeling that she is given less importance in comparison to other male counterparts in the family. She finds a similar situation in other families too and finally comes to the conclusion that her status is deemed to be low in comparison to that of the boys in the family. So a study was made among the adolescent girls in the age group of 13 to 16 years of age to measure the direction and intensity of their attitude towards the status of their own sex in the present Indian social set-up.

It was assumed that adolescent girls' intellectual level may have an effect upon the formation of their attitude towards their own sex. It was hypothesised that more intelligent girls have a more positive attitude towards the status of women. Those who are less intelligent (with average or below average I.Q.) do not have confidence upon their capabilities, nor do they understand the various complexities of life (specially their legal and economic rights), and therefore they estimate their status to be low, not realising that men too lack the same abilities.

Similarly girls with high n-achievement are expected to have a more positive attitude towards the status of women. They have a strong desire to compete with their male counterparts and do not think that women are deemed to have low status in society. It was therefore hypothesised that girls with high n-achievement have a more positive attitude towards the status of women. Those with low n-achievement feel relaxed and think that women's status is low in comparison to men. Kumar (1988), Nair (1988) and Karna, Manato & Panjiyar (1989) found that urban subjects and those from higher socioeconomic status have a more liberal attitude towards the status of women. It was found that even the constitutional guarantees for equality have not helped women to achieve their proper status. Hein (1989) and Diana (1990) found that men had an unfavourable attitude towards the status of women in comparison to women.

Based on this problem the following hypotheses have been formulated: (l) More intelligent and high n-achieving adolescent girls have a more positive attitudes towards the status of women. (2) Less intelligent and low n-achievement adolescent girls have a negative attitudes towards the status of women.

Method

Design: A2x2 factorial design was used to study the effect of the two independent variables, i.e., intelligence and need achievement and to study the interaction effect of these two upon the dependent variables, i.e., the attitude towards the status of women in India.

Sample: The sample consisted of 400 adolescent girls between the age range of 13 and 16 years, randomly selected from rural and urban areas of Agra, Manipuri and Etah in equal proportions. The sample included literature as well as illiterate adolescent girls who belonged to Brahmin, Kshatriya, Vaishya, Scheduled Castes and Backward Class groups.

Tools: Three test materials were used to collect data

1. Battery of Performance Tests of Intelligence by Bhatia (1955).
2. N-Achievement test by McClelland (1976).
3. Scale for measuring "Attitude towards status of Women" in India. This scale was prepared and validated by the investigator. The scale was based upon Thurstone's equal appearing intervals. The scale has the following five areas (1) Social, (2) Capabilities for taking decision and carrying out action, (3) Legal, (4) Responsibilities and (5) Economic.

Procedure: The investigator personally met the subjects in a group situation. They were explained the purpose of this test and the tests were administered individually. First Bhatia's Battery of Performance test was administered. The responses were recorded. Secondly McClelland's TAT N-Achievement test was administered. It is in the form of picture cards. The pictures were shown for 20 seconds and they were asked to write stories within five minutes time for each card. As soon as the task was over they were collected from the girls. The third test was the attitude side. It was the attitude towards the status of women. This was measured by an attitude scale developed by the investigator on the pattern of Thurtone's equal appearing intervals. The girls were asked to check the statements with which they agree. There were both positive and negative statements.

All the three scales were scored according to the procedure as given. The test manuals and the individuals scores were obtained. The scores were treated statistically and presented in tables and interpreted.

Results and Discussion

Table 1

Analysis of variance-effect of intelligence and N-achievement upon attitude scores

Source of variance	*Sum of squares*	*df*		*Mean square*	*F*
Intelligence (A)	1.46	1	1.46	9.48	p.01
N-Achievement (B)	0.0005	1	.005	0.032	p.05
A x B	0.13	1	1.05	6.82	p.05

The results in Table 1 indicate that intelligence has a significant effect upon the attitude towards the status of women. Girls who are more intelligent have a more positive attitude towards the status of women than the girls who are less in intelligence. But the effect of n-achievement upon the attitude was not found to be significant.

The effect of interaction of intelligence and n-achievement upon the attitude was tested and found that the interaction effects of n-achievement and intelligence are found to be significant at. 01 level.

Table 2
Showing the scores of the subjects on the intelligence test and the high and low achievement levels of the girls

		MeanMean	
	HighLow		
N-Ach.	High	5.044	5.025
	Low	5.139	4.916

The mean attitude scores in Table 2 indicate that highly intelligent girls had moderately high n-achievement and a high positive attitude towards the status of women. This means that highly intelligent girls with high n-achievement have the second high positive attitude. Girls with low n-achievement and low intelligence have a low attitude towards the status of women. It was found that among highly intelligent girls, with high n-achievement scores, they have greater opportunities to face the realities and they have a chance to achieve something better which may give them a better status in society equivalent to men. Therefore hypothesis one is accepted.

Highly intelligent girls with low n-achievement do not get much opportunity to face the realities of the world. Therefore, the girls with high intelligence and low n-achievement had slightly overestimated their status. In the case of less intelligent girls it was just the reverse. Girls with lower intellectual level having low n-achievement have easily accepted that the status of women is deemed to be low in society and therefore they underestimated their position. Hence hypotheses two is accepted.

References

Bhatia, C.M., *Performance Tests of Intelligence under Indian Conditions,* Bombay: Oxford University Press, 1955.

Diana, J., Palestinian women: The status, and roles of Palestinian Women in the West Bank, *Dissertation Abstracts International,* 1990, 49 (10).

Das, I. & Pandey, A Construction and standardisation of a scale measuring attitude towards status of women in India. Paper presented at the National Seminar organised by the Institute of Psychological Research at the Indian Institution of Science, Bangalore, 1992.

Garnett, P.E., Comparative study of male and female school board members' attitudes towards women, *Dissertation Abstract International,* 1985, 46 (12).

Karna N.L., Mahato, H.N. & Panjiyar J.P, Status of women in the eyes of women, A study in Mithilanchal paper presented at the 78th Session of the Indian Science Congress, 1989.

Kumar, S.K., Attitude towards the dowry system and social status of women: Review of the research report, *Indian Journal of Behaviour,* 10, 1988, (3), 31-35.

McClelland D.C.: Atkinson, J.W.: Clark, R.A. & Lowcll, R.L., *The achievement motive,* New York: John Wiley, 1976.

Nair; S.B., Link between women's status and quality, *Times of India,* 1988, Dec. 18.

CHAPTER 10

Family Background and Scholastic Achievements of Secondary School Students

M. Sarada Devi and Kavitha Kiran

Academic achievement has become the sole yardstick of self-worth and success and students are made to feel unworthy and guilty for performing low at school. Academic under-achievement is one of the major problems in the Indian educational system. The present study was taken up to find out the family factors associated with scholastic backwardness of secondary school children. Hyderabad city was selected for the study. The interview schedule was used to elicit family factors related to scholastic backwardness; 100 low achieving students (50 boys and 50 girls) of ninth and tenth classes from 10 private English-medium schools were taken as sample. Large family size, low educational status of parents, low parental involvement and low parental encouragement were found to be the major family factors associated with scholastic backwardness. To increase the academic performance of low achievement the quality of parent-child relationship should be strengthened and the children should be motivated and encouraged to perform better in the school. Parents should take sufficient interest in the education of their children.

INTRODUCTION

Education is a unique investment and academic achievement is a vital aspect in education. In this competitive world academic achievement is considered a key to judge one's potentialities and capacities. Hence educators are giving more importance to academic achievement. Academic underachievement, incidence of dropouts and failures at various levels of education are some of the major problems of the present education system. Low achievement may cause deterioration in personality, negative self-concept and social maladjustment.

A family has paramount influence on the child and is an important contributing factor for school achievement. Research on family and school showed that socioeconomic and cultural backgrounds have an impact on mental development and school achievement. Hence it becomes important to study the family factors responsible for scholastic backwardness of children. A study on secondary school children is necessary because the value of academic achievement is important during this age for further education and vocational placement. Hence this study was taken up to identify the family factors associated with scholastic backwardness of secondary school children.

Methods and Materials

A sample of 100 low achieving students (50 boys & 50 girls) were drawn from 10 private schools selected (each school 10) from all the five zones of Hyderabad city. Children who got less than 45 per cent of aggregate marks in previous annual examination were taken as underachievers.

An interview schedule was used to elicit information on family factors associated with scholastic backwardness of children.

The investigators personally met the subjects in the classroom situation and collected the data, and the treatment of the data are presented in tables.

Results and Discussion

The family factors associated with scholastic backwardness of the secondary school children were presented and discussed in the following:

1. Type of family
2. Size of the family
3. Educational status of parents
4. Occupation of parents
5. Relationship between family variables and academic achievement of low achievers.
6. Relationship of parents' education with parental involvement and parental motivation.
7. Association between parental involvement and parental motivation.

1. *Type of family:* Seventy-seven per cent of the children were from nuclear families and 23 per cent were from the joint families.

2. *Size of the family:* Details of the size of the family is given in Table 1.

Seventy-eight percent of the respondents had a family size of 5 to 10 members (Table 1). Through regression analysis it was found that family size had a significant influence on the scholastic backwardness of the respondents. Family size to a certain extent determines the distribution of materials and financial resources of the family. Adinarayana (1996) found that family size and father's education had a direct effect on the academic achievement of children.

Table 1: Size of the family

Family Size	*Percentage N = 100*	
3.4	22	
5.6	46	
7.8	15	78
9.10	17	

3. *Education of Parents:* The information on the educational status of the parents is given in Table 2.

Table 2: Educational level of parents

Educational level	*Percentage N=100*	
	Mothers	*Fathers*
Illiterate	17	1
Primary	59	12
S.S.C.	17	36
Intermediate	4	23
Graduate	3	21
Postgraduate	–	7

It is evident that most of the mothers had only primary education and fathers had up to intermediate level. It was found that parents' education has a positive significant relationship with parental involvement and motivation. Through regression analysis it was seen that the low educational status of mother was a significant contributing factor for low achievement. Educated mothers help the child progress in school (Stevenson and Baker, 1987). It was also found that father's low education was associated with scholastic backwardness.

Occupation of Parents

Majority (91%) of the respondents' mothers were housewives. Most of the respondents' fathers were low cadre government employees and small businessmen. Very few fathers were found in professional and executive levels. Low parental occupations are positively associated with scholastic underachievement of children.

Relationship between Family Variables and Academic Achievement of Low Achievers

Table 3 gives the relationship between family variables and low achievement.

Table 3
Relationship between Family Variables and Academic Achievement of Low Achievers

Family variables	*Maximum score*	*Minimum score*	*Mean+SD score*		*Academic achievement of low achievers*	
Family size	4	1	2.74 ±	0.98	-0.099	NS
Physical facilities	15	6	11.7	± 2.0	0.017	NS
Parental involvement	45	15	24.3	± 4.37	0.01	NS
Parent motivation	30	10	17.1	± 2.93	0.09	NS

NS - not significant

It was revealed through mean scores that children had a large family size and average physical facilities. It was also found that children had low parental involvement and low parent motivation. Family size had a negative relationship with academic achievement, but was not significant. Physical facilities, parental involvement and parental motivation had non-significant positive relationship with academic achievement of low achievers. This was because group consisted of only low achievers and they had low parental involvement and motivation. Osciala Esogwa (1981) found that underachievement is commonly associated with mild family dysfunction and accompanied by deficits in attention, memory, motivation and self-esteem. Chang & Chung-hising (1981) revealed that perceived parental expectations and students' own expectations were smaller in high achievers than in low achievers.

Relationship of Parents' Education with Parental Involvement and Parental Motivation

It is given in the Table 4.

It was revealed that both mother's and father's education were found to have positive significant relationship with parental involvement in their children's studies. It could be concluded that the more the parents are educated, the more they are involved in their children's education. Mothers education had a non-significant positive relationship with parental motivation but father's education had a significant positive relationship. In this study parents were less educated, hence less involved in their children's studies but when father's educational level was increasing, they were more involved and motivated their children to perform better. The present study reveals that low parental involvement was associated with scholastic backwardness which was in conformity with the findings of Grolnick and Slowiaczek (1994).

Table 4: Relationship of parents' education with parental involvement and parental motivation

Variable	*Mother's education*	*Father's education*
Parental involvement	0.446* *	0.4431* *
Parent motivation	0.162 NS	0.22*

** P –0.01
NS - not significant
* P 0.05

Relationship between Parental Involvement and Parental Motivation

The relationship is presented in Table 5.

Table 5
Relationship between parental involvement and parental motivation

Variables	*Parent motivation*
Parental involvement	0.26*

*P = 0.05

There exists a positive significant relationship between parental involvement and parental motivation. When the parents are more involved in the education of the child, they motivate the children to do better at school. Stevenson and Baker (1987), Barber and Bonnie (1988) found that parental involvement is related to the child's school performance. Authoritative parenting styles were positively associated with grades of children, Sandford (1987) & Steinberg (1989). Ginsburg and Phyllis (1993) found that parental surveillance of homework, parental reaction to grades were associated with high academic achievement of children.

From this study it could be concluded that family factors associated with scholastic backwardness were large family size, low educational status of parents, low parental involvement and low parent motivation.

Summary and Conclusions

Majority of the children studied were from nuclear families. Most of the mothers of the respondents had only primary education and few of them were illiterates. Large family size and low education of mothers were found to be significant leading factors for low achievement of the children. The educational status of parents determine their involvement and motivation in their children's education.

Hence, large family size, low educational status of parents, low parental involvement and low parental motivation were the major family factors associated with scholastic backwardness of the secondary school children.

References

Adinarayana, N., Family size and academic achievement of children. A study of urban high school students in Tamilnadu, *The Journal of Family Welfare,* 1996, (42), 46-50.

Backer, D & Stevenson, D., Mothers strategies for school achievement, *Managing the Transition to High School Sociology of Education,* 1986, (59), 156-167.

Barber & Bonnie, The influence of family demographic and parental teaching practices on Peruvians children's academic achievement, *Human Development,* 1988, (31), 370-377.

Chang & Chunghising Relationship between academic achievement and the discrepancies between student perceptions to parental expectations aid perceptions of their own performance, *Bulletin of Educational Psychology,* 1981, (14), 31-39.

Ginsberg, S.G. & Phyllis, B., Family factors related to children's intrinsic and extrinsic motivational orientation and academic performance, *Child Development,* 1993, (64), 1461-1474.

Grolnick, S.W. & Slowiaezek, Parents involvement in children's schooling, A multi-dimensional conceptualization and motivational model, *Child Development,* 1994, (65) 237-252.

Osciala Esogwa, Parental influence on academic achievement of students, *Asian Journal of Psychology and Education,* 1981, (7) 1-7.

Sanford, M.D., Relations of parenting styles to adolescents school performance, *Child Development,* 1987, (58), 244-1257.

Steinberg, H., Authoritative parenting, Psycho-social maturity and academic success among adolescents, *Child Development,* 1989, (60), 1424-1436.

CHAPTER 11

Influence of Family Socio-economic Status on Educational and Occupational Aspirations of High and Low Achieving Adolescents

Mahmood S. Khan **and** *Tsehaie Jemberu*

The present study was an attempt to investigate the influence of SES on the education and occupational aspirations of adolescents. The sample consisted of 80 students, selected from four groups-middle status/ high achieving, middle status/low achieving, lower status/high achieving, and lower status/low achieving. Occupational and educational aspiration scales were administered for data collection and the data were analysed by means of ANOVA. Results showed that while the impact of SES on educational aspirations was minimal, its influence on occupational aspirations was larger. Achievement highly influenced educational aspirations, but its impact on occupational aspiration was insignificant.

Introduction

Educational aspirations have been conceptualised as internalised advance estimates of eventual educational attainment (Phillips & Asbury, 1993). Occupational aspirations are the prestige levels of the occupations which a person desires to attain.

Aspirations develop as the child's identity develops (Iedema, Meeus & Goede, 1996). Gottfredson (1981) explained that people begin to circumscribe their occupational aspirations as they begin to develop concepts of themselves and of opportunities people like themselves can anticipate in life. Researchers have attempted to develop models that explain the influencing factors in the development of aspirations (e.g., Hossler & Stage, 1992; Walker & Sutherland, 1993). Farmer's (1985) model which is composed of background, personal and environmental factors is acclaimed to be one of the best models (Farmer & Chung, 1995).

Family SES, being a prominent background variable is reported to directly influence adolescents' educational and occupational aspirations. That is, the higher the SES, the higher was adolescents' aspirations (McDonald & Jessel, 1992; Wilson & Wilson, 1992). SES is also found to indirectly affect the adolescents' aspirations through family salience (Farmer & Chung, 1995) socialisation process (McDonald & Jessel, 1992). Parental expections (Solorzano, 1992), academic track (McCraken, Barcinas & Wims, 1991), Students' GPA (Hossler & Stage, 1992), school environment and quality (Wilson & Wilson, 1992), discussion with parents and teachers' expectations (Smith, 1999).

Academic achievement and ability are also reported to be strong predictors of educational/occupational aspirations. Adolescents possessing superior cognitive abilities and/or achievement held higher aspirations than the non-gifted and the disabled (Ramos & Sanchez, 1995). Gifted students showed higher levels of occupational aspirations and perceived fewer barriers than regular students (Kelly, 1992). Several other studies have also indicated strong positive relationships between ability/achievement and educational and/or occupational aspirations (Hossler & Stage, 1992; Owens, 1992; Rojewiski & Yang, 1997).

Positive relationships between family SES and academic achievement is explored by researchers (e.g., Karna & Panjiar, 1997). As SES rises, achievement level also rises and thus, higher levels of educational and occupational aspirations are expected.

In the light of the foregoing discussion, the question however is whether family SES influences the aspirations of high and low achieving adolescents similarly or not when the impact of SES on achievement is controlled. Identifying and understanding the pattern of the influence of factors on educational and occupational aspirations is an important endeavour for intervention programmes.

The present study was aimed at examining the influence of family SES on the educational and occupational aspirations of adolescents in the contexts of high and low achievements. It is hoped that this kind of research may contribute to the development of models that can explain and predict adolescents' educational/occupational aspirations.

Method

Sample: Eighty students of grade nine were selected from two schools in Aligarh city by employing the method of stratified random sampling. On the basis of the information furnished by the respondents to a demographic questionnaire and the report of class teachers the students were divided into four groups (high achieving/middle status, high achieving/lower status, low achieving/middle status, low achieving/lower status). From each group, 20 students were finally selected.

Variables and Instruments

The socioeconomic status (SES) was determined by the family monthly income, father's occupation and parents' education. Middle status was defined as a family monthly income of above Rs. 12,000, father's occupational status was independently rated to be above four (out of five) by two judges, and at least one of the parents' educational level is above bachelor's degree. Lower status was defined as a family monthly income below Rs. 6,000, father's occupational status is below two (out of five) as rated by two judges indepe-ndently and whose parents educational level is below bachelor's degree.

Achievement was defined in terms of class marks. High achiever is a student whose average class marks was above 70 per cent. Law achiever is a student with average marks below 45 per cent.

Occupational aspiration was measured by Grewal's (1975) Occupational Aspiration Scale (OAS), which is an eight-item multiple choice instrument. The scale is reported to be valid and reliable.

Educational aspiration was measured by an Educational Aspiration Scale (EAS) developed and validated by the present investigators. The scale consists of six items, each item containing six educational levels as options.

Procedure and Data Analysis: After securing the permission of school officials, participants were requested to complete the OAS and EAS. In each administration, around 10 students were called into a separate room, were given brief introduction and were assured of confidentiality.

Two-way ANOVA (SES and Achievement) were employed for the two dependent variables separately.

Results

Table 1

Two-way ANOVA summary table on educational aspirations

Source	*SS*	*df*	*MS*	F	*p*
A	145.80	1	145.80	5.97	<. 05
B	605.00	1	605.00	24.78	<. 01
AxB	42.00	1	42.00	1.72	NS
Within	1855.15	76	24.41		
Total	2647.95	79			

A = SES, B = Achievement

Table 1 indicates that there is a significant (p <. 05) main effect by the factor of SES. Middle status adolescents scored higher on EAS (mean = 28.6) than the lower status adolescents (mean = 25.9). This variable accounted for about 6% of the total variation in the EAS scores.

Table 1 also indicates that there is a significant (P <. 01) difference between high and low achievers. High achievers scored higher (mean = 30.0) than the low achievers (mean= 24.5) on EAS. This variable accounted for about 23 per cent of the total variability in EAS scores.

Table 2 indicates that there is a significant (p <. 01) main effect by the factor of SES. Middle status adolescents scored higher (mean = 58.1) on OAS than the lower status adolescents (mean = 53.9). This variable accounted for about 11 per cent of the total variation in OAS scores. The achievement variable influence on OAS scores was not statistically significant.

Table 2

Two-way ANOVA summary table on occupational aspirations

Source	*SS*	*df*	*MS*	F	*p*
A	340.32	1	340.32	9.496	<. 01
B	99.02	1	99.02	2.763	NS
AxB	12.00	1	12.00	.335	NS
Within	2723.65	76	35.84		
Total	31.74.99	79			

A = SES, B = Achievement

Discussion

The results indicated that SES had low influence on the educational aspiration of the sample. Rather it was academic achievement that accounted for the major proportion (23%) of the variability in the group's educational aspiration scores. In other words, the educational aspiration of lower SES/high achieving adolescents (mean = 28.0) was little affected by their social origins. In addition, middle SES/lower achieving students' educational aspirations (mean = 25.2) were not adequately raised due to their advantageous social status.

A number of path analytic studies have shown that SES and GPA/ability are correlated and influence aspirations (e.g., Hossler & Stage, 1992; Walker & Sutherland, 1993). But in the present study, when the effect of SES on academic achievement was controlled by sampling design, the role of SES as a major influencer of educational aspirations was highly diminished.

The higher educational aspirations of the lower SES/high achieving adolescents may be explained by the motivational effects of high achievement. The higher the academic achievement of the individual, the higher would be the self-efficacy, the expectations from parents and teachers and thus, higher educational aspiration levels. Another explanation could be that high achieving/low status adolescents may have differential exposure to the current educational norms as suggested by Smith (1981).

The resets also indicated that irrespective of the academic achievement, SES had significant influence on the occupational aspirations of the adolescents. The high achieving/ lower SES students, despite their high educational aspirations, aspired to lower status occupations when compared with their advantaged high and low achieving counterparts.

Several path analytic studies have shown achievement as one major influencing factor of occupational aspirations (Cook et al, 1996; Rojewiski & Yang, 1997). But, for the present sample, when the effect of SES on academic achievement was controlled by sampling design, achievement did not produce significant influence on occupational, aspirations.

The results obtained may be attributed to the perception of the opportunity structure, the systemic bias, social attitudes, cultural expectations and stereotypes, inadequate role models, lack of information which might lead to limited career alternatives and availability imposing lower status and devalued role in adolescents, irrespective of their abilities. This explanation falls in the line with status attainment theory (Hotchkiss & Borrow, 1996).

The findings of the present study need to be seen with caution. The sample was a select group as the proportion of high and low achievers were made equal from the two status groups.

The lower SES/high achieving group, which has high educational but low occupational aspirations needs special attention. Aspirations have serious implications in latter achievements and accomplishments. Any failure in providing adequate interventions may result in wasting talents in youth. Therefore, adequate interventions programmes are highly needed.

References

Cook, T D., et al. The development of occupational aspirations and expectations among inner-city boys, *Child Development,* 1996, 67, 3368-3385.

Fanner, H. S., Model of career and achievement motivation for women and men, *Journal of Counselling Psychology,* 1995, 32, 363-390.

Farmer, H. S., & Chung, Y B., Variables related to career commitment, mastery motivation, and level of aspiration among college students, *Journal of Career Development,* 1990, 21(4), 265-278.

Gottfredson, L.S., Circumscription and compromise: A development theory of occupational aspirations, *Journal of Counselling Psychology,* 1981, 28, 545-579.

Grewal, J.S., *Occupational Aspiration Scale*, National Psychological Corporation, 1975, Agra - 282 002.

Hossler, D., & Stage, E K., Family and high school experience on post secondary educational studies, *American Educational Research Journal,* 1992, 29(2), 425-451.

Hotchikiss, L., & Borrow, H. Sociological, perspectives on work and career development. In D. Drown & L. Brooks (eds.), *Career Choice Development* (3rd ed. pp. 281-334). San Fransisco: Jossey- Bass, 1996.

Iedema, J., Meets, W, & DeGoede, M., The effects of educational and relational mental incongruity on identity formation, *Social Behaviour and Personality,* 1996, 24(4), 393-404.

Karna N. L., & Panjiar, D., Environmental deprivation slid personality development, In Sinha, S.N. (ed). *Environmental Psychology* (pp. 43-52), Jaipur: Pointer Publishers, 1997.

Kelly, K., *Career maturity of young gifted adolescents: A replication study Journal for the education of the gifted*, 1992, 16(1), 36-45.

McCracken, J.D., Barcinas, D.T, & Wims, D., Aspirations of rural twelfth grade students in vocational, general and academic curricula in Ohio and South West Georgia, *Journal of Vocational Education,* 1991, 16(1), 51-77.

McDonald, J., & Jessel, J. C., Influence of select variables on occupational attitudes and perceived occupational ability of young adolescents, *Journal of Career Development,* 1992, 18(4), 239-250.

Phillips, C. P, & Asbury, C. A., Parental divorce/separation and the motivational characteristics and educational aspirations of African American University students, *Journal of Negro Education,* 1993, 62(2), 204-210.

Ramos, L., & Sanchez, A. R., Mexican-American high school students' educational aspiration, *Journal of Multicultural Counselling and Development,* 1995 23(4), 212-221.

Smith, E. S., Adolescent agreement with perceived maternal and paternal educational goals, *Journal of Marriage and the Family,* 1981, 43, 85-93.

Smith-Maddox, R., The social networks and resources of African American eighth graders: Evidence from the National Educational Longitudinal Study of 1988, *Adolescence,* 1999, 34 (133), 169-183

Walker, E. M., & Sutherland, M. E., Urban Black youths, educational mid-occupational goals, The impact of America's opportunity structure, *Urban Education,* 1993, 28(2), 200-220.

Wilson, P M., & Wilson, T. R., Environmental influences on adolescents educational aspiration: A logistic transform model, *Youth and Society,* 1992, 24(1), 52-69.

CHAPTER 12

Self-Concept and Scholastic Achievement of the Girls of Working and Non-working Mothers

Sadhna Mittal

The present study is aimed to compare the self-concept and scholastic achievement of the girls of working and non-working mothers. The sample consisted of 100 girls studying in twelfth class in Agra city. Bhatnagar's self-concept Inventory and Scholastic Achievement test were used to collect data. The investigator personally met the students and conducted the test. The data were statistically treated and the results show that there were no significant differences in any of the areas of self-concept and scholastic achievement.

Introduction

Psychologists, sociologists and educationists have unanimously documented the importance of the family on the development of the child. Family is the primary agency to transmit the sociocultural standards, family norms, values, discipline and various other qualities. These are transmitted by the family to the child through the process of socialisation. As Jemni, the author of *Brahmasutra*, puts it, "The child learns the beat lesson of citizenship between the kiss of the mother and cares of the father."

The Indian family has undergone and is still undergoing far reaching changes due to industrialisation, migration, modernisation, and technological changes. Adolescence, which is said to be the age of "stress and strain", "awkward age" and "problematic age" is a critical period in the life of the individual. As Margaret Mead puts it, adolescence may be stressful or smooth depending on how a particular society responds towards this group. Therefore parents should have proper understanding and education to guide and help the adolescent to grow into a healthy and competent individual in the society.

The entry of increasing number of women in the job market is creating changes in the family ecology which are important implications in scholastic achievement and in the development of self-concept of the children. Now, a question comes in our mind, whether working mothers are able to fulfil their duties perfectly or not.

Empirical studies in this context have yielded mixed results. Maternal employment encourages children to become self-sufficient and independent at an early age. Prasad and Prasad (1975) found that male children of working mothers are socially more participative than children of non-working mothers. Mody and Murthy (1988) observed children of working mothers as careless and slightly emotionally unstable in the early years but independent during later years as compared to the children of non-working mothers. They also reported low intelligence scores in children of working mothers at the age 12 years.

The available Indian studies have a number of problems and it is hard to draw any definite conclusion, therefore the present problem was chosen.

- *The problem:* The problem of this study is to compare the development of self-concept with scholastic achievement of the girls of working mothers and non-working mothers. On the basis of this a null hypothesis is formulated.
- *Hypothesise:* There is no significant difference between the scores of self-concept inventory and scholastic achievement of the schoolgirls of working and non-working mothers in the city of Agra.
- *Variables of the present study:* The dependent variables are the development of self-concepts anal scholastic achievement. The independent variables are the girls of the working mothers and non-working mothers, age level, and educational level.

Methodology

- *Sample:* The sample consisted of 100 girls studying in twelfth standard in Agra city. Their age ranged from 15 years to 17 years. The stratified purposeful sampling technique was used and the sample was selected. There were 50 girls, who were the daughters of working (teaching profession) mothers and 50 girls were the daughters of non-working mothers (educated up to P. G.). These two groups of girls were matched in education, age, sex and socio-economic status.
- *Tools:* Two test materials were used in this investigation. They were (1) Bhatnagar Self-Concept Inventory and (2) Scholastic Achievement test.
- *Bhatnagar Self-Concept Inventory:* For measuring the self-concept of the adolescent girls Bhatnagar's self-concept inventory was administered. This measures the self-concept of adolescents in five areas such as
- *The Scholastic Achievement test:* This test constitute the total marks of the girl students obtained in the U. P. Board High School Examination. The marks were taken as the scores.
- *Procedure:* All the selected subjects of the two groups were given the self-concept inventory. The instructions printed on the questionnaire booklet were read loudly to them. They took 30 minutes to complete the questionnaire. The personal data and high school marks in each subject were obtained from the school office records.

Results and Discussion

The scores of self-concept inventory and the scholastic achievement of girls of the working and non-working mothers were statistically treated and are presented in Table 1.

It was hypothesised that there is no significant difference between the self-concept of the girls of working mothers and non-working mothers.

The result as given in Table 1 shows the scores of self-concept in all five dimensions of the self-concept for the children of working and non-working mothers It is observed that there is no significant mean score difference between the girls of working and non-working mothers in any of the dimensions. As regards the achievement aspect of self concept the C.R. value is 0.86 which is not significant at any level between the two groups. While comparing the two groups on the dimension of self-confidence, the mean difference between them is very small (0.8) and not significant at any level. The girls of working women on the dimension of withdrawal tendency scored (43.24) higher than that of girls of non-working girls (38.86). The mean score difference between the two groups is not statistically significant (CR. 1.61.).

On the dimension, a feeling of inferiority the girls of non-working mothers scored (31.2) higher than their counterparts (30.96) but the difference (t-0.23) is not statistically significant. In the case of emotional instability there is very negligible difference (1.0) between the two groups and the mean scores did not yield any difference. The two groups are almost the same in emotional instability. The results show that the mother's employment seem to have some effect on the achievement of the girls (57.22) when compared to the girls of the non-working mothers (54.00). But the difference is not substantial. As far as scholastic achievement is concerned, the girls of non-working mothers were found to be little less than that of the girls of working mothers. Thus the results of this study support the hypothesis and therefore it is accepted.

Table 1

Showing the scores of the girls of working mothers and non-working mothers in self-concept and scholastic achievements tests

	Dimensions of self-concept	*Mean of W. Ms.*	*Mean of Nw. Ms. girls*	*Df. of mean girls N = 50*	*SEDm M_1–M_2 N = 50*	*Critical ratio*	*Level of sig.*
a)	Achievement	34.96	35.96	1.00	1.16	0.86	NS
b)	Confidence	30.94	31.74	0.80	3.07	0.26	NS
c)	Withdrawal	43.24	38.86	4.38	2.70	1.62	NS
d)	Inferiority feeling	30.96	31.20	0.24	1.06	0.23	NS
e)	Emotional instability	28.78	27.78	1.00	3.96	0.25	NS
f)	Scholastic achievement	57.22	54.00	3.22	7.79	0.41	NS

In conclusion, we can say that in the Indian context mothers play a key role in child-rearing practice, particularly during the early stage of development. But, at the adolescent stage the self-achievement, sibling relation, self-attitude, values seem to play a more effective role than the mother's care. In the present study the girls of non-working mothers were found to be relatively better in dimensions of achievement and confidence, but they had little more inferiority feelings than the children of the working mothers.

The sample was drawn from Agra city schools and the girls who were serving as subjects in this study were between 15 and 17 years of age. Since the girls of non-working mothers were educated up to the postgraduate level the girls were not lacking in their development of self-concept compared to the girls of working mothers. In fact, the girls of non-working mothers show little better development than the girls of the working mothers in the dimensions of achievement and confidence. But these differences are not real differences. Therefore we may conclude that there is no difference between the girls of working mothers and non-working mothers in the development of self-concept and scholastic achievement as revealed by this study in the Agra sample. The hypothesis should be verified with a wider sample of different socioeconomic status and geographical regions and with demographic variables.

References

Bronfenbrenner et al., Working and Watching: Maternal Employment Status and Parents Perceptions of their three year old children, *Child Development,* 1984, 55, 1362-1378.

Gold D, and Andres, D., Developmental Comparisons between adolescent children with employed and non-employed mothers, *Child Development,* 1978, 49, 75-84.

Hoffman, L.W., Effects of Maternal Employment on the child. A Review of the research, *Developmental Psychology,* 1974, 10, 204-228.

Mathur, K. and Migra, G., Influence of maternal employment on children's personality, *Indian Journal of Psychometry and Education,* 1994, 25 (102), 11-24.

Mody, S. N. and Murthy, V. N., The Study of mental health of children of working mothers, *Journal of Personality and Clinical Studies,* 1988, 4, 161-164.

Papalia, E. E., Old, S. W., *A Child's World Infancy through Adolescence,* New York: Mcgraw-Hill Book Co. 1975, 12-18.

Prasad, M.B., and Prasad, A., Social and emotional Development of Pre-school children of employed Mothers, *Journal of Social and Economic Studies,* 1975, 3, 78-87.

Scarr, S., and Hall, E., What's a Parent to do, *Psychology Today,* 1984, 18, 58-63.

CHAPTER 13

Adolescent Students' Achievement in Science Subjects in Secondary Schools— A Factor Analytical Study

Nimai Charan Das and *M. Rajamanickam*

The aim of this study is to discover the factors that are functioning in the school achievement of the adolescent students in the science subjects. It was observed that there was a continuous derath in the performance of the students with very low achievements. Therefore it is proposed to uncover the factors that are operating in this phenomenon. The sample of this study consisted of 328 secondary school adolescent students drawn from various parts of Bengal. Their age ranged from 15 to 19 years. A questionnaire was prepared involving 16 factors which could possibly elicit the causative factors. This was administered in the school situation by the investigator and the data were collected. The questionnaires were scored according to the procedure and they were treated statistically by applying the factor analysis. One centroid factor was extracted and there were high leadings in most of the variables. The adolescent students' low performance in science was elicited and is presented in Table 2.

Introduction

Though secondary schools maintain certain standards in administration, teaching and appointing competent persons as teachers, the adolescent students' performance vary considerably in various subjects, particularly the performance in science subjects which cause great concern both to the parents and teachers. This state of affairs should not continue for a long time. At one stage we must make an intensive study and disclose the causative factors and find out the remedy for this problem.

Adolescent students go to a school from various places for the study. They belong to different geographical areas, environments, socioeconomic backgrounds, culture and religion. The educational background of the family may vary considerably. The physical and mental make-up also vary considerably.

The school environment may have limited facilities, causing all kinds of inconveniences for the students to concentrate on their studies. The teachers who handle the classes may not be showing adequate interest in teaching the subjects. In some schools the teachers are not well qualified to teach secondary level subjects. All these factors and some other factors which are inherent must be the cause of the adolescent students school performance becoming poor.

Factor analysis is a highly sophisticated statistical method for determining the dimensions operating in the interrelationships (correlations) in a set of variables, and a set of reference vectors (factors) in terms of which the vectors representing the variables can be expressed (Fruchter, 1954).

The aim of this study is to discover the factors that contribute to the low achievement of secondary school students in general science by applying factor analysis to the obtained data. The hypothesis based upon the problem is, there are factors like, teacher's disinterestedness, administration defects in the school managements and emotional maladjustments of the student determine the students' low achievements in the schools.

Method

Sample: The sample consisted of 328 students studying in West Bengal. The age ranged from 15 to 19 years. They took part in this investigation. They were selected by the systematic random sampling method.

Tool: A questionnaire was constructed to find out the factors responsible for low achievement of secondary school students in general science by Das (1999, 2000). Item analysis of the questionnaire was done (Das, 1999). Reliability of the questionnaire was found to be 0.97. The validity of the questionnaire was observed to be 0.98.

There are 126 items in the final questionnaire. The three response categories, 'Yes', 'Do not know' and 'No' were assigned with a weight of two for Yes, one for Do not know, and zero for No. This is done according to the procedure of test development. The final form of the questionnaire consisted of 16 sub-tests.

Procedure: The investigator personally met the students in the classroom situation and after brief instructions the questionnaire was administered. The students have taken about 30 minutes to complete the questionnaire. As soon as they were completed they were collected from the students and the students were allowed to go away.

Method of Scoring: The questionnaires were scored according to the procedure. There were both positive and negative statements. The positive statements received the scores of 2, 1 and 0. The negative statements received the scores in the revised order as 0, 1 and 2.

Treatment of the Scores: The individual scores for all the variables were obtained and they were treated statistically. The important statistical treatment for verifying the hypothesis according to this study is the factor analysis. The basic data required for factor analysis is the intercorrelations among the scores of the variables or tests scores. They were worked out and are presented in Table 1.

Extraction of the First Centroid Factor: We are now entering into the task of extracting the First Centroid Factor. This is a laborious task. There are several techniques of factor analysis, such as P technique, Q technique and R technique. P technique deals with *occasions or times, Q technique deals with personality traits and* R *technique deals with the number of variables or tests. We apply here the* R *technique as there arc 16 subtests in this study There arc several steps in this. We are going step by step.*

First Step: The intercorrelations among the scores of 16 subtests were worked out and presented in Table 1. Intercorrelations between tests are the basic data in factor analysis. In the case of these 16 subtests the intercorrelations are:

$$\frac{N(N-1)}{2} = \frac{16(16-1)}{2} = \frac{16 \times 15}{2} = 120$$ Correlations Coefficients.

These correlations coefficients are always entered on the upper right portion of the matrix (Table 1). There may be both positive and negative correlations in the matrix. The highest positive correlation may be + 1.0 and the highest negative correlation may be –1.0. In this study there is no negative correlation coefficient. The correlation coefficients range from +.117 to +.821. The correlations are in rows and columns in a matrix.

Second Step-2: In the second step the correlation matrix is completed by entering the correlations in the lower left portion of the matrix with the same correlations found in Table 1. Now the correlation matrix is complete with the 16 diagonal cells empty (Table 2). In the extraction of factors, the diagonal cells should be filled with some values. Procedures are varied in filling up the diagonal cells. One procedure is to fill up all the diagonal cells with the largest correlation coefficient in the columns (Guilford, 1954). Another procedure is to put the highest possible correlation of 1.0 in the diagonal cells (Fruchter, 1954). A third procedure is suggested by Thurstone (1946). According to this, the highest correlation in columns is not inserted in the diagonal cells, but it is used as D value and added with the S value which is the total of the correlations in the columns.

The main aim of factor analysis is to identify the number of factors that are underlying in the performance of the students in common. The factors account for the levels of relationship among the test variables. Each test score has a loading in each of the factors and we are trying to identify the pattern to factor loading that is psychologically meaningful.

We can observe that the correlation coefficients themselves show the level of relationship between by any two test scores. But we do not know what amount of common relationship each test is having with every other test score in the battery. The factor analysis is done which would reveal the amount of relationship each test has with other test scores. Therefore in the second step of the factor analysis we must have a full correlation matrix (Table 2). At this stage the problem is the estimation of communality for each test. This we have already suggested. Rajamanickam (2001) states that the most convenient method in solving this problem is not entering the highest correlation in the diagonal cells, but to add it with total of the correlation in columns at the bottom.

Table 1

Inter-correlation matrix of the 16 subtest scores (N-328)

Sub-Test No.	*1*	*2*	*3*	*4*	*5*	*6*	*7*	*8*	*9*	*10*	*11*	*12*	*13*	*14*	*15*	*16*
1.	-	.712	.735	.428	.614	.544	.365	.500	.451	.500	.417	.445	.291	1.483	.253	.494
2.		-	.596	.361	.465	.409	.240	.304	.272	.305	.320	.223	.117	.296	.137	.348
3.			-	.460	.569	.654	.452	.600	.529	.560	.535	.511	.243	.582	.243	.531.
4.				-	.475	.440	.356	.387	.267	.359	.383	.415	.266	.431	..383	.468
5.					-	.520	.379	.515	.454	.471	.493	.467	.229	.491	.208	.549
6.						.-	.478	.624	.528	.583	.564	.598	.329	.597	.357	.643
7.							-	.704	.631	.591	.594	.519	.343	.510	.315	.368
8.								-	.821	.772	.735	.778	.491	.663	.390	.509
9.									-	.687	.643	.679	.410	.567	.307	.478
10.										-	.612	.651	.377	.551	.273	.495
11.											-	.662	.404	.576	.431	.478
12.												-	.669	.705	.459	.538
13.													-	.500	.557	.295
14.														-	.358	.556
15.															-	.358
16.																

Third Step: In the third step, the columns and rows are summed up and entered in the last row against S. Then the correlations in rows are summed up and entered in the last column under check sums. The sums of rows and columns should tally and check marks are made on each of the sum (Table 3). Further we must see that the sum of the sums should agree.

Fourth step: In the Fourth Step, the communalities (D values) are entered just below S values in the row against D. The 'D' value is the diagonal value and it is the highest correlation in each column. In this study the D value in the first column is. 735 and for the second column it is 712, for the 3rd column. 735, for the 4th,. 475, the for the 5th. 614, for the 6th. 654, for the 7th. 704, for the 8th. 821, for the 9th. 821, for the 10th. 772, for the 11th. 735, for the 12th. 778, for the 13th. 669, for the 14th. 705, for the 15th. 557 and for the 16th. 643. These values are entered just below the sum of S values and it is 112.897.

Fifth step: In the Fifth Step, the S values and D values in the rows are summed up and entered in the row below the D values against the formula $S_1 + D = E$. The sum of these two rows $(S_1 + D)$ are entered in the row.

Sixth step: In the Sixth Step, the sums of S_1 and the D values were added which was indicated by E, the sum of which was 124.027. This values is T. The T value is the grand total (Table 3).

Seventh step: In the Seventh Step, the root of T value was worked out. The formula for extracting the factor loading is $a_1 = \frac{\Sigma E\dot{\gamma}}{\sqrt{T}} = m\,E\dot{\gamma}$ where the root of T was 11.13674. Here a_1 referred to the factor loadings, E referred to the total value of $S_1 + D$ and *j* referred to the tests or variables. In this problem the number of tests were 16. T was the grand total of $S_1 + D$, the 'm' was the value of 1 divided by the root of T. The formula for m =. $\frac{1}{\sqrt{T}}$

Eighth step: In the Eight Step, the products of T are checked. The obtained root of T is $\frac{1}{\sqrt{T}}$ which is. 0897928 in this problem. It is to be verified that the root of T is equivalent to the equation mT. In this study it is 11.13674. These two values T = 11.13674 and the mT value 11.13674 are the same. All these values in the last column are checked with check marks. It is important according to the procedure that these values are always presented in five decimal digits (Table-3).

Ninth step: In the Ninth Step, we have extracted the complete centroid factor loadings. Generally factor extracting is made by multiplying every E value by the root of T and dividing the product by T (124.027). But we have simplified this work by using a constant 'm' which is obtained in the equation $\frac{1}{\sqrt{T}} = m$. In this study the constant 'm' is 0.0897928. The formula for extracting the factor loadings at this state is $a_1 = mE$. Therefore, here we have multiplied each E by the constant 'm'. Thus we have obtained the factor loadings for the test 1, (mE) 0.0897928 x 7.927 = 0.771. In the same manner the factor loadings are worked out for all the 16 subtests and we have the first centroid factor loadings as:. 711,. 522,. 771,. 570,. 674,. 765,. 677,. 863,. 767,. 768,. 721,. 816,. 552,. 761,. 502, and. 696 (Tables 3 and 4). The sum of factor loadings are found to be equal to the root of T =

Table-2: Inter-correlation matrix of the 16 Subtest Scores (N-328)

Sub-Test No.	*1*	*2*	*3*	*4*	*5*	*6*	*7*	*8*	*9*	*10*	*11*	*12*	*13*	*14*	*15*	*16*
1.	-	.712	.735	.428	.614	.544	.365	.500	.451	.500	.417	.445	.251	.483	.253	.494
2.	.712	-	.596	.361	.465	.409	.240	.304	.272	.305	.520	.223	.117	.296	.137	.348
3.	.735	.596	-	.460	.569	.654	.452	.600	.529	.560	.535	.511	.243	.582	.243	.531
4.	.428	.361	.460	-	.475	.440	.356	.387	.267	.359	.382	.415	.266	.431	.383	.468
5.	.614	.465	.569	.475	-	.520	.379	.515	.454	.471	.493	.467	.229	.491	.208	.549
6.	.544	.409	.654	.440	.520	-	.478	.624	.528	.583	.564	.598	.329	.597	.357	.643
7.	.365	.240	.452	.356	.379	.478	-	.704	.631	.591	.594	.519	.342	.510	.315	.368
8.	.500	.304	.600	.387	.515	.624	.704	-	.821	.772	.735	.778	.491	.663	.390	.509
9.	.451	.272	.529	.267	.454	.528	.631	.821	.-	.687	.643	.679	.410	.567	.307	.478
10.	.500	.305	.560	.359	.471	.583	.591	.772	.687	-	.612	.651	.377	.551	.237	.495
11.	.417	.320	.535	.382	.493	.564	.594	.735	.643	.612	-	.662	.404	.576	.431	.478
12.	.445	.323	.511	.415	.467	.598	.519	.778	.679	.651	.662	-	.669	.705	.459	.538
13.	.251	.117	.243	.266	.229	.329	.342	.491	.410	.377	.404	.669	-	.500	.557	.295
14.	.483	.296	.582	.431	.491	.597	.510	.663	.567	.551	.576	.705	.500	-	.358	.556
15.	.253	.137	.243	.383	.208	.357	.315	.390	.307	.273	.431	.459	.557	.358	-	.358
16.	.494	.348	.531	.468	.549	.643	.368	.509	.478	.495	.478	.538	.295	.556	.358	-

Table-3: Inter-correlation matrix of the 16 Sub test Scores (N-328)

Sub-Test No.	*1*	*2*	*3*	*4*	*5*	*6*	*7*	*8*	*9*	*10*	*11*	*12*	*13*	*14*	*15*	*16*	*Check sums*
1.	-	.712	.735	.428	.614	.544	.365	.500	.451	.500	.417	.445	.251	.483	.253	.494	7.192
2.	.712	-	.596	.361	.465	.409	.240	.304	.272	.305	.520	.223	.117	.296	.137	.348	5.103
3.	.735	.596	-	.460	.569	.654	.452	.600	.529	.560	.535	.511	.243	.582	.243	.531	7.800
4.	.428	.361	.460	-	.475	.440	.356	.387	.267	.359	.382	.415	.266	.431	.383	.468	5.878
5.	.614	.465	.569	.475	-	.520	.379	.515	.454	.471	.493	.467	.229	.491	.208	.549	6.902
6.	.544	.409	.654	.440	.520	-	.478	.624	.528	.583	.564	.598	.329	.597	.357	.643	7.868
7.	.365	.240	.452	.356	.379	.478	-	.704	.631	.591	.594	.519	.342	.510	.315	.368	6.844
8.	.500	.304	.600	.387	.515	.624	.704	-	.821	.772	.735	.778	.491	.663	.390	.509	8.793
9.	.451	.272	.529	.267	.454	.528	.631	.821	-	.687	.643	.679	.410	.567	.307	.478	7.724
10.	.500	.305	.560	.359	.471	.583	.591	.772	.687	-	.612	.651	.377	.551	.237	.495	7.787
11.	.417	.320	.535	.382	.493	.564	.594	.735	.643	.612	-	.662	.404	.576	.431	.478	7.296
12.	.445	.323	.511	.415	.467	.598	.519	.778	.679	.651	.662	-	.669	.705	.459	.538	8.319
13.	.251	.117	.243	.266	.229	.329	.342	.491	.410	.377	.404	.669	-	.500	.557	.295	5.488
14.	.483	.296	.582	.431	.491	.597	.510	.663	.567	.551	.576	.705	.500	-	.358	.556	7.766
15.	.253	.137	.243	.383	.208	.357	.315	.390	.307	.273	.431	.459	.557	.358	-	.358	5.029
16.	.494	.348	.531	.468	.549	.643	.368	.509	.478	.495	.4T	.538	.295	.556	.358	-	7.108
S_1	7.192	5.103	.800	5.878	6.902	7.868	6.844	8.793	7.724	7.787	7.296	8.319	5.488	7.766	5.029	7.108	112.897
D	.735	.712	.735	.475	.614	.654	.704	.821	.821	.772	.735	.778	.669	.705	.557	.643	11.130
S_1+ D=E	7.927	5.815	8.535	6.353	7.516	8.522	7.548	9.614	8.545	8.559	8.031	9.097	6.517	8.471	5.586	7.751	124.027

=T/ÖT= 11.13674

mE = a_1	0.711	0.522	0.771	0.570	0.674	0.765	0.677	0.863	0.767	0.768	0.721	0.816	0.552	0.761	0.502	0.696

m=1/ÖT = 0.0897928

mT =

11.13674 = 11.136

11.136 (three decimal points). Since these values agree with each other, the factor loadings are correct. According to the procedure we are to extract 16 factors in this study as there are 16 sub-tests or variables. But we have extracted only one factor to assess the level of the students' performance in science subjects.

Interpretation of the Results and Discussion

The first factor in all the variables has high loading ranging from 0.500 to 0.863. It looks like a common factor of the performance in general science. The factor loadings on the whole are higher for the subtests in teaching deficiencies and disinterestedness of the teachers (.863), the administrative drawbacks (0.816), and unsympathatic teachers (.768) and inefficient teachers (.767). The emotional maladjustment of the students (.771), dearth of study materials (.765), defective teaching methods (.761), defective syllabus (.721), lack of study habits among the students (.711) have high loadings. These variables may be stated as the first main causes for the low performance of the students.

The other important variables as revealed by the factor analysis are undesirable home environment (.696), inexperienced teachers (.677) the influence of anti-educational force (.674).

Table 4: Extraction of the first centroid factor loadings (N-328)

No.of sub-tests	*Short description of subtest*	*Factor loading*	*Communality* h^2
1.	Want of study habits of the students	.711	.505
2.	Poor abilities (General and specific) lack of alertness of the students	.522	.272
3.	Emotional maladjustment of students	.771	.594
4.	Malnutrition of students	.570	.325
5.	Influence of anti-educational forces	.674	.454
6.	Dearth of books, papers, pen, pencil	.765	.585
7.	Inexperienced teachers	.677	.458
8.	Disinterested teachers	.863	.745
9.	Inefficient teachers	.767	.588
10.	Unsympathetic teachers	.768	.589
11.	Defective syllabus and unscientific examination system	.721	.519
12.	Administrative drawbacks	.816	.767
13.	Infrequent use of teaching aids and appliances of science	.552	.305
14.	Defective teaching methods	.761	.579
15.	Socioeconomic and political orises	.502	.252
16.	Undesirable home environment	.696	.484
	11.136		

The other variables are lack of teaching aids (.552), lack of alertness (abilities) of the students (.522), and socioeconomic and political crises (.502). These factors are supposed to be the causes of low performance of the students in science subjects in secondary schools as revealed by this study. Generally, it is very difficult to assess the behaviour and the mode of study of the present day adolescent students. They temperamentally differ from place to place and from time of time. But a general view can be obtained from a larger sample and from very wider areas. An important observation is that a class should not consist of more than 40 students in higher secondary schools. Since the students are in a transitory stage from adolescance to adulthood and they are with full of imagination, the classroom becomes an important place at the stage. The teacher is the important person who should be endowed with valuable information and knowledge, and who can attract the students in the classroom with his scholarly approach of the subjects taught.

Particularly in the case of teaching science subjects, the teacher should explain every small matter with proper demonstrations and practicals. Events seen and heard might be easily registered in the memory of the students. In most of the secondary schools this type of approach is lacking. Properly trained or well informed teachers should be appointed in the schools. The teacher on any account should not aspire for engaging private tuition to the students. This is one of the unacademic practices prevailing in most of the secondary schools. The school management should carefully see to it that such practices are not followed by the teachers of the schools.

In this study it is found that the teachers' roles in the classroom were found to be the important factors, apart from other factors, in the low performance of the adolescent students in science subjects in secondary schools These problems can be solved to some extent by the school management if they are really interested in providing good education to the students. Students' maladjustment problem can be reduced by keeping the students properly engaged in curricular activities.

Conclusions

Therefore it is concluded that since the factor loadings in all the variables strongly support the hypothesis that the students' low performance in schools in science subjects was due to teachers' disinterestedness in classroom, administrative drawbacks, teachers' attitudes, emotional maladjustment of the students, dearth of study materials, defective teaching methods, defective syllabus and the examination system and other factors. Further study on a larger sample from different areas may facilitate for still better results for generalising these results.

References

Das, N.C., A study of item validity of a questionnaire, *Advance Abstracts of the Section of Psychology and Educational Sciences*, 86th, Session of Indian Science Congress, Chennai, 1999.

Fruchter, B., *Introduction to Factor Analysis,* 1st., ed., D.Van Nostrand Company INC., Princeton, New Jersey, U.S.A., 1954.

Garrett, H.E., *Statistics in Psychology and Education,* 4th ed., Longmans, Green & Co., INC.55, Fifth Avenue, New York., 1954.

Guilford, J.P., *Psychometric Methods,* 2nd ed., Bombay: Tata graw-Hill Publishing Co., Ltd., Bombay, 1954.

Harman, H.H., *Modern Factor Analysis*, 2nd ed., Rev, The University of Chicago Press, Chicago., 1970.

Rajamanickam, M., *Statistical Methods in Psychological and Educational Research,* New Delhi; Concept Publishing Company, 2000.

Thurstone, L.L., *Multiple-Factor Analysis, a Development and Expansion of The Vectors of Mind,* 1st., ed., Chicago, University of Chicago Press, 1947.

CHAPTER 14

Relative Efficiency of Piagetian Conservation Abilities and Academic Achievement in Science

H.M. Kasinath

The purpose of the study is to explore the relative efficiency of Piagetian conservation abilities and academic achievement in sciences. A sample of 198 students studying in eighth standard was selected using random sampling technique. Piagetian type tests were developed by the investigator using scientific procedure to measure conservation of age, classification, liquid, solid, weight, number, length, area and volume. The stability coefficient and consistency coefficient using split-half method with odd and even items of the entire tool were 0.8273 and 0.776 respectively. The range of intrinsic validity coefficients was between 0.8809 to 0.9096. Aitken's method was used to calculate regression coefficients. Relative contributions were obtained by multiplying regression coefficients (b) with the corresponding correlation coefficients (G). The study revealed that the contributions of conservation of length, number, classification and solid in predicting the academic achievement in science are relatively high. Conservation of length and classification are the good predictors in case of boys, girls, urban and rural samples.

Introduction

The research pursued in the areas like nature and course of development of cognitive processes; the qualitative and quantitative aspects of development of cognitive processes; the direction of development of the cognitive processes; the relative importance of biological and cultural influences on cognitive development; and the organization of cognitive abilities have posed a number of debatable issues. Nevertheless, the study of cognitive processes is considered to be of great importance in the sphere of education. Research findings indicate that learning, retention and problem-solving depend considerably on the level at which the information is processed and on the strategies that are used. Promotion of effective learning, memory and problem solving skills among students is one of the important goals of education. Since these skills are largely acquired by students through strategic functioning in learning situations, the study of cognitive processes seems to have very positive consequences for educational achievement of students of different age, grade, SES, cultural and educational background.

a) Rationale to the Approach

Among various approaches to the study of cognitive development, Piaget's approach has been widely used to comprehend the nature of changes in cognitive processing. According to Piaget, conservations of length and number are attained between the ages of six and seven; area, mass and liquid between the ages of seven and eight; weight between the ages of nine and ten; and volume between the ages 11-12 (Wadsworth, 1978, p. 18). Rath and Patnaik, (1979) noticed that as age increased training had much greater effect both in respect of conservation of volume and length. Padmini (1980) showed that the action programme based on Piagetian theory consisted of instructional situations, focused on concepts such as length, area, volume, weight, etc., and was more effective in fostering cognitive development. Shukla (1980) reported that all the indices of relationship between the different dimensions of scientific creativity and conservation of mass, weight and volume were found to be significant. Jha (1981) found that age factor seemed to play an important role in the attainment of conservation tasks and the mass was conserved first followed by volume and number. Amin (1982) revealed that intelligence was moderately but positively correlated with conservation of length and area. Shukla (1988) noted that concepts of weight, volume and density were fully conserved at the age of 10+, 15+ and 16+ respectively.

Kumari (1990) found that high intelligent children showed an earlier conservation of mass, weight, volume, seriation and classifications than low intelligent children. Agrawal (1997) found that the concept of conservation of continuous quantities (liquid and clay) develops through invariant sequence of stages. Shanbhag (1999) found that the combined interaction effects of sex, caste and age on conservation of age, seriation, multiple classification, liquid, solid, weight, number, length, area and volume in disadvantaged children were not significant.

It is evident from the review that a number of studies have been done on comparison of attainment of conservation abilities and impact of cultural factors on conservation abilities. However, studies on exploring the relative efficiency of conservation abilities in predicting academic achievement are very rare. Therefore, the present study would assume its relevance and significance.

b) Objective

To determine the relative efficiency of the different Piagetian conservation abilities in predicting the academic achievement of science in: (i) total sample, (ii) boys, (iii) girls, (iv) urban sample, (v) rural sample.

Method

Sample: A total of 198 students studying in eighth Standard were selected using random sampling technique from seven schools of Dharwad taluka. It consisted of 75 boys, 123 girls, 98 urban students and 100 rural students whose age ranged from 13 to 16 years.

Tools: Piagetian type tests were developed by the investigator to measure the conservation of age, classification, liquid, solid, weight, number, length, area and volume using scientific procedure. Each conservation task had three situations and each situation had three questions of judgement, prediction and explanation. Correct responses were scored as one and incorrect responses as zero. Thus, for each child there was a total possible conservation score of 9.

The stability coefficient of the test by test-retest method was 0.8273 (n=50) and consistency coefficient by the split-half method using odd and even items was 0.776. Intrinsic validity of the test ranges from 0.8809 to 0.9096 (Guilford, 1954, p. 399). The content validity of the test was established by referring it to five experts in the field.

Collection of Data: All the subjects were interviewed individually in their local language over a period of 60-90 minutes. The subject was regarded as a full conserver if he/she made no error in judgement, predicted correctly and gave correct reasons for his/her judgement. Thus, there were three judgements, three predictions and three explanations for each conservation task. If the subject gave all nine correct responses, he/she was regarded as a full conserver.

Academic achievement in science, which was considered as dependent variable in the study was measured by taking the students' annual examination marks in science at the eighth standard. In order to get the marks from different schools comparable, the raw scores were converted into T scores before subjecting them to analysis. The annual question paper in science which was set by the District Board of Secondary School Teachers was commonly used in all the secondary schools of Dharwad district. The content validity of the question paper was also established by giving it to five science teachers. It was found to be comprehensive and relevant by the judges.

Statistical Techniques: Aitken's method of calculating regression coefficients (Ferguson, 1971, p. 396) was employed. The relative contributions of conservation abilities to variance in achievement in science were determined by multiplying corresponding regression coefficients (b) with the correlations of independent variable with the dependent variable (G).

Results

a) Conservation Abilities and Academic Achievement in Total Sample

It is observed that, about 9.731 per cent of the criterion variable is accounted for by the variance in Conservation of Length scores, about 4.958 per cent by the Number, about 4.612 per cent by the classification, about 4.187 per cent by the Solid and about 2.299 per cent by the Weight respectively. Nearly 25.162 per cent of the total variance in academic achievement in science is due to selected predictors. Thus, it seems that Conservation of Length, Number, Classification and Solid are good predictors of the academic achievement in science in case of total sample. The negative sign with regard to Conservation of Liquid and Volume indicates suppressing effect on achievement in science (Table 1).

Table 1
Relative contributions of the conservation abilities in predicting academic achievement in science — total sample (n=198)

Predictors	*b values*	*'G' values*	*b × G*	*Percentage of contribution*
Age	0.0019	0:043	0.00008	0.008
Classification	0.1721	0.268	0.0461	4.612
Liquid	-0.0541	0.159	-0.0086	-0.860
Solid	0.1434	0.292	0.0418	4.187
Weight	0.0871	0.264	0.0229	2.299
Number	0.1381	0.359	0.0495	4.958
Length	0.2476	0.393	0.0973	9.731
Area	0.0796	0.161	0.0128	1.282
Volume	-0.0986	0.107	-0.0105	-1.055
Total				25.162

b) Conservation Abilities and Academic Achievement in Boys

While assessing the emservation abilities and academic achievements of girls, it is observed that about 9.884 per cent of the criterion variable, i.e., the academic achievement in science is accounted for by the conservation of solid, about 9.850 per cent by the Length and about 3.966 per cent by the classification. Thus, about 22.545 per cent of the total variance in academic achievement in science among boys is best predicted by Conservation of Solid, Length and Classifcation. But the achievement of boys in science is suppressed by Conservation of Liquid and Weight (Table 2).

Table 2
Relative contributions of the conservation abilities in predicting academic achievement in science — Boys (n=75)

Predictors	*b values*	*'G' values*	*b × G*	*Percentage of contribution*
Age	0.0099	0.0867	0.0008	0.085
Classification	0.1789	0.2217	0.0396	3.966
Liquid	-0.0316	0.1873	-0.0059	-0.591
Solid	0.3488	0.2834	0.0988	9.884
Weight	-0.1663	0.1601	-0.0266	-2.662
Number	0.0361	0.2542	0.0091	0.917
Length	0.3135	0.3142	0.0985	9.850
Area	0.0820	0.1142	0.0093	0.936
Volume	-0.1760	-0.0091	0.0016	0.160
Total				22.545

c) Conservation Abilities and Academic Achievement in Girls

Table 3 Relative contributions of the conservation abilities in predicting academic achievement in science — girls (n=123)

Predictors	*b values*	*'G' values*	*b x G*	*Percentage of contribution*
Age	0.0091	0.0172	0.0015	0.015
Classification	0.1779	0.3288	0.0584	5.849
Liquid	-0.0829	0.1353	-0.0112	-1.121
Solid	0.0349	0.2985	0.0104	1.043
Weight	0.2132	0.3677	0.0783	7.839
Number	0.2117	0.4609	0.0975	9.757
Length	0.2534	0.4813	0.1219	12.196
Area	0.0681	0.2066	0.0140	1.406
Volume	-0.0806	0.1908	0.0153	-1.538
Total				35.446

d) Conservation Abilities and Academic Achievement in Urban Sample

The data presented in Table 4 reveal that, about 8.1056 per cent of the criterion variable is accounted for by the variance in Conservation of Classification; about 4.0794 per cent by the Number and about 2.7018 per cent by the Length respectively. About 18.999 per cent of the total variance in academic achievement in science is by the selected Conservation abilities. Thus, it is found that the academic achievement in science among urban students is best predicted by Conservation of Classification, Number of Length. However, Conservation of Area acts as a suppressor of achievement in science in urban sample.

Table 4 Relative contributions of the conservation abilities in predicting academic achievement in science—Urban sample (n=98)

Predictors	*b values*	*'G' values*	*b x G*	*Percentage of contribution*
Age	0.0355	0.0478	0.0016	0.1696
Classification	0.2630	0.3082	0.0810	8.1056
Liquid	-0.1305	-0.0154	0.0020	0.2009
Solid	0.0471	0.1893	0.0089	0.8916
Weight	0.0624	0.1485	0.0092	0.9266
Number	0.1566	0.2605	0.0407	4.0794
Length	0.1375	0.1965	0.02701	2.7018
Area	0.0072	-0.0094	-0.00006	-0.0067
Volume	0.1275	0.1514	0.0193	1.9303
Total				18.999

e) Conservation Abilities and Academic Achievement in Rural Sample

The data as presented in Table 5 reveal that, about 30.7971 per cent of the criterion variable, i.e., change in academic achievement in science among rural students is accounted for by the nine selected Conservation abilities. About 16.1472 per cent is accounted for by the Conservation in Length, about 5.8662 per cent by the Solid, about 3.4739% by the Classification, about 3.4420 per cent by the Number, and about 2.2738 per cent by the Area. Thus, it is noticed that Conservation of Length, Solid, Classification, Number and Area are the best predictors of academic achievement of science in rural sample. However, the achievement in science among rural students is lowered by Conservation of Age, Liquid and Volume.

Table 5
Relative contribution of the conservation abilities in predicting academic achievement in science — Rural sample (n=100)

Predictors	*b values*	*'G' values*	*b × G*	*Percentage of contribution*
Age	-0.0210	0.0408	-0.0008	-0.0856
Classification	0.1357	0.2560	0.0347	3.4739
Liquid	-0.0186	0.2344	-0.0043	-0.4359
Solid	0.1732	0.3387	0.0586	5.8662
Weight	0.0534	0.3107	0.0165	1.6591
Number	0.0881	0.3907	0.0344	3.4420
Length	0.3531	0.4573	0.1614	16.1472
Area	0.0951	0.2391	0.0227	2.2738
Volume	-0.1887	0.0818	-0.0154	-1.5436
Total			30.7971	

Conclusions and Implications

The results of this study indicate that the best predictors of academic achievement in science among eighth standard students are Conservation of Length, Number, Classification and Solid.

Further, Conservation of Classification, Length and Solid are found to be the best predictors of academic achievement in science among boys. The good predictors of academic achievement in science among girls arc Conservation of Length, Number, Weight and Classification.

The Conservation of Classification, Number and Length have contributed to the academic achievement of science in urban sample, whereas, in rural sample, the contributions of Conservation abilities like Length, Solid, Classification, Number and Area have been effective in contributing to the academic achievement of students in science. However, Conservation of Liquid and Volume have a suppressing effect in all the treatment groups.

The results of the study suggest for the provision of adequate experiences relevant to Conservation of Age, Liquid, Weight, Area and Volume since they have failed to predict changes in academic achievement in science. Therefore, it is for the educators to think of relevant instructional packages and child-centred activities for catering the needs of children at different levels of reasoning.

Children's learning of science concepts is developed from their actions on 'concrete' objects. Comprehension of scientific knowledge and principles cannot be derived solely from reading about science and listening to lectures. The major criticism of most conventional science instruction from a Piagetian point of view is that it takes place largely through books and lectures instead of being based on the actions of the child. Teaching methods that deal primarily with representations of knowledge are ineffective.

The principle of Conservation of Age, Liquid, Weight, Area and Volume can be taught by using simple explanations and concrete materials and by allowing children to manipulate the materials. This needs the nurturing the process of cognitive growth at any particular stage by presenting lessons in a form that is consistent with but slightly more advanced than the students existing schemes.

The findings suggest that cognitive development can be accelerated if instruction is provided at the right time and in the right way is consistent with the ideas of Lev Vygotsy, a Russian Psychologist. He emphasized more than Piaget the influence of social experience on cognitive development. He maintained that the various things we learn, such as facts, concepts, rules, problem-solving skills and attitudes are strongly influenced by the kinds of social interactions that typify over culture.

References

Agrawal, R., A Comparative Study of Concept of Conservation of Continuous Quantities in Primary Level Students of English and Hindi Medium Schools, *Indian Journal of Educational Research,* 1997, 16(2), 27-31.

Amin, N., A Study of Relationship Between Spatial Egocentrism and Conservation of Length and Area in Delhi School Children, Ph.D. Edu., JMI, 1982.

Ferguson, G.A., *Statistical Analysis in Psychology and Education,* N.Y.: McGrawHill, 1971.

Guilford, J.P., *Psychometric Methods,* New Delhi: Tata McGraw-Hill Publishing Co. Ltd., 1954.

Jha, T., A Study of Conservation Among Tribal and Non-tribal Children, D. Phil. Psy, All. Uni., 1981.

Padmini, T., Fostering Cognitive Development in First Standard Pupils – An Experimental Study, Ph.D. Edu., My. Uni., 1980.

Rath, R. and Patnaik, N., *Effect of Training on Some Cognitive Abilities*, Dept. of Phy, Utkal Uni., 1979.

Shanbhag, S.P, A Multiple Cross-Sectional Study of Logical Reasoning among Disadvantaged Children, Ph.D. Edn., Kar. Uni., 1999.

Shukla, J.P and Sharma, V.P., Conservation of Substances: Effect of Sex, *Indian Educational Review,* 1988, 23(4), 105-109.

Shukla, J.P., Conservation and Scientific Creativity Through Cultures During the Period of Formal Operation, Ph.D. Psy, RSU, 1980.

Wadsworth, B.J., *Piaget for the Classroom Teacher,* New York: Longman Inc., 1978.

Part III
Adolescents' Perception of Issues and Problems

It is observed that the way in which the parents bring up their children becomes one of the causes of adolescent problems. The nature and characteristics of child-rearing practices adopted by the parents vary from family to family and also from one child to another. It is true that some children in some families are deprived of proper care and attention by the parents and some children are overprotected. When the deprived children reach the adolescent stage, they think of their childhood state and introspect into the past and see how they were deprived of many things and sometimes react to it. Adolescents now and then face several personal problems which may be specific to the individual and he has to evolve strategies to solve them. In Indian culture women are respected equally on bar with men. But there are instances occurring, that women are badly treated by men. In spite of so much political struggles and educational and occupational status women are looked down upon. How do the present generation of boys and girls perceive the status of women? This is one of the problems the general public ignored. Psychologists tried to study this problem by conducting investigations. The adolescents are very sensitive to the issues and problems, irregularities and injustices. They never hesitate to protest against such things. They organise strikes and processions and show their protest by all means. These instances are taking place in various places nowadays.

CHAPTER 15

Adolescent's Perception of Child-rearing Practices of the Parents and Delinquency Proneness

Kanwal Nalwa and Vidhu Mohan

The present study is an attempt to see whether there is any relationship between what the adolescent perceives to be the parental rearing practices and tendencies of delinquency prone behaviour. In order to study this, 420 boys and 330 girls in the adolescent group, were administered the Jesness Inventory. On the basis of this high and low delinquency prone Ss were identified using 1/2SD+/- Mean on the scale. The sample thus consisted of 524 of which 165 males and 111 females in the high delinquency prone group and 124 males and 124 females in the low delinquency prone group. These Ss were then administered the Perception of Mother's / Father's Child Rearing Practices Scale (PMFCRPS). The results obtained showed that delinquency proneness was a significant factor in the negative perception of the parental child rearing practices. The perception of the high delinquency prone group was significantly poorer in the area of academic interest, social interaction, recreation, nutrition and clothes for both the parents. However, the same group perceived that the preparation for puberty development was done better by both the parents of this group in comparison with the low delinquency prone group. This implies that parents should be trained to practice healthier ways of rearing up their children. Major sex differences also emerge snowing that the girls perceived the parenting methods to be better than the boys. The differences were found to be significant in the areas of economic support, nutrition, clothes, puberty development, demonstration of love, health care and overall perception.

Introduction

Juvenile delinquency is a complex social problem, the rapid increase of which is becoming a threat to the very basic structure of society. It is rife in all communities and countries and has emerged as a serious social evil with the passage of time. According to Sarkar (1987) the rapid social reconstruction, increase in social mobility, deteriorating moral values and the changing family structure resulting in the weakening of traditional systems of social control which regulated behavioural patterns of children have led to social disorganisation, instability and maladjustment.

Indian society, though essentially rural with old cultural traditions cannot escape the global influences that are invading its social set up. The emerging trend among the youth is to gravitate towards the external grandeur of western trends. In a country like India, the problem of delinquency has serious implications. In a developing country, progress depends to a large extent on the proper canalisation of human energy and talent. Since independence, there has been tremendous scientific advancement and industrial growth in India. The fast changing India society; with the new face of nuclear families, consumerist culture and working couples has brought about a situation where the parents are under stress and as a consequence their children also experience stress. When parents get less time to spend with the child, they try to assuage their guilt by pandering to her/his whims and demands while they are with her/him. It is becoming increasingly fashionable to blame the society; poverty; lack of proper facilities, unemployment etc. for child criminals. However, the basic truth is that it is the individuals who constitute the society (Sodhi, 1994).

Juvenile delinquency is deviant behaviour exhibited by persons of a tender age. Erratic acts depicting the defiance of norms, riles and regulations and violations of law, committed by them are not only injurious to individuals and groups, but also blur the future of the society and nation. (Lavania, 93). Delinquent behaviour must be a concern of the entire community and not just dismissed as a problem to be tackled by the police, courts or professional agencies. Parent's involvement is essential to eradicate this social evil. A combined effort would help foster a non-crimogenic milieu. Hetherington and Parke (1986) have very rightly said that the beliefs, values and attitudes of the culture are filtered through parents and presented to the child in a highly personalised selective fashion.

There are various external and personal factors that play a role in the development of delinquent behaviour, one of the most prominent being the FAMILY. The family is the first institution in which the child is socialised and it exerts a decisive influence on the developmental process. It is the backdrop where the child learns to deal with his emotions and drives and handle his problems in a socially acceptable manner. An adequate home encourages growth, confidence, frankness, all ability to face reality and results in the development of a healthy and well-adjusted personality. Dislocation in a youth's family, the absence of the family's potentially positive effects or any severe disturbance in one or both parents can produce devastating negative impacts, juvenile delinquency being one. Failure by parents to foster a child's skills, to model and encourage normative values and to provide a caring environment places a child at risk for delinquency (Snyder and Patterson, 1987). Lykken (1994) opined that the root cause of crime and violence is the unwillingness or inability of parents to socialise their children adequately Harmony in the family has emerged time and again as an essential prerequisite to harmony in the society

a) *Parental Rejection:* Incidence of delinquency is much greater under conditions of child rearing where parents are rejecting and neglectful and make the child feel unloved, unwanted and insecure in affectional relationships. The delinquency pattern may first originate when such children discover that the only way they can get some attention is by participating in disapproved behaviour. Low parental involvement, thwarting of the need to be loved, parental rejection are all associated with delinquent attitudes and early conviction. (Mohan & Singh, 1982; Elliot et al. 1985; Simons et al. 1989; Farrington & Hawkins, 1991; Jain & Panwar, 1992). Sodhi (1994) opined that in the final analysis of the factors responsible for turning children into criminals it is obvious that what is lacking is quality time spent with the child helping him with his problems.

b) *Broken Homes and Family Tension:* Disruption in the family at an early age and lack of cohesiveness or a sense of mutual affection and cooperation between family members tend to contribute towards delinquent behaviour. A significantly greater number of delinquents than non-delinquents come from broken, unaffectionate or disorganised homes (Browning, 1960; Patterson & Becker, 1965; Chilton & Markle, 1972). Minty (1987) found that there are strong' associations between descriptions of critical and hostile parents or parents who were generally arguing and sons who later became delinquent. Johnson and Pandina (1991) found parental warmth and hostility significant factors contributing to variations in delinquency.

c) *Relationship with Parents:* The warm relationship between a child and his parents is of great significance in developing a wholesome set of ideals. Defective parents child relationship is a handicap for the growing child because it fosters a feeling of insecurity and rejection. Delinquents generally come from families where normal communication between fathers and sons are blocked, there are high rates of defensive communication and lower rates of supportive communication more disjointed and disorganised conversations, unhealthy parent-child relationships, and negative parent-child interaction (Alexander, 1973; Thilagaraj, 1983; Barron & Earls, 1984). Tygart (1990) reported that the strongest association with delinquency was not with parental status but with the amount of time parents spend with the children over other family related factors i.e. divorced parents, single parents, step parents etc. Problem behaviour results when the parents, especially the mother, fail to produce a pattern of secure attachment.

d) *Child-rearing Practices:* There is consistent evidence that child centred effective parenting practices such as nurturance, involvement, positive reinforcement, non-punitive practices and consistency in child rearing are each associated with positive developmental outcomes in children (Patterson, 1982; Pulkkinen Maccoby & Martin, 1983). There has to be a balance between nurturance and discipline for the development of a healthy personality. Child-rearing practices, particularly those reflecting achievement pressure and conditional approval are related to emotional and behaviour problems among adolescents (Denoff, 1988). Shaw & Scott (1991) found inductive parenting to be associated with decrease in juvenile crime whereas punitive parenting was associated with increase in delinquency Newson et al. (1993) opined that it is the capacity of the parents to alter their child-rearing strategies appropriately in respect to the transition from childhood through adolescence and into young adulthood that appears important in keeping youngsters out of trouble.

e) *Perception of Parental Child-rearing Practices*: According to Kuzma (1981), "the important thing is not just how a parent loves a child but how the child perceives this love". The child's perception of his parents is dependent on his early experiences with them as they try to inculcate in him, their ideas of desirable behaviour. The behaviour of the child is an indication of his perception. It is a reflection of what he receives from the significant others in his life i.e., his parents. The child tries to emulate the values, principles and standards of his parents as he perceives them. The child's perception of his parents also depends on how his parents view him. If parents are meticulous in the modes of socialisation, the child develops a feeling of self-worth and confidence. If they provide a warm and supportive environment where they set limits for their children as well as are responsive to their needs and requirements, the feelings of trust and security are developed. A child, reared in such a climate which fosters maximal growth and development, will perceive his parents as rational and facilitating whose rearing techniques are effective and organised. Adequate satisfaction of physical, recreational and psychological needs will lead to the favourable perception of parental hill rearing practices. Research has shown that delinquents have a negative perception of their father, regarded their fathers as unacceptable of emulation and defective in the use of praise (Andry, 1950; Glueck & Glueck, 1950; Andry, 1960). Medinnus (1965) found non-delinquents to have a more favourable perception of their parents and the difference between the two groups was greater regarding perception of the father than that of the mother. The unfavourable attitude of the delinquents towards their fathers was especially marked on the, Neglecting and Rejecting' scales. Singh (1981) compared delinquents and non-delinquents on a picture story task. The delinquents harboured a negative parental picture whereas non delinquents had a positive parental picture. Lai (1983) investigated the differences in perceived parent-child relationships between delinquents and non-delinquents. Results revealed that delinquents had less opportunity to talk with their parents, seemed to be less understood by their parents and had worse relationships with their parents causing them to feel indifference and even hostility towards their parents.

Kroupa (1988) found that delinquent subjects reported their mothers to he more rejecting/neglecting than non-delinquents. Brand et al. (1990) fouled 51% of the variation in emotional adjustment accounted for by parental inconsistency as perceived by adolescents. Adolescents with conduct and oppositional disorders perceive their parents as less caring than normal adolescents (Rey & Plapp, 1990). Adolescents who characterised their parents as authoritative scored highest on measures of psycho-social competence and lowest on measures of psychological and behavioural dysfunction, the reverse was true for adolescents who described their parents as neglectful (Lamborn et al. 1991).

Saxena (1992) found that children who perceive maternal rejection tend to indulge in negative attention-seeking class room behaviour. If such behaviour persists over a period of time, they are likely to indulge in antisocial acts. Lau and Leung (1992) found poorer perceived relations with parents to be associated with higher frequency in committing delinquent acts in both boys and girls. Saxena (1993) found delinquent adolescents to perceive greater maternal rejection than their non-delinquent counterparts.

Objectives of the Present Study

The present study was conducted to ascertain whether delinquency proneness is related to the perception of parental child-rearing practices of adolescent boys and; girls. The orientation of using behavioural indices in measuring child-rearing practices is of relatively new origin, developed by Mohan and Kaur in 1989. The scale developed by Mohan and Kaur (1989) and subsequently modified in 1992 does not study parental attitudes but areas of importance in rearing related to aspects of the child's interaction with parents.

In the light of the studies reviewed the following hypotheses are formulated.

1. *High delinquency prone adolescents' perception on the behavioural indices of parenting:* academic, social, recreation, economic, nutrition, clothes, puberty development, demonstration of love, personality development, health as well as overall perception is poorer than that of low delinquency prone adolescents.
2. *Females perception on the behavioural indices of parenting:* academic, social, recreation, economic, nutrition, clothes, puberty development, demonstration of love, personality development, health as well as overall perception is better than that of males.

Method

Design: In an attempt to study the relationship between delinquency proneness and perception of parental child-rearing practices, two extreme groups on delinquency proneness were studied. An initial sample of 750 adolescents (420 males and 330 females) were administered the Jesness inventory (Jesness, 1966). On the basis of the total scores obtained on the Jesness inventory, two groups were identified viz., that of high delinquency prone and low delinquency prone using ½ S.D ± Mean as the criterion for selection. The selected sample was administered the Perception of child-Rearing Practices Scale (Mohan and Kaur, 1989) for both mother and father.

Sample: The initial sample for the present study consisted of 750 adolescents (420 males and 330 females). From this sample, a selection of high delinquency prone and low delinquency prone males and females was made on the basis of their total scores on the Jesness inventory. The selected sample was of 524 subjects with 165 males and 111 females in the high delinquency prone group and 124 males and 124 females in the low delinquency prone group. All the subjects were in the age group of 13 to 18 years from an urban background and intact families.

Tests Used: 1) The Jesness. inventory (Jesness, 1966): The Jesness inventory is a personality test designed to distinguish delinquents from non-delinquents, to provide a basis for classification into personality type and to seine as a measure of attitude change. The scale consists of 155 items to which the subject responds 'true' or 'false'. The items are scored on 10 sub-scales social maladjustment, value orientation, immaturity, alienation, autism, manifest aggression, withdrawal, social anxiety, repression and denial.

2. The Perception of Mother's % Father's child-Rearing Practices Scale (developed by Mohan & Kaur (1989) and subsequently modified in 1992): The Perception of Mother's/Father's Child-Rearing Practices Scale is a measure of the child's perception of his/her parental child-Rearing practices in Indian settings. It consists of 40 items relating to ten behavioural indices of child rearing with respect to the child's interaction with the parents which are:

- *Academic:* refers to the parental interest in the child's academic pursuits, reading habits, etc.
- *Social:* refers to the parental interest in the child's social relationships, friendships, etc.
- *Recreation:* refers to the parental interest in the child's leisure time activities, games, etc.
- *Economic:* refers to the parental interest in the child's financial needs and demands.
- *Nutrition:* refers to the parental interest in the child taking a balanced and nutritious diet.
- *Clothes:* refers to the parental interest in the child's wardrobe.
- *Puberty development:* refers to the parental interest in the development changes and problems associated with them.
- *Demonstration of love:* refers to the parental expression of love and affection.
- *Personality development:* refers to the parental efforts in the development of a well moulded personality.
- *Health:* refers to the parental interest in the child being physically fit and healthy.

The subjects are required to respond to the items on a five point rating scale which varies from very often, quite often, moderately; seldom and never. The range of scores is 40 to 200, with higher scores indicating a more positive perception of parental child-rearing practices. The PMFCRP scale deals with the different dimensions of nurturance which are manifested in the different areas of parental child-rearing practices as perceived by adolescents.

Results and Discussion

The present study was conducted to ascertain whether delinquency proneness is related to perception of parental child-rearing practices of adolescent boys and girls.

Table 1

Summary of 2 X 2 Anova on the Behavioural Indices of the Perception of Mother's and Father's Child Reading Practices in Relation to Deliquency Proneness and Sex

Source of Variance	df	1. Academic				2. Social				3. Recreation				4. Economic			
		Mother's		*Father's*		*Mother's*		*Father's*		*Mother's*		*Father's*		*Mother's*		*Father's*	
		MSS	*F*	*MSS*	*F*	*MSS*	*F*	*MSS*	*F*	*MSS*	*F*	*MSS*	*F*	*MSS*	*F*	*MSS*	*F*
Delinquency (A) (High/Low)	1	1.24	14.40**	1.11	13.16**	0.85	10.46**	1.46	14.78**	0.75	8.66**	1.11	11.89**	0.09	1.07	0.28	3.07
Sex (B) (Male/Female)A	1	0.25	2.86	0.07	0.82	0.06	0.71	0.14	1.44	0.30	3.49	0.08	0.84	0.90	10.30**	0.88	9.52**
AXB	1	0.02	0.23	0.00	0.00	0.00	0.04	0.02	0.19	0.03	0.38	0.06	0.64	0.04	0.41	0.41	4.42*
WSS	520	0.09		0.08		0.08		0.10		0.09	0.09		0.09				
		Mean	*SD*	*Mean*	*SD*	*Mean*	*SD*	*Mean*	*SD*	*Mean*	*SD*	*Mean*	*SD*	*Mean*	*SD*	*Mean*	*SD*
High Delinquency Prone		14.51	3.36	14.58	3.52	12.93	3.27	12.32	3.78	13.83	3.43	14.07	3.55	14.29	3.54	14.08	3.62
Low Delinquency Pronc		15.66	3.29	15.85	3.01	13.87	3.16	13.57	3.28	14.74	3.23	15.13	3.33	14.71	3.15	14.76	3.31
Males		14.78	3.62	15.38	3.48	13.22	3.36	12.69	3.72	13.98	3.39	14.40	3.45	14.05	3.34	13.94	3.54
Females		15.38	3.02	15.22	3.13	13.55	3.09	13.19	3.44	14.61	3.32	14.77	3.52	15.03	3.33	14.96	3.34

(Contd...)

		5. Nutrition				6. Clothes				7. Puberty Development				8. Demonstration of Love				
Source of		*Mother's*		*Father's*		*Mother's*		*Father's*		*Mother's*		*Father's*		*Mother's*		*Father's*		*Variance df*
		MSS	F	*MSS*	F	*MSS*	F	*MSS*	F	*MSS*	F	*MSS*	F	*MSS*	F	*MSS*	F	
Delinquency (A)1	0.27	4.86*	0.12	1.29	0.82	10.73**	0.52	6.04**	1.32	11.59**	1.57	16.44**	0.04	0.30	0.02	0.13		
(High/Low)																		
Sex (B)	1	0.21	3.80	0.76	7.88**	0.66	8.66**	0.19	2.27	20.87	182.98**	0.23	2.36	1.20	9.40**	1.01	7.59**	
(Male/Female)A																		
AXB	1	0.03	0.57	0.03	0.32	0.00	0.05	0.00	0.02	0.06	0.50	0.05	0.50	0.06	0.46	0.01	0.09	WSS
520	0.06		0.97		0.08		0.09		0.11		0.10		0.13		0.13			
		Mean	*SD*	*Mean*	*SD*	*Mean*	*SD*	*Mean*	*SD*	*Mean*	*SD*	*Mean*	*SD*	*Mean*	*SD*	*Mean*	*SD*	
High Delinquency																		
Prone		15.71	2.77	13.62	3.71	14.90	3.47	14.14	3.49	10.11	4.59	7.74	3.90	13.14	3.99	11.67	4.02	
Low Delinquency																		
Prone		16.26	2.56	14.04	3.33	15.88	2.75	14.90	3.09	9.38	4.24	6.45	2.98	13.02	4.17	11.89	4.28	
Males		15.75	2.68	13.42	3.57	14.96	3.26	14.27	3.29	7.77	3.44	7.40	3.32	12.61	4.16	11.32	4.17	
Females		16.25	2.66	14.31	3.44	15.86	3.02	14.78	3.36	12.21	4.31	6.81	3.81	13.67	3.88	12.33	4.06	

To test the significance of difference between the two groups, analysis of variance of the order 2*2 was applied having two levels of delinquency proneness- high and low and the two sexes — males and females on the 10 behavioural indices of the perception of parental child-rearing practices academic, social, recreation, economic, nutrition, clothes, puberty development, demonstration of love, personality development, health as well as overall perception, the results of which are presented in Table 1.

a) Perception of Parental Child-rearing Practices

Results of the present study (Table 1) reveal that low delinquency prone adolescents perception of their mothers and fathers child rearing practices is significantly better than that of the high delinquency prone adolescents on the behavioural indices — academic, social, recreation, and clothes. Another area where this difference emerged was nutrition in the case of the mother only. However, in the case of puberty development, high delinquency prone adolescents perception was better of both mother and father.

The significant interaction (delinquency proneness x sex) on the economic index reveals that the high delinquency prone males perception of the father is poorest of this index. (Table 2)

Table 2
Contingency table showing interaction between Delinquency Proneness (High/Low) and Sex on the behavioural Index: Economic

	Males	*Females*
High Delinquency Prone	13.44	15.02
Low Delinquency Prone	14.61	14.91

Results of the present study reveal that the high delinquency prone adolescents perception of both the parents child-rearing practices are conceptualised along similar lines. Their perception on the puberty development scale is better than that of the low delinquency prone adolescents with reference to both the parents. May be high delinquency prone adolescents lack any inhibitions in discussing sex related issues with their parents.

The adjustment of a child is influenced by parental regulations and interactions which help the child to develop the ego and superego controls that enable them to become self-disciplined instead of coming under the influence of their impulses (Levine & Kozak, 1979). Loeber & Dishion (1983) opined that composite measures of family management techniques are most predictive of delinquency Reiterating the significant role of parents in the child's life, Lykken (1994) opined that the root cause of crime and violence is the unwillingness or inability of parents to socialise their children.

Parents who provide the child with a home where there is a healthy interpersonal network of relationships with reciprocal trust, respect and understanding facilitate the proper personality development of the child. Meaningful and positive caring and communication are important factors in delinquency causation (Alexander, 1973; Snyder & Patterson, 1987; Campbell, 1987). Faulty parenting can have drastic effects on the growth and development of the child. His world view gets moderated by parental attitudes, his personality imbibes the parental distortions (Mohan, 1994).

Delinquents have been reported to perceive their parents negatively and as rejecting (Imperio & Chabot, 1980; Singh, 1981, Lai, 1983; Kroupa, 1988; Lamborn et al. 1991; Lau & Leung, 1992; Saxena, 1993; Lavania, 1993). Families of delinquents have less provision for wholesome recreation. Avocational activities serve to help the individual in developing a healthy and well adjusted personality (Ganguly & Maitra, 1966). Agnew & Peterson (1989) found delinquency to be negatively related to time spent in organised leisure activities.

Children need both the parents to be involved in their lives. Effective fathering is of vital importance to the growing boy as all experience which promotes maturation and social adaptation (Anderson, 1968). Parke (1981) found that if fathers were involved in the dally care of their infants during the first eight weeks after childbirth, the babies were more socially responsive and capable of withstanding stressful circumstances during their school years. Though fathers cannot imitate a mother's nurturing care of her child, fathers have an essential nurturing function that is distinctly, their own (Pr uett, 1993). The paternal presence is a vital force in their growing up.

The results of the present study reaffirm the necessity of establishment of an affectionate and trusting relationship between the adolescents and their parents, so that they can conform to the rules, regulations and demands of society. (Medinnus, 1965; Shukla, 1983). Parents must employ attentive and nurturant child-rearing techniques to alter the deviant perceptions of children and develop socio-ethical personalities. When adolescents perceive their parents as disinterested or inefficient in their child rearing techniques their appraisal of the self and the environment play get distorted and this play lead to antisocial behaviour. Effective rearing techniques and subsequently their perception as adequate would foster successful coping strategies to overcome delinquency in adolescents. The earlier work on parenting (Maccoby and Martin, 1983; Jensen and Kingston, 1986) emphasised primarily the attitude with which the parents dealt with their children. However, these studies did not, indicate the behavioural indices through which these attitudes could be manifested. In the present work, the focus is on behavioural indices with respect to the child's interaction with the parents.

b) Sex differences on Perception of Parental Child-rearing Practices

Sex differences emerged in the perception of parental child rearing practices with the females showing more appreciation of parental inputs. Females perceived the mother's child-rearing practices significantly better (Table 1) on the behavioural indices of economic, clothes, puberty development, demonstration of love, health as well as overall perception. In the case of perception of father's Child-rearing practices, results (Table I) show that females perception was significantly better on the behavioural indices - economic, nutrition, demonstration of love, health as well as overall perception. For both the parents the overall perception was better of the females with special emphasis on the behavioural indices-economic, demonstration of love and health. Research has revealed that girls perception of their parents attitude towards theirs and their child rearing practices is more favourable and positive than that of the boys (Wadkar & Palsane, 1987; Mohan & Kaur, 1989; Adjukovic, 1990; Kaur, 1992; Mohan & Nalwa, 1996).

Child-welfare is important for building up human resources as ail essential component of national development. It is on the children and their well-being that the future of the country rests. The proper rearing and upbringing of the child and the opportunities for growth and development are of paramount importance and pave the way for a strong and healthy society and country. Effective parenting techniques lead to the development of a well moulded personality. It is the parents responsibility not only to help the child survive but also to look after his social, emotional and psychological needs and in addition, provide an environment conducive for his psycho-social growth. When parents sire perceived as neglecting, rejecting and disinterested, children arc more susceptible to external influences. They may develop ties with antisocial elements and indulge in delinquent activities. To curb antisocial and delinquent tendencies in children and help them realise their potential to the maximum, supportive and nurturant parent-child interactions and relationships are essential.

References

1. Adjukovic, M., Differences in Parents Rearing Style Between Female and Male Pre-delinquents and Delinquent Youth, *Psychologische Beitrage,* (1990) 32 (1-2), 7-15.
2. Agnew, R & Peterson, D.M., *Leisure and delinquency Social Problems,* (1959) 36 (4), 332-350.
3. Alexander, J.F., *Defensive and Supportive Communication in Normal and Deviant Families, Journal of Consulting & Clinical Psychology;* (1973) 40, 223-231.
4. Anderson, R.E., Where' s Dad? Paternal Deprivation and Delinquency, *Archives of General Psychiatry,* (1968) 18, 641-649.
5. Andry R.G., Faulty Paternal and Maternal Child Relationships, Affection and Delinquency, *British Journal of Delinquency,* (1950) 1, 34-48.
6. Andry R.G., *Delinquency and Parental Pathology,* London; Metheun, 1960.
7. Barron, AT & Earls, E., The Relationship of Temperament and Social Forces to Behaviour Problems in Three Year Old Children, *Journal of Child Psychology & Psychiatry,* (1984) 25, 23-33.
8. Brand, H.J. Bernhardt, H. & Hanekom, J.D., Perceived Inconsistency as a Factor in the Emotional Development of Behaviour Disordered Children, *Psychological Reports,* (1990), 66(2), 620-622.
9. Browning, C.J., Differential Impact of Family Organisation on Male Adolescents, *Social Forces,* (1960), 8, 37-44.
10. Campbell, A., Self-reported Delinquency and Home Life: Evidence from a Sample of British Girls, *Journal of Youth & Adolescence,* (1987), 16 (2), 167-177.
11. Chilton, R.J. & Markle, G.E., Family Disruption, Delinquent Conduct & the Effect of Sub-classification, *American Sociological Review,* (1972), 37, 93-99.
12. Denoff, M., An Integrated Analysis of the Contribution made by Irrational Beliefs and Parental Interaction to Drug Abuse, *International Journal of the Addictions,* (1988), 23, 655-669.
13. Elliot, D;S.; Huizinga, D. & Ageton, S.S., Explaining Delinquency and Drug Use, *Beverly Hills,* CA: Sage Publications. (1985).

14. Farrington, D.P., & Hawkins, J.D., Predicting Participation, Early Onset and Later Persistence in Officially Recorded Offending, *Criminal Behaviour & Mental Health,* (1991), 1(1), 1-33.

15. Ganguly D. & Maitra, A.K., *Some Environmental Correlates of Juvenile Delinquency Indian Journal of Social Work,* (1966), 27, 205-210.

16. Glueek:, S. & Glueck, E., *Unravelling Juvenile Delinquency* Cambridge, Mass: Harvard University Press. (1950)

17. Hetherington, E.M. & Parke, S.D., *Child Psychology,* New York: Harper & Row, (1986).

18. Inlperio, A.N. & Chabot, D.R., Male Delinquents Perception of their Parents: A Factor Analysis, *Perceptual & Motor Skills,* (1980), 51, 829-830.

19. Jain, S & Panwar, S., A Study of Criminal Behaviour as a Function of Parents Acceptance, *Indian journal of Criminology;* (1992), 20 (2), 107-111.

20. Jensen, L.C. & Kingston, M., Parenting. Chicago: Holt Rinehart and Winston, (1986).

21. Jensen, C.F., *Manual of the Jesness Inventory Palo Alto*, California, Consulting Psychologists Press: (1966)

22. Johnson, V & Pandina, R.J., Effects of the Family Environment on Adolescent Substance Use, Delinquency and Coping Styles, *American Journal of Drug & Alcohol Abuse,* (1991), 17 (1), 71-88.

23. Kaur J., Perception of Child-rearing Practices, Adjustment and Academic Achievement of Children of Working and Non -Working Mothers, *Unpublished Doctoral Thesis,* Panjab University; Chandigarh, (1992)

24. Kroupa, S.E., *Perceived Parental Acceptance and Female Juvenile Delinquency Adolescence,* (1988), 23 (89), 171-185.

25. Kuzma, K., Working Mothers – How You Can Have A Career and be a Good Parent Too, New York: Harper & Row, (1981)

26. Lai, P., A Study of the Parent-Child Relations of Delinquents in Taiwan, *Japanese Journal of Criminal Psychology,* (1983), 20 (1), 33-42.

27. Lamborn, S.D.; Mounts, N.S.; Steinberg, L. & Dornbusch, S.M., Patterns of Competence and Adjustment among Adolescents from Authoritative, Authoritarian, Indulgent quid Neglectful Families, *Child Development,* (1991) 62, 1049-1065.

28. Lull, S. & Leung, K., Relations with Parents and School and Chinese Adolescents Self-concept, Delinquency and Academic Performance, *British Journal of Educational Psychology;* (1992) 62, 193-202.

29. Lavania, S., *Juvenile Delinquency,* Jaipur: Rawat Publishers, (1993)

30. Levine, E.M. & Kozak, C., Drug and Alcohol Use, Delinquency and Vandalism among Upper Middle Class Pre and Post Adolescents, *Journal of Youth & Adolescence,* (1979) 8 (1), 91-101.

31. Loeber, R. & Dishion, T., Early Predictors of Male Delinquency: *A Review, Psychological Bulletin,* (1983), 94 (1), 68-99.

32. Lykken, D.T., On the Causes of Crime and Violence: A Reply to Aber and Rappaport, *Applied & Preventive Psychology*, (1994) 3 (1), 55-58.

33. Maccoby, E. & Martin, J., Socialization in the Context of the Family: Parent Child Interaction, In E.M. Hetherington (Ed.), PH. Mussen (Series Ed.), Handbook of Child Psychology: Vol. 4, *Socialization, Personality and Social Development,* New York: Wiley, (1983)

34. Medinnus, G.R., Delinquents Perception of their Parents, *Journal of Consulting Psychology* (1965) 29 (6), 592-593.

35. Minty, B., *Child Care and Adult Crime,* Manchester, U.K., Manchester University Press, (1987).

36. Mohan, V "Women - education and Child-rearing" , *In The Indian Girls* (Edss.) V R. Dhoundiyal et al., Almora, India: Shri Almora Book Depot. (1994)

37. Mohan, V & Kaur, J., Perception of Child-rearing Practices by children of Working and Non-Working Mothers, *Indian Journal of Community Guidance Service,* (1989) 6 (1), 1-12.

38. Mohan, V & Nalwa, K., Perception of Child-rearing Practices of Deprived and Non-deprived Adolescent Students, *Journal of Community Guidance & Research,* (1996) 13 (2), 191-206.

39. Mohan, V & Singh, S., General Adjustment as Related to Personality. *Personality Study & Group Behaviour*, (1989) 9 (1), 23-28.

40. Newson, J. Newson, E. & Adams, M., *The Social Origins of Delinquency Criminal Behaviour & Mental Health*, (1993) 31 (1), 19-29.

41. Parke, R., Fathers, Cambridge, M.A., Harvard University Press, (1981).

42. Patterson, G.R., Coercive Family Process, Eugene, OR: Castalia, (1982)

43. Peterson, D.R. & Becker, W.C., Family Interaction and Delinquency. In H.C. Quay (Ed.) Juvenile Delinquency: Research and Theory Princeton, N.J: Van Nostrand, (1965).

44. Pruett, K.D., The Paternal Presence, Families in Society, *The Journal of Contemporary Human Services,* (1993) January, 37-41.

45. Pulkkinen, L., Self Control and Continuity from Childhood to Adolescence, In P.B. Baltes & O.G. Brim (Eds.), *Life-Span Development and Behaviour,* Vol. 4. New York: Academic Press. (1982)

46. Rey, J.M. & Plapp, J.M., Quality of Perceived Parenting in Oppositional and Conduct Disordered Adolescents, *Journal of the American Academy of Child & Adolescent Psychiatry,* (1990) 29 (3), 382-385.

47. Sarkar, C., Juvenile Delinquency in India (An Etiological Analysis), New Delhi: Daya Publishing House, (1987)

48. Sexena, V., Perceived Maternal Rejection as Related to Negative Attention Seeking Classroom Behaviour among Primary School Children, *Journal of Personality & Clinical Psychology,* (1992), 8, 129-135.

49. Saxena, V., Perceived Maternal Acceptance- Rejection among Delinquents and Non-delinquents, Indian Journal of Psychology, (1993), 68, 99-103.

50. Shaw, J.M. & Scott WA., Influence of Parent Discipline Style on Delinquent Behaviour: The Mediating Role of Control Orientation, *Australian Journal of Psychology*, (1991), 43(2), 61 - 67.

51. Shukla K.S., Juvenile Delinquency and Parental Roles, *Indian Journal of Criminology & Criminalistics,* (1983) 3 (1).

52. Simons, R.L., Robertson, J.E. & Downs, W.R., The Nature of Association Between Parental Rejection and Delinquent Behaviour, *Journal of Youth & Adolescence,* (1989), 18 (3), 297-310.

53. Singly A.., Personality of Juvenile Delinquents: A Comparison of NSQ & EPI scores, *Indian Journal of Clinical Psychology,* (1981), 8, 177-181.

54. Snyder, J.J. & Patterson, C.R., Family Interaction and Delinquent Behaviour, In H.C. Quay (Ed.) Handbook of Juvenile Delinquency, New York: John Wiley & Sons, (1987)

55. Sodhi, H. Child Criminals: who is to blame? The Tribune, Chandigarh, (1994), July, 17.

56. Tilagaraj, R., Parent-Child Relationship and Juvenile Delinquency, *Social Defence,* (1983), 19 (73), 20-26.

57. Tygart, C.E., Self-reported Delinquency and Natural Parents, Step-Parent Youth Relations, *Journal of Divorce,* (1990), 13 (4), 89-99.

58. Wadkar, A.J. & Palsane, M.N., Sex Differences in Child's perception Parent-Child Relationships, *Journal of Psychological Researches,* (1987), 31 (3), 160-165.

CHAPTER 16

Perception of Child-rearing Practices of Deprived and Non-deprived Adolescent Students

Vidhu Mohan and Kanwal Nalwa

The present study was conducted to ascertain whether deprivation has any influence on the parental child-rearing practices as perceived by adolescents. The Prolonged Deprivation Scale (PDS) was administered to 415 boys and 331 girls. On the basis of the scores on the deprivation scale two groups were identified, namely, that of deprived and non-deprived using ½ SD ± Mean as the criterion for selection. The sample thus selected was of 424 subjects having 141 males and 72 females in the deprived group and 122 males and 89 females in the non-deprived group. The selected sample was administered with the Perception of Mothers' Child Rearing Practices Scale (PMCRP). Non-deprivation has emerged as a significant factor contributing to a more positive perception of parents' child rearing practices of adolescents on all the factors, i.e., academic, social, recreation, economic, nutrition, clothes, puberty development, demonstration of love, personality development, health and on the total PMCRP scale.

Sex differences also have emerged, with the females perceiving the parental child rearing practices significantly, being more congenial on the factors of recreation, economic, nutrition, clothes, puberty development, demonstration of love, personality development, health and total on the PMCRP scale than the males. While comparing the parental child-rearing practices it was found that only mother's child rearing practices were perceived to be significantly more positive on the factors of nutrition, clothes, puberty development, demonstration of love, personality development, health and total on the PMCRP scale than that of fathers.

INTRODUCTION

Human beings live in a complex, multifaceted environment comprising geophysical, social and psychological space. Their adjustment largely depends on the extent to which they can cope with their biological demands, personal requirements, and social obligations within the framework of environmental facilities and restraints. The word 'deprivation' is derived from the verb, 'to deprive', which means to dispossess or strip and it implies a 'felt loss'. According to Nurcombe (1970), "deprivation refers strictly to a dispossession or loss of privileges, opportunities, material goods and the like." It may occur with reference to three interrelated sets of basic needs i.e. physical, psychological and sociocultural. Langmeir (1972) viewed deprivation as a general phenomena and defined the same as 'insufficient satisfaction of basic needs for a prolonged period'. In his conceptualisation, he emphasized four things, i.e., lack of stimulation, lack of cognitive structure, lack of specific attachment and lack of individualisation. The reference is to certain deficiencies in the environment which are not there but are also experienced as such by the individual and which have an impact on the functioning of the individual (Sinha, Tripathi & Misra, 1982). According to Misra (1983), deprivation is employed interchangeably with other terms like cultural deprivation, psychological deprivation, environmental deprivation and social disadvantage to denote deficient environmental conditions, impoverished experiences as well as certain personal characteristics of the members of disadvantaged groups.

Deprivation can therefore be considered as a prolonged process relative to a defined, social setting. Sociocultural life in any social setting can be conceptualised as a continuum at one end of which lie those who have all the psychological, physical, social, economic and other facilities for fulfilment of their needs biogenic and sociogenic, leading to varied experiences in life, while on the other end lie those who are materialistically, socially, and psychologically handicapped in the fulfilment of their needs and acquisition of diverse experiences. Deprivation, as conceived here, is a hypothetical construct referring to all possible aspects of experiential input an individual has received during his lifetime. In view of the fact that accumulation of experiential variety and the extent is an outcome of relatively longer periods in a natural setting, it is referred to as prolonged deprivation (Misra & Tripathi, 1980). The concept of prolonged deprivation refers to a number of environmental and organismic variables constituting the basic sources of experiences to the living organism. The concept of prolonged deprivation aims at characterising the variations in psychological functioning of an individual in terms of his total experiential background.

Prolonged Deprivation and the Indian Scene

India is a third world country and poverty is a very major syndrome. All social segments do not get equal opportunity of undergoing enriched experiences. There are entensive variations in the degree of exposure to the variety of environmental conditions that are conducive to proper cognitive functioning, adjustment and self-enhancement of the individual (Misra & Tripathi, 1980). The Indian political system has many substates which have multiplicity of subcultures, the Aryan and Dravidian being the main two cultural streams. These are further ramified into states which have their levels of prosperity or lack of it. For example, Punjab, Haryana, Gujarat and Maharashtra are relatively prosperous states and Uttar Pradesh, Bihar and Orissa would be classified as having surplus quota of below poverty line population. Overpopulation, overcrowding and ecological cramming have their psychological deficits in terms of perceived deprivations. It is not only economic deficit but its perception in terms of deprivation which has an effect on various behavioural indices.

Effect of Deprivation on Behaviour

Individuals in different social groups are exposed to different experiences which are the basic factors affecting the growth and development of cognitive structures.

a) *Prolonged Deprivation and Cognitive Functions:* Cognitive processes or cognitions refer to all the processes involved in apprehending environmental stimulations encountered by the organism. According to Misra & Tripathi (1980), cognitive processes "can be rightly viewed as processes with the help of which we know, act and understand our environment". They also found that the observed variation in cognitive and intellective functions can be accounted for in terms of the prolonged deprivation as measured by PDS. Unstimulating environments result in poorer performance on intelligence tests and cognitive skills (Sinha, 1985).

b) *Prolonged Deprivation and Motivation:* Although man's basic psychological requirements are less readily identified than his requirements for food, water, sleep and the like, there is widespread agreement that psychological needs must be met if the individual is to maintain his personality integration and to function effectively. Summerlin (1972) found disadvantaged subjects to function at a lower level in Maslow's hierarchy of needs than non-disadvantaged subjects. Misra & Tripathi (1980) found a negative relationship between prolonged deprivation and achievement motive. Dubey (1984) in a comparative study of scheduled caste (deprived) and non-scheduled caste adolescents found scheduled caste adolescents to have significantly lower needs for achievement, interception and aggression and significantly higher needs for affiliation, succorance, abasement and nurturance.

c) *Prolonged Deprivation and Personality:* Impoverished living environment affects the personality development of the individual which results in inadequate behaviour patterns. The roots are traced to parental interactions and the general process of socialisation which the child in the impoverished environment undergoes (Sinha, 1985). The environment of the deprived child has greater incidence of stress and strain and lack of satisfaction of physical and psychological drives leading to anxiety. Mohan & Gill (1988) and Mohan & Verma (1990) found deprived subjects high on neuroticism and low on extraversion as compared to the non-deprived subjects.

d) *Prolonged Deprivation & Parent-Child Relationship:* The child holds the key to the future of a nation as tomorrow's citizen. The care and protection, the opportunities for growth and development, the proper rearing and upbringing of the child is of paramount importance and paves the way for a strong and healthy society and country. According to Thompson (1965), parents are varied in their rearing practices and frequently unpredictable. Their interactions with children are often tinged with odd combinations of tradition, personal prejudice, emotional regard and rule-of-thumb procedure. Hess & Shipman (1965) have stated that "the behaviour leading to deprivation is socialised in early childhood, the main quality involved in the effect of cultural deprivation is a

> lack of cognitive meaning in mother-child communication system, and the growth of cognitive processes is fostered in family control system. In the context of deprived families the nature of the control system relating parents to children imposes restrictions on number and kind of alternatives for action and thought available for the child."

If parents provide optimal climate for the maximal growth of their children they may be perceived by their children as having effective and organised parenting techniques. Children whose parents child rearing practices and techniques are warm, supportive and confident, reflect high achievement and responsible traits. They set high standards of excellence for their children, they do not expect perfection unless their children are realistically capable of achieving such a goal. They just push them to operate at the peak of their abilities (Jensen & Kingston, 1986).

Objectives of the Present Study

Research in the past has focused primarily on sex differences, effect of parental deprivation and economic deprivation on children's perceptions of parental attitudes.

Mothers are rated as more affectionate, friendlier, less punitive, less dominant and less threatening than fathers (Kogan, 1956), more loving, less ignoring and neglecting (Droppleman & Schaefer, 1963). Goldin (1969), in a review of children's reports of parents' behaviour concluded that mothers are perceived as more accepting, fathers were judged as more punitive. Boys perceived their parents as less accepting and loving, more psychologically controlling and demanding and more punitive than do girls. Singh (1984) found secondary school students to perceive mothers as more loving, more protecting and less domiant, rejecting and punishing than the fathers. The fathers were more disciplinarian than the mothers. Seigal (1984) opined that economic deprivation may exacerbate conflict in the family, diminish children's perceptions of parents and give rise to problem behaviour in boys. Evidence also suggested that deprivation may be an antecedent of poor psychological well-being in adults and of child-abuse. Ambast (1986) assessed six to 12-year-old boys' and girls' perceptions concerning their parents' child-rearing behaviour. Eleven of the subjects indicated that their mothers are friendlier, less punitive, less dominant and less threatening than their fathers.

The orientation of using behavioural indices in measuring child-rearing practices is of relatively new origin, developed by Mohan and Kaur in 1989. The scale developed by Mohan & Kaur (1989) and modified by Kaurl (1992) does not study the parental attitudes but areas of importance in rearing related to aspects of the child's interaction with parents. Mohan & Kaur (1989) studied the perception on the behavioural indices of child-rearing of 120 female and male adolescents of working and non-working mothers. Sex differences emerged on puberty development, as well as overall perception, where girls' perception was significantly better. Working mothers' sons' perception was significantly better on the behavioural indices of academics and demonstration of love as well as overall perception than that of non-working mothers' sons. No significant differences emerged in the perception of girls of working and non-working mothers.

Mohan & Grewal (1990) found children of high PMT mothers to perceive the rearing practices of their mothers to be poorer in comparison to low PMT mothers in the areas of academic, social, recreation, demonstration of love, personality development as well as overall perception.

The present study is an attempt to investigate if prolonged deprivation has any effect on the perception of parental child-rearing practices in adolescents. In the light of this and studies reviewed, the following hypotheses are formulated for the present study.

1. The perception of the deprived adolescents of the behavioural indices of, parental child-rearing practices is less congenial than that of non-deprived adolescents.
2. The perception of the girls of the behavioural indices of parental child-rearing practices is more congenial than that of the boys.
3. The perception of the adolescents of the behavioural indices of the mothers' child-rearing practices is more congenial than that of fathers.

Method

Design: The present study was conducted to ascertain whether deprivation has any influence on the parental child-rearing practices as perceived by adolescents. A 2x2x2 factorial design was employed having two levels of deprivation, boys and girls and perception of child-rearing practices of fathers and mothers.

Sample: The sample for the present study consisted of 746 adolescents, of which 415 were boys and 331 girls. Their age ranged from 14 to 19 years and they were studying in Central Schools in Chandigarh. The Prolonged Deprivation Scale was administered to them. On the basis of the scores on the deprivation scale two groups were identified, viz., that of deprived and non-deprived using ½ SD ± Mean as the criterion for selection. The sample thus finally selected was of 424 subjects of which 141 were males and 72 females in the deprived group and 122 males and 89 females in the non-deprived group. These selected 424 subjects were administered the Perception of Mothers's Child Rearing Practices Scale.

Tests

1) *Prolonged Deprivation Scale (PDS):* This scale was designed and developed by Misra & Tripathi (1977) to measure the level of deprivations. The PSD aims at a quantitative measurement of prolonged deprivation experienced by individuals in Indian settings and includes all possible measurable items of deprivation. In this scale 15 aspects of natural settings with special reference to life experiences in India are included which have been split into 96 items on a five-point scale. The range of scores is from 96 to 480, with higher scores indicating greater deprivation.
2) *Perception of Mothers' Child-rearing Practices Scale (PMCRP):* This scale was originally designed and developed by Mohan & Kaur (1989) and later on it was modified by Kaur (1992) and used to measure the adolescents' perception of their parental child-rearing practices. This scale consists of 40 items relating to 10 behavioural indices of child-rearing with respect to the child's interaction with the parents. The behavioural indices are academic, social, recreation, economic, clothes, nutrition, puberty development, demonstration of love, personality development and health with four items pertaining to each index. The subjects are required to respond to the items on a five-point rating scale which varies: very often, quite often, moderately, seldom and never. The range of scores is from 40 to 200, with higher scores indicating a more favourable perception of parental child-rearing practices.

Procedure: The data were collected from adolescent students studying in Central Schools in Chandigarh. The subjects were personally contacted and the PDS was administered to them in groups of 20 to 25 subjects. The method of responding was demonstrated using the first item as an example. After scoring the PDS forms according to the procedure given in the manual, cut-off points were obtained using 1/2 SD ± Mean (14.84 + 191.86) as the criterion. Subjects scoring 207 and above were identified as deprived and those scoring 177 and below were identified as non-deprived. The subjects who fell in the extreme groups were contacted again and the PMCRP scale was administered to them in small groups of 20 to 25 subjects. The response sheets of the PMCRP scale were scored according to the procedure given in the manual. Scores were obtained on each behavioural index which ranged from 4 to 20 with higher scores indicating congenial perception. The raw scores of the deprived and non-deprived adolescents on the behavioural indices of the PMCRP scale were computerised for the suitable statistical analysis used in the study. To test the significance of differences between the two groups, analysis of variance of the order 2x2x2 was applied having two levels of deprivation (deprived/non-deprived), sex (male/female) and parents (mother/father).

Results and Discussion

The present study was conducted to ascertain whether deprivation has any influence on the parental child-rearing practices as perceived by adolescents. A 2x2x2 factorial design was employed having two levels of deprivation, boys and girls and perception of parents' child-rearing practices.

I. Deprivation and Perception of Parental Child-rearing Practices

It is observed in this study that non-deprivation has emerged as a significant factor contributing to congenial perception of parental child-rearing practices on all the behavioural indices, i.e., academic, social, recreation, economic, nutrition, clothes, puberty development, demonstration of love, personality development and health. The overall perception was also significantly more favourable in the case of non-deprived adolescents. The environment in which the deprived child is reared is characterised by stress and strain, inadequate facilities and lack of satisfaction of physical as well as psychological needs. The anxiety provoking situation caused by lack of basic amenities in which parents of deprived children bring them up, leads to an impoverished-psychological space for the child to grow up. Paucity of psychologically satisfying experience can further lead to negative perception of parental contributions. The anger that a deprived condition evokes in a child is usually projected on the parent. Deprivation of all types hinders proper socialisation and development of children. This is exactly what has emerged in the present study. The interactions "which were significant for recreation, economic and health areas" also show that the deprived male adolescents perceived that deficit to the maximum level. The non-deprived female seemed to perceive her parental child-rearing indices as the best. These results support hypothesis one and therefore hypothesis one is accepted. The contingency table (Table 2) given below shows the respective mean perceptions in the different cells. Seigal (1984) opined that economic deprivation may exacerbate conflict in the family, diminish childrens' perceptions of parents and give rise to problem behaviour in boys. Evidence also suggested that deprivation may be an antecedent of poor psychological well-being in adults and of child-abuse.

Perception of Father's and Mother's Child-rearing Practices

While comparing the parental child-rearing practices it was found that mothers child-rearing practices were perceived to be significantly move positive on the behavioural indices of nutrition, clothes, puberty development, demonstration of love, personality development, health as well as overall perception. Results also showed that girls perceptions of the mothers' child-rearing practices were the most favourable whereas the boys' perception of the fathers' child-rearing practices were most unfavourable. This also reflected daughter's intimacy, trust and faith in the mother.

Overall boys' perception of both father and mother was less congenial than that of daughters. The result seems to support hypothesis 2 and therefore hypothesis 2 is accepted. Droppleman & Schaefer (1963), Golding (1969) and Singh (1984) also found mothers were rated more affectionate, more loving, more accepting, less punitive, less dominating and less threatening than the fathers. The perception scores of boys and girls are found to be more for mother (136.11, and 149.64) than for fathers (130.97 and 137.39). This means, both boys and girls have more congenial perceptions toward mothers than fathers. Therefore hypothesis three is accepted.

Table 1

Summary of 2 X 2 X 2 analysis of variance (unequal) on the factors of the PMGRP scale

Source of variance Academic		*Social*			*Recreation*			*Economic*					
main effects	*df*	*SS*	*MSS*	*F*	*SS*	*MSS*	*F*	*SS*	*MSS*	*S*	*SS*	*MSS*	*F*
Parents (A) (Mother/Father)	1	0.008	0.008	0.07	0.21	0.21	1.70	0.09	0.09	0.80	0.02	0.02	0.22
Sex (B) (Male/Female)	1	0.12	0.12	1.08	0.06	0.06	0.50	0.60	0.60	0.41*	3.69	3.69	35.74**
Deprivation (C) (Non-deprivated/ Deprived)	1	6.88	6.88	59.77**	9.66	9.66	78.25**	10.48	10.48	95.23**	9.80	9.80	94.99**
Interaction effects													
AxB	1	0.20	0 20	1.76	0.00	0.00	0.00	1.10	0.10	0.93	0.02	0.02	0.18
AxC	1	0.11	0.11	0.96	0.09	0.09	0.76	0.08	0.08	0.74	0.11	0.11	1.09
B x C	1	0.00	0.00	0.00	0.01	0.01	0.12	0.38	0.38	3.50*	0.68	0.68	6.62**
A x B x C	1	0.04	0.04	0.36	0.00	0.00	0.00	0.005	0.005	0.05	0.002	0.002	0.03
BSS	7	7.37	1.05	01.04	1.43	11.74	1.68	14.33	2.05				
WSS	840	9575.45	0.12	10.26	1.71	0.12		9151.52	0.11		8577.95	0.10	
Parents (A) (Mother/Father)	1	7.77	7.77	84.25**	1.65	1.65	16.91**	13.53	13.54	101.71**	4.11	4.11	24.27**
Sex (B) (Male/Female)	1	2.04	2.04	22.15**	0.58	0.58	5.90*	4.92	4.92	36.98**	3.51	3.512	20.73**
Depriavation (C) (Non-deprivated/ Deprived)	1	7.84	7.84	85.07**	15.43	15.43	158.38**	3.89	3.89	29.21**	12.46	12.46	73.61**
Interaction effects													
AxB	1	0.20	0 02	0.26	0.10	0.10	1.02	12.71	12.71	95.48**	0.009	0.009	0.05
AxC	1	0.03	0.03	0.35	0.03	0.03	0.27	0.11	0.11	0.82	0.000	0.000	0.006

B x C	1	0.11	0.11	1.22	0.02	0.02	0.16	0.16	0.16	1.20	0.22	0.22	1.29
A x B x C	1	0.04	0.04	0.41	0.006	0.006	0.06	0.37	0.37	2.78	0.00	0.00	0.00
BSS		7	17.37	2.55		17.80	2.54		35.70	5.10		20.30	2.90
WSS	840	7663.12	0.09		8102.28	0.10		11066.34	0.13		14070.34	0.17	

(Contd...)

Source of variance		*Personality*			*Health*			*Total on PMCRP*			
main effects	*df*	*SS*	*MSS*	F	*SS*	*MSS*	F	*SS*	*MSS*	F	
Parents (A) 1	3.83	3.83	40.59**	0.42	0.42	4.37*	152.29	152.29	38.18**		
(Mother/Father)											
Sex (B)	1	0.58	0.58	6.16*	2.22	2.22	22.99*	133.22	133.22	33.39**	
(Male/Female)											
Depriavation (C)	1	9.14	9.14	96.80**	1.96	1.96	20.24**	823.73	823.73	206.50**	
(Non-deprivated/											
Deprived)											
Interaction effects											
AxB	1	0.01	0.01	0.11	0.02	0.02	0.19	25.89	25.89	6.49*	AxC
1	0.009	0.009	0.09	0.09	0.09	0.98	0.38	0.38	0.09		
B x C	1	0.13	0.13	1.42	0.39	0.39	4.12*	0.13	0.13	0.03	
A x B x C 1	0.01	0.01	0.12	0.49	0.49	0.51	0.08	0.08	0.02		
BSS	7	13.72	1.96		5.16	0.74		1135.72	162.24		
WSS	840	7848.86	0.09		8039.92	0.09		331642.10	3.99		

* Significant at 0.05 level. ** Significant at 0.01 level

Sex Differences on Perception of Parental Child-rearing Practices

Sex: Differences emerged, with the females perceiving the parental child-rearing practices significantly better on the behavioural indices of recreation, economic, nutrition, clothes, puberty development, demonstration of love, personality development, health as well as overall perception. One interaction was found to be significant, viz., that of puberty development (Table 4). Girls perceived maximum closeness with their mothers and lowest with their fathers. In the Indian situation, sex and issues related to it are held as a taboo. Puberty development means growth of sex-related physical dimensions. In girls menarche is a major trauma and also in most homes a matter of secrecy and shame. In such a situation it is with the mother that the girl can share her apprehensions rather than the father. Boys, it seems, get the brunt from both the parents, as seen from the low score of 7.67, and 7.58. They cannot share their problems of puberty development neither with the mother (being opposite sex) nor with the father who perhaps has little time for intimacy.

Goldin (1969) found boys to perceive their parents as less accepting and loving, more psychologically controlling and demanding and more punitive than girls. Mohan & Kaur (1989) found that girls perceive the overall mothers' child-rearing practices with special emphasis on aspects of puberty development to be significantly better than the boys.

The present work has contributed by making some interesting revelations which have salient consequences for training to be better parents. The behavioural indices of child-rearing patterns have a great impact on the subsequent perception of children about their parental child-rearing practices. The present findings unequivocally show that the mother is perceived to have greater inputs in rearing than the father. The myth that 'daughters love fathers' has been dispensed with. Girls are consistently showing better perception of mothers' inputs in all the areas.

Table 2
Contingency tables showing interaction between sex (males/females) and deprivation (deprived/non-deprived)

	Recreation		*Economic*		*Health*	
Group	*Males*	*Females*	*Males*	*Females*	*Males*	*Females*
Deprived	13.20	13.30	12.44	14.38	13:98	15.47
Non-deprived	15.04	16.03	15.24.	16.01	5.411	16.02

Table 3
Continquency table showing interaction between sex (males/females) and parents (father s/mother s) on overall perception

Parents	*Males*	*Females*
Mothers	136.11	149.64
Fathers	130.97	137.39

Table 4
Contingency table showing interaction between sex (male/female) and parents (mother s/father s) on puberty development

Parents	*Males*	*Females*
Mothers	7.67	11.92
Fathers	7.58	6.73

This has implications for counselling fathers for making improvement in their inputs for their children. Girls have a more positive outlook for mothers in delicate issues like puberty development, whereas boys seem not to have many pleasant perceptions in this area. Lack of proper adjustment in this area can lead to serious maladjustment in one's life. Better sex education and sharing of experiences, development of intimacy are a must for boys. Fathers being of the same sex can play a greater role.

Deprivation has a serious influence on parental child-rearing, as has been visible in the perceived scores of children. Enrichment of environment, not only in terms of tangible amenities, but also in terms of psychological inputs is a must for better adjustment in life. Overall the girls have a more healthy, adjusted, positive outlook and appreciation for parental inputs. If boys coming from deprived homes have very uncongenial perception of parental rearing practices, then this can have a serious effect on their behavioural adjustment. Sometimes delinquent, violent and negative behaviour can be an outcome of such a negative outlook. In India one finds that violence amongst young boys is on the increase. Perceived love, nurturance and care can undo the negative behaviour in life.

References

Ambast, R. Parents: Perceived by the child, *Perspectives in Psychological Researches,* 1986, vol. 9 (1), 47-49

Droppleman, L.F., & Schaefer, B.S., Boys' and girls' reports of maternal and paternal behaviour, *Journal of Abnormal and Social Psychology*, 1963 Vol. 67, 648-654.

Dubey, S.N., Characteristic need patterns of scheduled caste Indians, *Psychology in the Orient*, 1984, Vol. 27(2), 122-124.

Goldin, P. C. A review of, children's reports of parent behaviours, *Psychological Bulletin*, 1969, Vol. 71 (3), 222-236.

Cordon, E.A., Review of Compensatory Education, *American Journal of Orthopsychiatry,* 1965, Vol. 35, 640-651.

Hess, R. & Shipman, V., Early experiences and the socialisation of cognitive modes in children, *Child Development,* 1965, Vol. 36, 869-885.

Jensen, L.C. & Kingston, M., *Parenting,* Chicago: Holt, Rinehart and Winston, 1986.

Kagan, J., The child's perception of the parent, *Journal of Abnormal and Social Psychology,* 1956, Vol. 53, 257-258.

Kaur, J., Perception of Child-Rearing Practices, Adjustment and Academic Achievement of Children of working and Non-Working Mothers, Unpublished Doctoral Thesis, Panjab University, Chandiarh, 1992.

Langmier, J., Personalities of Deprived Children, In F.J., Monks et al. (Eds.), *Determinants of behavioural development,* N Y: Academic Press, 331-348, 1972.

Misra, G., Deprivation and Development: A review of Indian studies, *Indian Education Review,* 1989, Vol. 18(1), 12-32.

Misra, G., & Tripathi, L.E. *Manual of the Prolonged Deprivation Scale,* Agra: National Psychological Corporation 1977.

Misra, G., & Tripathi, L.P., *Psychological Consequences of Prolonged Deprivation*, National Psychological Corporation, Agra, India, 1980.

Mohan, V., & Gill, N., Personality differences of socially deprived and non deprived school children, *Journal of Psychometry,* 1988, Vol. 9. 23-27.

Mohan, V., & Grewal, R., Perception of Child Rearing Practices of Mothers with High Premenstrual Tension Syndrome, *Journal of the Indian Academy of Applied Psychology*, 1990, Vol. 16 (2), 23-29.

Mohan, V., & Kaur, J., Perception of Child-Rearing Practices by Children of Working and Non-working Mothers, *Indian Journal of Community Guidance Service*, 1989, Vol. 6, 1-12.

Mohan,. V., &. Verma, S., Social deprivation, intelligence and personality correlates, *Indian Journal of Community Guidance Service,* 1990, Vol. 7. 25-36.

Nurcombe: B., Deprivation: An essay in definition with special consideration of the Australian aboriginals, *Medical Journal of Australia,* 1970, Vol. 2, 88, 92.

Seigal, M., Economic deprivation and the quality of parent-child relationship: A trickle down framework, *Journal of Applied Developmental Psychology,* 1984, Vol. 5(2), 127-144.

Singh, R.A., Perception of Maternal and Paternal, Child-Rearing Behaviour in Secondary School students, *Indian Journal of Psychology,* 1994, Vol. 59.

Sinha, D., Cognitive and motivational correlates of deprivation and their implications for the education of scheduled caste children, *Journal of Personality and Clinical Studies,* 1985, Vol. 1, 11-16.

Sinha, D., Tripathi, R.C., & Misra, G., *Deprivation: Its Social Roots and Psychological Consequences,* Concept Publishing Company, New Delhi, 1982.

Summerlin, C.G., An Analysis of Occurrence and Intensity of Masolvian Needs of Disadvantaged and Non Disadvantaged Students, *Dissertation Abstracts International,* 1972, Vol. 33, No. 4A.

Thompson, G.G., *Child Psychology: Growth Trends in Psychological Adjustment,* Times of India Press, Bombay, 1965.

CHAPTER 17

Personal Problem Solving: The Perception and Strategies of the Adolescent Girls

Mukul Bhalla **and** *Pallavi Bhatnagar*

An attempt has been made in this study to explore the phenomena of personal problem solving skills with cognitive approach. The sample consisted of 45 higher secondary girl students studying in the Loreto Convent Intermediate College at Lucknow. The age of the girls ranged from 16.5 to 17.5 years. They all belonged to middle socioeconomic status families. It was an incidental sampling. The respondents were given five formal intellectual problem-solving tests. The first was to transfer a pile of three coins to any one of the three pegs in some limited moves. The second had four coins instead of three. The third problem was to transfer the globes proportionately to the size of the three monsters. The fourth was with three executives having different levels of competence. Here the executives replace the monsters. The task was to assign the skill according to the competence of the executive. The fifth problem was with three water-jugs of different structures: 8 litre, 5 litre and 3 litre and to distribute 8 litre water in the 8 litre, 5 litre jugs evenly. The experiment was conducted and scored according to the procedure.

From the results, the problems were classified as inconveniences, frustrations involving someone else, situation out of one's control, decisions and personal disabilities. The respondents had accurate and complete perception of the problems in the beginning, but the goal status were less complete. Few problems were completely perceived and less than half of the problems had potentially successful solution. The respondents showed a higher success rate on the formal intellectual problems than on the personal problems.

Introduction

If we were able to categorise problem types, as Greeno (1978) says, "Look, there are essentially 5 (or 10 or 15, or whatever) types of problems. Any problem you name can be categorised as one of these types or some combination of them." We could devote our research efforts for understanding the strategies used by people who were successful in solving them, and hence be able to carry out the correct strategies for all classes of problems, as also suggested by Kahney (1986). The developing of this ability would aid people, at large to cope effectively with their problems. Thus classifying problems is the first in the series of steps which could lead to some goal. But it is clear that not all problems are the same, and differ along various continua, viz. the routine-creative, formal-informal, well-defined, ill-defined, real life-hypothetical, specified unspecified actions, tangible-intangible goals, etc. (Heppner and Krauskopf (1987) thus making the task of classifying problems difficult. This is evidenced in the fact that not much is known about how people cope with their real life and problem difficulties (Sternberg, 1982). Though there is no dearth of literature dealing with formal intellectual problem solving (Simon and Hayes, 1972 Reed et al., 1974; Egan and Greeno, 1974; Newell and Simon, 1974, 1976; Luger and Bauer, 1978. Pitts, 1983) little attention has been paid to personal problem solving, whether real or hypothetical.

In the context too, there exists a serious gap in the psychological literature dealing with personal problem solving, considering its importance in helping a person to cope with his daily life problems and face stressful situations effectively. It should be interesting to study whether the Indian adolescent differs from his Western counterpart, both in the perception of his personal problems as well as the strategies he employs in coping with these problems. Some differences are anticipated, due in part to variations in the life scripts, parental training methods, cultural value, social norms, etc., all of which will influence, in turn, how the individual perceives the problem, as well as the way he evolves different strategies to cope with his problem.

Once the individual realises that a problem exists, he has to further analyse to the best of his ability, questions regarding his problem—What happened? What I am worried about? What might I do about it? and so on (Leigh, 1983). This is essential, since completeness and accuracy of defining the problem (or encoding) affects the subjects performance in later problem-solving activities, such as generating alternatives and decision making.

It is apparent that this ability to detect a problem is seemingly the most significant at no other stage in life than in adolescence — the 'age of crisis', 'a' period of stress and storm (Hall, 1904). The adolescent encounters a large gamut of problems during this stage, and the Indian adolescent is no different. The question that arise are: How aware would female Indian adolescent be of her problems? How complete and accurate would her perception be of the various personal problems? How does she envisage herself solving these problems? The strategies that a subject evolves for solving her problems are clearly dependent upon the completeness and accuracy of the perception she has for the problems. Miller (1960) pointed out that there is a great deal of uncertainty in an actual problem-solving situation than in its lab counterpart. Would this factor of uncertainty have a differential effect on the S's performance in formal intellectual problems? These were the questions that intrigued the researchers to take up the present study. The main purpose of the study is to gauge the completeness and accuracy in the perception of the Indian adolescent girls for their personal problems, pertaining to different content area. A secondary aim was to study the adequacy of probable strategies evolved by them to cope up with these problems. Besides, a comparison was also attempted between the performance of formal intellectual and personal problems.

Method

Sample: The sample consisted of 45 higher secondary female students from Loreto Convent Intermediate College, Lucknow. Their age ranged from 16.5 to 17.5 years. They all belonged the middle socio economic-status families and the method of sample selection was incidental sampling.

Materials: The personal problems were generated by the respondents themselves and prior to that following five formal intellectual problems solving tests were given to them.

The first problem test was the Towers of Hanio transformed into coin problem for facilitating administration. This has been one of the most popular problem-solving tests (Newell & Simon 1972, Simon & Hayes 1976, Kahney 1986). Here, the S was to transfer a pile of three coins (smallest on the top, largest at the bottom and medium-sized coin in the middle) from Peg A to B or to C. The S could move only one coin at a time and should not place a larger coin on a smaller one. The S has to place the coins only on any one of the three pegs during the task and not on the table, floor or hold it in his/her hand and should complete the task with minimum number of moves.

The second problem-solving test (the isomorphic problem with the identical task) had increased level of difficulty with four coins instead of three. The third and fourth problem solving tests were homomorphic, that is, had similar but not identical underlying structure, more akin to the real-life situation.

The third problem-solving test thus had three monsters (large, medium and small) holding medium, large and small globes respectively. The S's task was to shift globes so as to have the monsters holding the globes proportionate to their own sizes. The conditional rules were that one globe could be shifted at a time and a monster holding two globes had to transfer the larger of the two, a globe could not be transferred to a monster holding a larger globe.

The fourth test was a self-devised problem in which, used, three executives having maximum, moderate and minimum competence, in place of the three monsters. Tasks requiring three degrees of skills assigned to those executives substituted the globes. The S had to reassign the tasks such that the task requiring maximum skill was to be given to the most competent executive and the one requiring least skill to the executive with minimum skill, thus allotting the tasks as per the skill required and the competence of the executive. The problem had to be approached according to the rules for solving it which were corresponding to the third problem.

The fifth problem was the water jug test with a different structure altogether. There were three jugs of 8, 5 and 3 litres capacity with 8 litre jug being full of water. The S's task was to transfer the water back and forth among the jugs so as to end up with 4 litre in each of 8 and 5 litres jugs.

Procedure: Since verbalising about personal problems entails imparting information of a sensitive nature, close personal rapport was first established with each subject individually. The subjects were first given five formal intellectual problems to work on, which included four problems based on the Tower of Hanoi problem (two isomorphic and two homomorphic) and one problem with a changed problem structure (the water-jug problem). The Ss were asked to give a verbal account of all that they were thinking while solving each of the problem. Elicting information about the problem-solving process through verbal protocols not only gave a clearer insight into the process but also provided a good opportunity of interaction between the researcher and the Ss, thus establishing a rapport. After the solution of the five problems each S was introduced to the part of the study regarding personal problems. Each subject was given the following instructions:

"We are interested in seeing what problems are generally encountered by young Indian girls in their daily life. We would like you to tell us about problems that you might be facing, however small or trivial. Describe the problem as fully as you can, telling us how you would like the problem to be solved and what are the goal states you aim to achieve regarding these problems. Also try and give us the way you go about solving them, the methods you employ. You should try and describe everything. All the information that you give will be kept absolutely confidential, so be frank". While some subjects spoke out aloud, most of them felt inhibited in doing so, and preferred to write down their accounts, and were given paper and pen for the same. In this way detailed accounts of personal problems were obtained from each of the 45 adolescent students.

Results and Discussion

Each day each one of us faces many problems ranging from simple problems of fixing a flat tyre to the challenging problems of science. But perhaps the most crucial are those of a personal nature—dealing with relationships, decision making, etc., because it is the effective coping of such problems that our well being depends. For this end, it is the cognisance of the problem that paves the way for the satisfactory solution of a problem. In the present study, we find in the subjects, a fair degree of awareness of the problems facing them. From the verbal accounts of problems encountered by the subjects in daily life, a total of seven broad categories of problems were identified.

Table 1

Showing the categories of personal problems and their relative percentages

S.No.	*Problem category*	*Percentage*
1.	Inconvenience	6.74 %
2.	Frustration involving someone else	11.24 %
3.	Situation out of one's own control	15.73 %

4.	Decisions	37.08 %
5.	Personal inhibitions and weaknesses	5.62 %
6.	Frustration Involving others — out of one's control	21.24 %
7.	Inconvenience — out of one's control	2.25 %

The classification was in line with the four factors dominant in personal problems as described by Fallahi (1983). The classes thus obtained were:

a) *Inconveniences:* These are problems that are not too serious and are more likely tiresome, troublesome and easily surmountable, viz., Transport Problem —"I don't have a fixed vehicle and so have a tempo some day and a rickshaw another day".

b) *Frustrations involving someone else:* These are problems encountered by the subjects, caused by the thwarting of the subject's progress towards his desired goal by some-one else. "I have a lot of arguments with my father and when they get heated up, I leave the room, lest I be rude."

c) *Situations out of one's control:* This includes problems which fall beyond the subject's capacity to deal with directly, viz., "Prescribed books of U.P. Board are not in English, so it creates problems for us English Mediums."

d) *Decisions:* These are problems involving making choices between alternatives, viz., "I want to be independent financially and take up a job, but I am in the process of deciding on a job, and find it difficult to make up my mind."

   Besides these, two more categories are distinguishable, derived from combination of, 'b' and 'c' categories which is categorised here as 'e'.

e) *Frustrations involving someone else out of one's own control*: Problems which arise basically out of a blocking of progress towards one's goal by someone else, about which the subject is unable to do anything much. "Implementation of the Mandal Commission and its repercussions on my career prospects."

   *Then a combination of 'a' and 'c' denoted here as category 'f'.

f) *Inconvenience — Out of one's control*: There are inconvenience about which the subject is not very capable of doing anything, viz., "I live far from college and have to take 2 tempos and then walk 15 minutes and waste one hour coming and going each. Finally, a seventh category was also observed.

(g) *Personal inhibitions and weaknesses:* These are problems which arise from a negative self-evaluation, viz., "I am very sensitive and feel hurt at the most trivial things."

Of the total number of 89 problems, generated by the 45 subjects, Table 1 shows the relative percentage of each of the seven categories. We find that problems regarding decisions make for the single largest class of problems as encountered by the adolescent females (37.08%). This is the age when the individual is making some of the most important decisions of his or her life, and he or she has to decide how to schedule his time to its best utility. Figure 1 further elaborates the breakup of these seven categories and the relative percentage also.

A major portion of the decisions problems is of Time Management (Figure 1) which implies dividing time most effectively and efficiently between various activities, like studies, co-curricular activities, etc. The immediate personal and very important problem of the choice of a career is another important decision for the adolescent, which affects his future, which also finds support from Grinder (1973).

The second largest group of problems is of frustrations involving others—out of one's own control (Table 1, 21.24%) reflecting the special characteristic of the age — the tendency to think in terms of 'oughts' and 'shoulds' as Hurlock (1973) refers to it as the 'age of idealism'. Six sub categories of the problems can be identified in this category (Figure 1). The Mandal Report, affecting the career prospects of the youth, supersedes the other five categories of disturbance in studies due to the arrival of unexpected guests; overprotection by parents; crank calls on the phone; and disturbance by others; and the miscellaneous class, consisting mainly of concern over the Babri-Masjid-Ram Janmabhoomi issue.

The third category is of situations out of one's own control (15.3%) which includes vast courses at college; securing good marks in the exams; erratic electric supply; noise pollution; non-availability of books in English; and miscellaneous problems.

About 11.24 per cent is the contribution of the problems related to Frustrations Involving Someone Else of which the largest sub-category is of Overprotection by parents; followed by Differences in the value systems of the subjects with their parents; Lack of communication amongst family members; and miscellaneous problems, as lack of close friends, imposition of a career choice, etc. (Figure 1).

Inconveniences: These consist mainly of problems due to transport difficulties; differences in food preferences among family members; paucity of finances, etc. (Table 1, 6.74%, Fig. 1).

Personal inhabitation and weaknesses: These contribute in a small measure to the total (5.62%) and include the tendency to be shy and sensitive or of being unable to exercise adequate control over one's feelings —"Flying off the handle pretty fast," as one subject put it (Figure 1).

Inconveniences out of one's own control: These make the smallest contribution to the entire set of problems (2.25%) and consist mainly of transport problems. But a mere awareness of the problem is not enough. The problem must be received in its entirety and the more complete the perception, the higher will be the probability of success of the strategy evolved for it.

Perception of the personal problems: In line with Day's (1988) contention, representation of the problem would seem to be related to its perception. Only when the person could perceive the problem clearly could he give it an adequate representation and complete perception of the problem. Perception of the problem can be analysed from two points of view—the completeness of the initial state and the completeness of the goal state. In well defined problems, the starting point or the initial state of the problem is clear, as is the goal point or goal state. An ill defined problem, on the other hand, has an ambiguous initial and goal states (Wessels, 1982).

From Table 2 we find that the subjects had a clear idea of the existing state of affairs giving rise to the problem, for almost 84 per cent of the problems, as 74 out of 89 problems had complete and structured initial states, while only 15 problems had incomplete and unstructured initial states.

Table 2: Showing the perception of personal problems

Perception of Initial State	
Complete and structured initial state	Incomplete and unstructured initial state
74	15

But as regards the goal state perception, 55 out of 89 problems were not clearly perceived, and for 14 problems, the goal state was clearly undefined. Only 20 problems have been clearly stated, with complete and structured goal states (Table 3).

Table 3

Showing the categories of perception of goal states

Perception of goal state		
Complete and structured goal state	Incomplete and unstructured goal state	Undefined goal
2	55	14

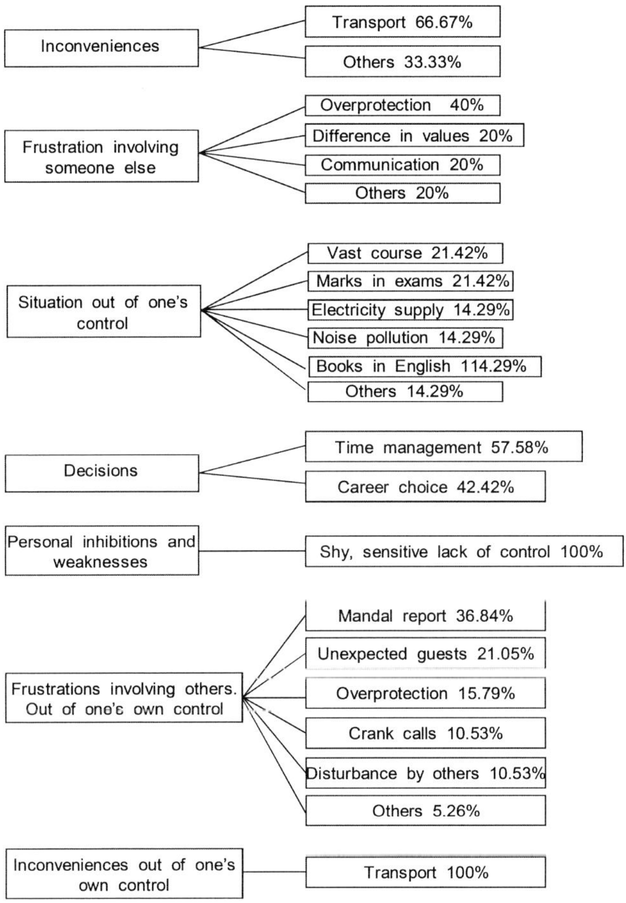

Figure 1 Schematic representation of the seven major problem areas and their sub-categories

Thus the picture that emerges is that though the subjects are able to perceive the problem situation quite clearly, for most of the difficulties, they are not very explicit about what they would consider as the ideal, tension free state, i.e., the goal state. The injunctions and scripting messages given from childhood to strictly adhere to the modelled behaviour of the significant persons become the guidelines for the youth, more so in India. He or she is on the threshold of adulthood, but is still treated as a child, and told that he is not old enough to deal with things on his own without the aid of his parents and others, adding to his inadequacy in dealing with his problems. This speaks for the incomplete perception of the problems. Thus, ambiguity in the situation acts as the main obstacle in evolving viable solution for the problems generated. Besides, another reason for the same would be the typical female stereotype to build up more on tolerance, dependence, obedience, etc. Few opportunities are given to the young girl to try dealing with problem situation autonomously, leaving her inadequate to deal with problems on her own, when the need arises.

Strategies Suggested as Potential Solutions to Personal Problems

Table 4 shows the success rate of the subjects at personal problems. Since they cannot be solved within a specified time limit, we can judge their perspective success or failure through the strategies evolved by the subjects to help them. There emerge four such categories of problems: 'A' - strategy related to the problem complete; 'B' - strategy related to the problem-incomplete; 'C' - strategy unrelated to the problem; 'D' - No strategy stated.

Table 4

Showing the success rate of personnel problems

S.No	*Problem*	*No.of Subjects reporting the problems*	*Success A*	*Failure B*	*C*	*D*
a.	Inconvenience	6	4			2
	Transport	4	–	4	–	–
	Others	2	–	–	–	2
	Frustration					
b.	Involving someone else	10	5	5		
	Overprotection	4	–	1	–	3
	Difference in values	2	–	1	–	1
	Communication	2	–	2	–	–
	Others.	2	–	1		–
c.	Situation out of one's own control	14		7		6

	Vast course	3	1	–	1	1
	Marks in exams	3	–	–	–	3
	Electricity supply	2	1	1	–	–
	Noise pollution	2	–	2	–	–
	Books in English	2	–	1	–	1
	Others	2	-	1	–	1
d.	Decisions	33	12		21	
	Time management	19	1	6	–	12
	Career	14	3	2	–	9
	Personal					
e.	Inhibitions and weaknesses	5	0	5		
	Shy, sensitive, lack of control	5	–	–	–	5
f.	Frustrations involving others out of one's own control	19	12			7
	Mandal	7	–	4	1	2
	Unexpected guests	4	–	3	–	1
	Overprotection	3	–	1	–	2
	Crank calls	2	–	2	–	–
	Disturbance by others	2	–	–	–	1
	Others	1	–	1	–	–
	Inconveniences out of one's own control	2		0		2
g.	Transport	2	-	-	-	2

A: Strategy related to the problem — complete,
B: Strategy related to the problem — incomplete
C: Strategy unrelated to the problem
D: No strategy stated

The figures indicate that there are few problems (7) for which the subjects have been able to evolve complete and relevant strategies, e.g., for the problem arising from excessive power cuts, one subject offers that "one would study with a lamp, or candles, don't study at all and sit idle, or if possible study during the day", thus, providing a fairly comprehensive solution.

Incomplete strategies make up the bulk of the relevant solutions offered for the problems (33), e.g., one of the subjects, worried about the Mandal Report, suggests organising rallies, writing articles in newspapers and recommends agitation to leave the Prime Minister to reconsider his decision, as will be noticed, these steps may not lead to the solution of the problems by themselves, but they are relevant to the problem even though they might not be considered complete solutions.

We find that the strategies unrelated to the problems are rare and only two such solutions are offered, e.g., regarding the mandal report, a subject holds, "V.P. Singh should resign", a suggestion that will not lead to a solution of the problem. By far the largest category is that of "No strategy stated" constituting nearly half of the total problems as mentioned before, lack of an unambiguous perception of the problem, as well as inexperience at handling problems independently, can account for the fact that the subjects find themselves at a loss when it comes to suggesting, "I don't know what to do exactly, but I am trying my best."

The Mandal Report has become an intensely emotional issue. This has influenced the adequacy of its solutions, in keeping with the contentions of Everall (1935) and Patricle (1934) that emotional reactions reduce flexibility and that of Lants (1945), that frustration reduces fluency. Similar reactions are also observed for other problems as overprotection and marks in examination, etc.

From Table 3 we see that of the seven broad categories of problems the greatest success was achieved at "Inconveniences" and four out six problems can be expected to be solved successfully. Nearly the same proportion (amount) of success is seen for "Frustration involving others - out of one's own control" (12 out of 19) paradoxical but again reflecting on adolescence as being the 'age of idealism'. Solution were in terms of "Guests should come after giving prior information so we can plan accordingly."

More than a third of the decisions problems show successful solutions as well as the greatest number of complete relevant strategies, as compared to the other categories. For both "Frustrations involving others" and "situations out of one's own control", successful solutions are suggested for 50 per cent of the problems. While the subjects seem fairly capable of solving most of the problems in these two categories', 'Overprotection' in the former and educational concerns in the latter seem more difficult to deal with. The remaining two categories' Personal Inhibitations and Weaknesses' and 'Inconveniences out of one's own control' contribute only five and two problems respectively to the total but they fail to show viable solutions and strategies for them.

Formal Intellectual and Personal Problems Compared

It is on this very dimensions of uncertainty and lack of structure that personal problems differ perceptibly from the formal intellectual problems. A formal intellectual problem is a complete and structured problem of the "to find" or "to prove" character, which contains specified details about the problem, the initial state, possible operators to solve the problem, the essential restrictions as well as the goals, e.g., String Problems (Maier, 1931). Chess Problems (Chase & Simon, 1975) Tower of Hanoi (Simon, 1975; Egan & Greeno, 1974; Newell & Simon, 1972); Maths Problems (Marshall, 1982), Anagrams (Davis, 1966) and Analogies (Stenberg, 1985) — all these problems tend to consist of well defined parameters and have objective means of determining the adequacy of the solution.

Personal problems are of the informal kind, involving real-life problem or decisions, with poorly specified characteristics, which do not have a clearly-stated initial state, goal state, operators or the restrictions. The question that arises is. Would the formal intellectual and personal problems differ in their success rates as guaged by the strategies evolved for solving them? The 45 subjects were taken for the two sets of problems. Formal Intellectual and Personal Problems, and then their performance on both was analysed to see whether any difference would exist in their problem-solving abilities as related to the differences in structuredness of the two different types of problems. It was found that the subjects performed better when the problem was structured, i.e., it had a clearly defined initial state, goal state, operators and restrictions, rather than when it was structured, and it was left to the individual to work out the initial state, goal state operators and restrictions.

Table 5 Showing the success rate of formal intellectual problems

S.No.	*Problem number*	*Success*	*Failure*
1.	Problem I	44	01
2.	Problem II	30	15
3.	Problem III	20	25
4.	Problem IV	24	21
5.	Problem VI	34	11

Table 5 shows the number of problems solved in the formal intellectual set (Bhalla & Bhatnagar, in press). In comparison the performance on the two sets brings out the fact (Figure 2) that about 67 per cent of the formal-intellectual problems, were solved by the 45 subject, only 45 per cent successful solutions were obtained for the personal problems.

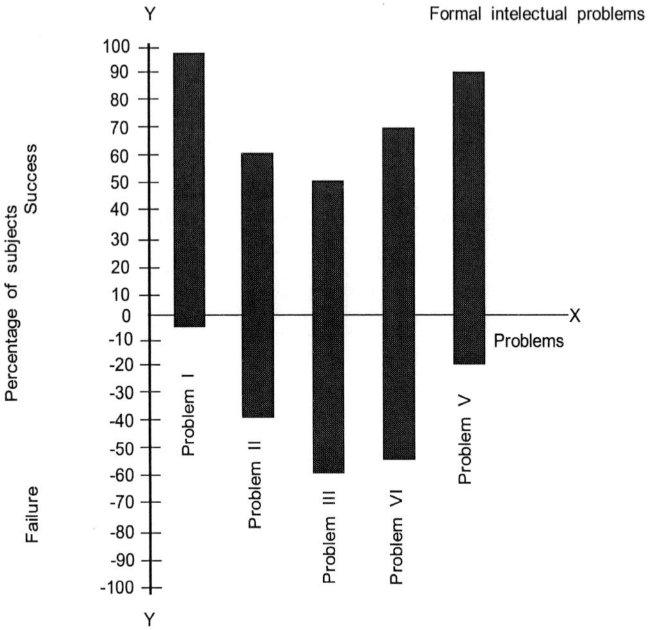
Formal intelectual problems
Y
Percentage of subjects
Success
Failure
100
90
80
70
60
50
40
30
20
10
0
-10
-20
-30
-40
-50
-60
-70
-80
-90
-100
X
Problems
Problem I
Problem II
Problem III
Problem VI
Problem V

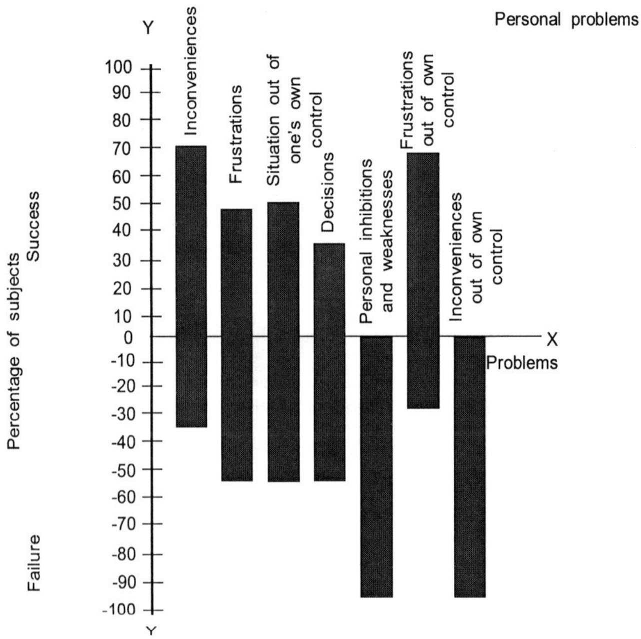
Personal problems
Y
Percentage of subjects
Success
Failure
100
90
80
70
60
50
40
30
20
10
0
-10
-20
-30
-40
-50
-60
-70
-80
-90
-100
X
Problems
Inconveniences
Frustrations
Situation out of one's own control
Decisions
Personal inhibitions and weaknesses
Frustrations out of own control
Inconveniences out of own control

Since the subjects could not perceive clearly what exactly the problem was, they could not devise successful solutions to them. Again, in the personal problems, we find that sometimes (as for problems with "Personal Inhabitation and Weaknesses" and "Inconvenience out of one's own control") the subjects were unable to give any solution at all, indicating a failure to arrive at even a single viable solution, but for the formal intellectual problems, this was never the case, and even on the third problem which shows the smallest number of correct solutions, at least 45 per cent of the subjects managed to solve it (Figure 2).

The solutions for formal intellectual problems point towards the building up of a scheme, an organised framework of knowledge about the underlying structure of the problems (Bhalla and Bhalanagar in Press). Thus, after they had gone over the first problem, the subject had some idea as to the specific strategy to use, the sub-goals to reach, etc., but in the case of the personal problems, this was not possible, due to the lack of structure and due to the vast differences among the personal problems themselves. Thus, the inability to perceive problem relatedness is expected to affect the problem-solving ability, as also held by Silver (1988).

It is seen that in the formal-intellectual problems the success rate falls due to an increase in the difficulty level (Problem l to 2) and the change from the theoretical to the applied aspect (from Problems 1 and 2 to Problems 3 and 4). But as familiarity with the problem increased, so did the number of subjects able to solve the problems correctly (from 20 to 24 for Problems 3 and 4 respectively).

For the personal problems also, we find that the difficulty level influences the solutions to the problems (Fallahi, 1983) amongst those for which some success was attained, difficulty level nevertheless determined the solution rate 'Inconveniences' are the simplest problems to solve and show the maximum success (66.67%) while 'Decisions' the most difficulty, show the least success (36.33%) and the problems involving 'Frustrations involving others' and 'Situations out of one's own control' fall in the middle ranges with 50 per cent of successful solutions being evolved for each category. The ability to see the basic structure of the problem and to represent it so that it clearly points out the initial state, goal state, operators and restrictions seems to be crucial in solving the problems effectively. The female adolescent in India faces restraints and restrictions and the stereotypical female role fosters a degree of dependency in her which hinders the development of independent problem-solving capacity later in life, while her male counterpart is encouraged to be independent and to develop his skills at autonomous thinking, reasoning and analysis. It should be interesting to study whether this gives rise to any significant differences in their problem-solving skills. It would also relevant to study whether these differences, if any, continue to persist even later in life, and the conditions to which they are subject.

References

Bhalla M, and Bhatnagar P., *State Space Analysis of Isomorphic, Homomorphic and Changed Problem Structure* (In Press).

Day, R.S., "Alternative Representations", *Psychology of Learning and Motivation* 1988, 22, 261-305.

Egan D.W. & Greeno, I.G., Theories of rule induction knowledge acquired in concept learning, serial pattern learning and problem solving, In Gregg, W.G. (Ed) *Knowledge and Cognition*, Hillsdale, N.J.: Lawrence Earlbaum Asso: Inc. 1974.

Grinder, R.E., *Adolescence*, New York: John Wiley & Sons Inc., 1973.

Hall, S.G., *Adolescence*, New York: Appleton Century Crofts, 1904.

Heppner and Krauskopf, "An Information Processing Approach to Personal Problem Solving, *Counselling Psychologist,* 1987, 15, 3 (July), 371-447.

Hurlock, E.B., *Adolescent Development,* New York: McGraw Hill 1973.

Kelley, H., *Problem Solving: A Cognitive approach*, Milton Keynes, Philadelphia: Open University Press 1986.

Kelley, H., Adolescence: A suppressed Minority Group, *Personnel Guide Journal 1969 47,* 634-642.

Leigh, A., *Decisions, Decisions: A Practical Guide to Problem Solving and Decision Making,* 1983.

Lugar, & Bauer, "Transfer effects in Isomorphic Problem situations, *Acta Psychologia"* 1978, 34, 121-131.

Miller, G.A., Galanter, E. & Pribraum, K.H., *Plans and the Structure of Behaviour,* New York: Holt, Rinehart & Winston 1960.

Newell, A. Simon, H.A., *Human Problem Solving,* Englewood Cliffs, N.J.: Prentice Hall 1972.

Pitt, R.B., Development of General Problem Solving Schema in Adolescence and Early adulthood, *Journal of Experimental Psychology* (General), 1983, 112, 4, 547-584.

Reed, S.K., Ernest, G.W. & Baney R., The role of analogy in transfer between similar problem states, *Cognitive Psychology*, 1974, 60, 436-50.

Silver E.A., Problem perception, problem schemata and problem solving, *Journal of Mathematical Behaviour*, 1982, 3, 2, 169-181.

Simon, H.A. and Hayes J.R., The Understanding Process of Problem Isomorphs, *Cognitive Psychology,* 1976, 8, 165-190.

Stenberg R.J., "*Beyond I.Q.,* Cambridge: Cambridge University Press, 1985.

Wessells, M.G., *Congitive Psychology*, N.Y.: Haper Row Pub. 1982.

CHAPTER 18

Adolescents' Perception of Indian Women's Position in Different Areas

Anjana Sharma, Ira Das, and S.P. Sinha

An attempt has been made to assess the adolescents' perception of Indian women's position in different areas. The sample consisted of 76 male and 76 female students. Their age ranged from 16 to 20 years. They were from both high and low socioeconomic groups. An attitude scale constructed on the pattern of Thurstone Scale Technique was administered to the students. The scoring was made according to the procedure. The scores were treated statistically and presented in tables. The results of this study show that the adolescent males perceived the women's position more negatively than the female students. The lower income group perceived the woman's position more negatively than the high income group in areas like legal, capability, social and economic.

Introduction

In the Vedic period women held a position equal to that of men. Girls and boys were required to undergo *upanayanam* ceremonies and according to Vedic hymns husbands as well as wives were joint owners of the property. They took share in sacrifices and religious duties. They were also considered as intellectual companions of their husbands. Hindu wives were honoured and respected in ancient times. But the position of women in India deteriorated from the fourth century, when Alexander the Great invaded India. Modern society has come to treat the rights and position of women only in relation to man's daughter, wife and mother.

India seems to be occupying a significant position in terms of quantity and diversity of material in women's studies. Parikh (1991) studied the influence of self-awareness and women's capabilities upon the attitude towards the status of women, and found that high self-awareness group of women were found to have a more favourable attitude towards the status of women than its counterparts. Similarly, the career of women did play a crucial role in the attitude towards the status of women.

In India, women's studies should be considered both as an instrument for women's development and as a necessary step to develop the knowledge base of various disciplines. The scenario of Indian women is different from Western countries. Various studies have been done to study the position, role, rights, etc., of women in Japan, Florida, Kuwait, Atlanta, Virginia and Western countries.

In the present study, an attempt has been made to study the perception of adolescents towards Indian women in different areas (social, legal, responsibility, capability and economic). The present research would help to indicate if there is any difference in the attitude of adolescents towards the position of women. If there exists a difference, efforts should be made to minimise them otherwise this would lead to maladjustment within a family structure. Efforts should be made to promote awareness among adolescents to develop and utilise women's full potential as resources for national development in its economic, political and sociocultural aspects. In the same way adolescents from different income groups (low & high) should be taught to form a more correct and realistic attitude which would ultimately form a healthy society.

Method

Sample: The sample consisted of 76 male and 76 female students aged 16-20 years. They were from low and high income groups. Stratified random sampling was used.

Tool: An attitude scale by Das & Pandey (1992) was constructed on the lines of Thurstone's scale, to measure an attitude towards the position of women. It was based on the principles of equal appearing interval scale. It consisted of 70 statements showing positive, negative or neutral attitude towards the women. Items were concerned with social conditions and economic rights of women. The reliability of the scale was found to be 0.74 by test-retest method.

Procedure: After selecting the sample and the tool the investigator administered the attitude scale among the subjects. The subjects were asked to answer with two response categories, i.e., ü or X. The subject marks a ü for a statement with which he or she agrees and a

X mark with which he/she does not agree. There was no limitation of time. Each subject was asked to give details regarding his age, educational qualifications, income of parents, locality to which he beloned, in the answer sheets.

Results and Discussion

The obtained data were statistically treated and presented in tables.

The results indicate that there are significant differences among the four different (i.e., social, capability, legal, economic) areas in their mean scores. The 't' value of four different areas are 2.2, 5, 5.31, 9.1 respectively. In the economic area boys perceive women as burdens on their family. Boys underestimate the capabilities of women. Boys think that women should not have equal legal rights. In the social area, boys have a more negative attitude towards women in the society (Table 1).

Table 1
Mean attitude score and 't' value of boys and girls in different areas

	Boys			*Girls*			*'t' value*
	N	*Mean*	*S.D.*	*N*	*Mean*	*S.D.*	
Social	76	4.67	0.64	76	4.89	0.62	2.20*
Capability	76	5.47	0.54	76	5.92	0.60	5.00 **
Legal	76	5.60	1.14	76	6.45	0.91	5.31**
Responsibility	76	9.54	0.10	76	9.50	0.41	0.80
Economic	76	3.09	0.46	76	4.-00	0.79	9.10**

*p<0.05; **p<0.01

Table 2
Mean attitude score and 't' value of economic status in different areas

	Low economic group			*High economic group*			*'t'value*
	N	*Mean*	*S.D.*	*N*	*Mean*	*S.D.*	
Social	76	4.58	0.47	76	4.99	0.69	4.56**
Capability	76	5.59	0.56	76	5.79	0.67	2.00**
Legal	76	5.93	1.02	76	6.31	1.09	2.23*
Responsibility	76	9.54	0.25	76	9.49	0.41	1.00
Economic	76	3.32	0.48	76	3.62	0.68	3.00**

*p<0.05;**p<0.01

The results in Table 2 show that there exist significant differences in the four different areas (i.e., social, capability, economic and legal) in the mean scores of the low and high income groups. It depicts that the high income group members do not make much discrimination between boys and girls. The low income group underestimates the position of the women in the society. The high income group thinks that women have legal rights, whereas the low income group thinks that women do not have equal legal rights. The low income group underestimates the capabilities of Indian women. No significant difference exists in the responsibility area.

According to the results the adolescents perceive the position of women to be lower in society. From their viewpoints women do not get equal status and respect in the society. They are not given equal rights as are given to menfolk. They are not even considered eligible to do certain duties. They are not provided by their family members equal opportunities for receiving education and doing jobs. The cause of such type of difference may be the mode of their upbringing, the child-rearing practices and parental attitudes towards the position of women. The findings are consistent with the findings of Linda (1979); Garnett (1085).

In the present study the subjects were classified under two income groups, viz., low income group and high income group. The subjects whose parents' income was less than Rs. 4,500 p.m. came under the low income group, while the subjects whose parents' income was more than Rs. 8,000 p.m. came under the high income group. In India, the low income group thought, girls were considered as a burden on menfolk, ever since their birth until death. The main cause behind this is their economic dependency and lack of education. As a result of this women are unable to take decisions on crucial matters and are unable to implement them. Therefore they are dominated by the male members of their family. On the other hand, economic prosperity leads to the removal of a number of stresses. Affluent persons spend money in the form of dowry, etc., to gain social prestige. For them the female child in the family is not a big problem. Therefore, female members in such families receive love, affection, recognition and respect. The study by Kumar (1988), Das et.al. (1994) lends support to these results.

Thus, it can be concluded that the adolescent males and lower income group adolescents perceive the position of women negatively in different areas (legal, capability, social and economic), according to this study.

References

Das, I., & Pandey A., "Construction and standardisation of an attitude scale towards status of women in India", Paper presented at the national seminar organised by the Institute of Psychological Research, at the Indian Institute of Science, Bangalore, May 7 & 8, 1992.

Garnett, P.E., Comparative study of male and female school board members attitudes towards women, *Dissertation Abstract International,* 1985, 46(12), 4687-A.

Kumar,. S.K., Attitude towards the dowry system and social status of women, *Psychological Abstract,* 1998, 75 (4), 10702.

Linda, W., Attitude towards the rights and roles of women in society, *Dissertation Abstract International,* 1979 40(4), 2789-A.

Mandal, E.S., Weiss, I.N., Hein, A., Attitude towards the position of women, *Hindustan Times,* Aug. 20., 1994.

Parikh, J.C., Women status in context of self-awareness of career, Paper presented at the 28th annual conference of the India Academy of Applied Psychology at the Centre of Advanced Study in Psychology, Utkal University, Bhubhaneshwar, July 10-12, 1991.

Thurstone, L.L., & Chave, C.J., *The measurement of attitude*, Chicago, 1927.

CHAPTER 19

Perception of Feminine Worth and Its Relation to Fear of Success in Adolescents with Army and Civilian Backgrounds

Vidhu Mohan and *Monica Bali*

The present study was conducted to ascertain whether fear of success, which is an aspect of self-esteem, has any relation to the perception of Feminine Worth in adolescents of army and civilian backgrounds. The sample consisted of 155 adolescents, which included 41 civilian boys, 40 army boys, 34 civilian girls, and 40 army girls in the age range of 12 to 16 years, from the state of Haryana. The tools used were the Fear of Success Scale by Zuckerman and Allison and the Feminine Worth Scale by Mohan et al. A 2 x 2 ANOVA was used to test the difference, if any, amongst the scores of Fear of Success Scale (FOSS) and Feminine Worth Scale (FWS) and the 13 variables. The correlation coefficients were computed between the scores of Fear of Success Scale and Feminine Worth Scale for males and females and for the total sample. The results show that there was sex difference and the females perceived the overall feminine worth and in other 12 variables, such as, birth of a girl-child, education, social status, marriage, dowry, marital adjustment, marital ethics, wife battering, widow remarriage, divorce, work, finance, and flesh trade, significantly better than the males, and the army and civilian backgrounds caused no difference. The correlation coefficients between FWS and FOSS were insignificant for the total sample. However, a different trend was perceived for males and females. There were significant negative correlations for females, between the scores of FOSS and some variables of Feminine Worth Scale, namely, dowry, work and finance while a significant positive correlation was found between FOSS and variables of flesh trade and a significant negative correlation for males between FOSS and variables of education, and a positive correlation between FOSS and issues relating to finance.

Introduction

Women are the important resources of human potentials. Their emancipation and growth are essential for the development of the country. In the post-independent India, women have easy access to higher education, better employment opportunities and better human rights. Though our country had a woman Prime Minister at the helm of affairs for over a decade, it is by no means reflective of the position of women in this country. Only a small percentage of women occupy important decisionmaking positions in the government, administration, industry and in public life. A woman is worshipped as "Shakti", the epitome of strength and inner resilience but is rarely given opportunities to realise her potential. Rather, the traditional attitudes still assign the sexes to stereotypical roles. "Feudal" attitudes are still prevalent and are reinforced on women. Females are viewed as home-makers-affiliative and less competent while males are seen as competent, achieving and the master of the house.

Thus while external barriers like discriminative governmental policies have disappeared, women still face tremendous socially imposed conflicts (Mukherjee, 1985) and internal psychological barriers that prevent them from adopting independent achieving orientations. They still face many role-related conflicts in the home as well as the place of work (Mohan &c Kapur, 1985). It may even make their self-esteem lower and the sense of self-worth poorer.

Horner (1968) proposed the concept of Fear of Success (FOS) or Motive to Avoid Success (MAS) as a psychological barrier to achievement because of the negative consequences of social rejection and/or loss of femininity that results from success. Though this construct was postulated as more characteristic of women, rather than men, subsequent research showed that MAS is not sex-linked but occurs in both men and women (Zuckerman & Wheeler, 1975). However, it is to be recognised that to be successful in a male-dominated society, women may be perceived as less attractive. In a country where marriage is seen as the only logical step for females, this may be threatening and also creates undesirable situation.

Behaviour and attitudes are reciprocal and prior attitudes affect subsequent behaviour as experience shapes later attitudes. Stafford (1984) found that attitudes towards women's roles are significantly correlated with the amount of labour force attachment, and the woman's roles are factor distinguishing, homemakers, job holders and careerists. Kumar (1986) found that a women's readiness to work is inextricably tied to the extent of their work being congruent with their gender identity. Thus, the way women are viewed may their own sex and the opposite sex would determine their roles in their society. Some issues are deeply linked with a woman's identity and determine her role in society. These issues related to feminine worth are: acceptance of the female child at birth, her right to education, her social status, marriage, the issue of dowry, marital adjustment, divorce, marital ethics, wife battering, widow remarriage, women and their right to work, financial independence of women and flesh trade (Mohan et al., 1994).

Birth: In India a female child is considered inauspicious and a financial burden on her parents. Foeticide, infanticide, neglect, physical violence and lack of medical care-all result in higher mortality rates for girls than boys. However there are indications of welcome attitudinal changes regarding the birth of female children (Chaudhary 1988, Mohan et al., 1994) as perceived by women.

Education: Even today the strongest social support for female education comes only from its increasing demand in the marriage market (Joshi, 1973). Education is the most viable instrument to help achieve equality for women and has to become relevant to the future role expectation of Indian women.

Social status: The social status of Indian women has deteriorated down the centuries. Government policies and programmes attempt to provide social dignity to women but attitudinal changes are required. Mohan et al. (1991) report desirable changes with younger women holding more favourable views than older women on the social status of women.

Marriage: Modern education has had a significant effect on marriage values in the country with preference for increased age at marriage, a desire to gain higher education and economic independence before marriage and preference for greater participation in the decision-making process (Punia & Punia, 1985, Ahuja, 1994) but issues related to marriage and the role of the girl in the decision-making process still receives less significance as compared to other issues (Mohan et al. 1991, 1994).

Dowry: The commercialisation of the economy has fuelled the dowry system and women are still treated as a commodity at the time of marriage. Younger women do express more emancipated opinions on dowry issues than their older counterparts. (Mohan et al., 1991). Even the younger generation of males view dowry as one of the most important issues relating to a women's worth (Mohan et al., 1990).

Martial adjustment: In Indian society males continue to display greater dominance while women show more and more succour and abasement within the marital relationship (Mohan & Nalwa, 1993). Mohan et al. (1994) reported significant sex differences in the area of marital adjustment with females in favour of more equality within the marital relationship.

Marital ethics: With the breakdown of moral value systems, there is greater acceptance of immorality within the marital relationship. Mohan et al. (1991 & 1994) report that marital ethics consistently ranks as one of the least preferred variables on feminine worth.

Wife battering: Physical abuse of a woman within the family is increasing around the world. It destroys a woman's dignity and self-esteem. Research indicates (Mohan, 1989) that support for the cause of battered women is increasing.

Widow remarriage: In India, where a husband is an integral part of a woman's self-concept, widowhood can be devastating particularly because of the inauspiciousness associated with it. However, today increasing numbers support the cause of widow remarriage (Chaudhary, 1988, Mohan et al., 1991).

Divorce: Women in India still do not regard divorce as an easy way out of a bad marriage, and though the right of a woman to seek divorce is supported (Chaudhary, 1988), the issue remains one of the least preferred variables on feminine worth (Mohan et al., 1994).

Women and work: While women are trying to utilise employment as a means of raising their status, they still experience considerable socially imposed role conflicts (Mohan &. Kapur, 1985). Mohan et al. (1994) report significant sex differences on this variable with females more favourably inclined towards this issue.

Finance: Most of the working Indian women do not have access to their own earnings. Mohan et al. (1991) reported that though women in the older age group accept the financial dominance of men, younger women are emerging with very favourable views toward economic independence.

Flesh trade: The practice of prostitution and the "objectification" of women under the garb of, modernisation flourishes. This issue continues to receive least support among the variables on Feminine Worth (Mohan et al., 1994).

The present work is an attempt to see whether fear of success (FOS), which is a salient aspect of self-esteem, has any relation with the perception of feminine worth. For this purpose all the aforesaid areas of feminine worth are being studied in relation to Fear of Success in adolescents from army and civilian background. One's socialisation is often affected by one's psychosocial surroundings. These can also play a major role in determining one's attitudes towards various issues.

Method

Design: The present study was undertaken to, ascertain whether the perception of Feminine Worth has any relation to fear of success. A 2 x 2 factorial design was employed having males and females from army and civilian background. Besides, the correlation was also computed between Fear of Success and the 13 issues of Feminine Worth Scale.

Samples: The sample for the present study consisted of 155 adolescents in the age range of 12 to 16 years studying in Army School, Ambala Cantonment in the state of Haryana. They came from both army and civilian background. The break-up was as follows — 81 boys out of which 41 were from civilian background and 40 were from army background and 74 girls out of which 34 were from civilian background and 40 were from army background.

Tests: Two scales were used in this study to collect data.

1. *Fear of Success Scale (FOSS):* This was developed by Zuckermann and Allison (1976), consisting of 27 items on a five-point scale ranging from Strongly Agree to Strongly Disagree. The range of scores is from 27 to 189 with higher scores indicating greater fear of success.
2. *The Feminine Worth Scale (FWS):* This scale was designed by Mohan et al. (1991) measuring 13 issues relating to feminine esteem. The issues taken up in the scale are: (a) birth of a girl child, (b) her education, (c) her social status, (d) her

participation in marriage process, (e) dowry issues, (f) marital adjustment, (g) marital ethics, (h) wife battering, (i) divorce, (j) widow remarriage, (k) women and work, (l) financial independence and (m) flesh trade. The range of scores is from 52 to 260 with four items for each of the 13 issues. Responses are made on a five-point scale ranging from Strongly Agree to Strongly Disagree. The higher the scores, the greater is the perceived worth.

Procedure: The data was collected from adolescents studying in Army School, Ambala Cantonment. The subjects were personally contacted and the two scales were administered to then in groups of 20 to 25 subjects. The method of responding to each of the scales was demonstrated using the first items as an example. The scoring for each of the scales was done according to the procedure given in the scoring keys of the scales. The raw scores of the males and females from army and civilian background, on the Fear of Success Scale and the Feminine Worth Scale were computerised for the suitable statistical analysis. A 2 x 2 ANOVA was employed to test the significance of difference between means for the two sexes from army and civilian background on Fear of Success Scale and Feminine Worth Scale with its 13 issues. The correlation was also computed between the scores of Fear of Success Scale and the scores of 13 issues of Feminine Worth Scale for total sample and separately for male and female groups.

Results

The raw scores on FOSS and FWS were analysed to find out means and dispersions for Fear of Success and the 13 issues of Feminine Worth for two sexes of the army and civilian backgrounds. These values are presented in Table 1. In order to test the significance of difference amongst the various means a 2 x 2 ANOVA was done for FOSS and FWS. The F values and significance are reported in Table 2. The final phase of treatment was to find out the correlation coefficients between FOSS and the 13 issues of FWS. Since there were highly significant sex difference on the FWS, the correlations were separately computed for males and females and are presented in Table 3.

Table 1: Means and SDs of scores on feminine worth scale (FWS) aad fear of success (FOS)

Variables	*Males (81)*		*Female (74)*		*Army (80)*		*Civilian (75)*		*(Total 155)*	
	Means	*SD*	*Means*	*SD*	*Means*	*SD*	*Means*	*SD*	*Means*	*SD*
Fear of Success	102.99	12.59	106.53	12.43	104.14	12.95	105.25	12.27	104.68	12 56
FWS (Total)	171.74	13.43	193.35	13.46	182.65	17.47	181.43	17.06	182.06	17 17
1. Birth	15.83	2.35	17.91	2.11	1701	2.49	16.61	2.43	16.82	2.46
2. Education	13.57	2.09	15.92	1.85	14.84	2.39	14.53	2.20	14.69	2 29
3. Social	13.16	2.45	15.66	2.26	14.58	2.55	14.12	2.78	14.35	2.66
4. Marriage	10.07	2.22	12.69	2.66	11.06	2.73	11.60	2.79	11.32	2.75
5. Dowry	14.37	2.88	15.05	1.99	14.86	2.39	14.52	2.64	14.70	2.50
6. Marital adjustment	14.04	2.61	15.28	2.44	14.80	2.55	14.47	2 65	14.64	2.59
7. Marital ethics	11.77	2,79	13.50	2.79	12.75	3.03	12.52	2.71	12.64	2 86
8. Wife battering	14.23	2.59	16.30	2.54	15.23	3.02	15.21	3.47	15.22	2.75
9. Widow remarriage	14.33	1.89	15.16	1.31	14.65	1.71	14.81	1.67	14.73	1.68
10. Divorce	11.00	2.38	12.00	2.43	11.30	2.31	11.67	2.59	11.48	2.44
11. Work	14.09	2.08	15.65	1.79	14.58	2.25	15.11	1.89	14.83	2.08
12. Finance	15.06	2.28	16.91	2.38	16.41	2.64	15.44	2.24	1 5.94	2.49
13. Flesh trade	10.21	3.10	11.23	2.97	10.59	3.01	10.81	3.15	10.70	3.06

Table 2: ANOVA for sex and army/civilian for FWS and FOSS

Source of Variance		*FOSS*		*FWS*		*Birth*		*Education*		*Social*		*Marriage*		*Dowry*		*Marital Adjustment*	
	df	*MSS*	*F*	*MSS*	*F*	*MSS*	*F*	*MSS*	*F*	*MSS*	*F*	*MSS*	*F*	*MSS*	*F*	*MSS*	*F*
					**		**		**		**		**				**
Sex	1	12.98	3.16	465.47	99.97	4.27	32.49	5.49	53.40	6.14	42.27	7.02	45.65	.47	2.87	1.52	9.12
Background	1	1.66	.40	.42	.09	.09	.69	.04	.37	.12	.84	.44	2.87	.09	.53	.07	.41
Sex X Background	1	.01	.002	.28	.06	.002	.01	.01	.004	.05	.34	.005	.04	.13	.79	.11	.67
Error	151	4.11		4.66		.13		.10		.15		.15		.16		.17	

Source of variance	*df*	*Marital Ethics*		*Wife battering*		*Widow remarriage*		*Divorce*		*Work*		*Finance*		*Flesh Trade*	
		MSS	*F*	*MSS*	*F*	*MASS*	*F*	*MASS*	*F*	*MASS*	*F*	*MASS*	*F*	*MASS*	*F*
			**		**		**		**		**		**		*
Sex	1	3.31	17.08	5.22	24.52	.68	9.64	1.06	7.02	2.49	25.85	3.18	23.47	1.11	4.63**
Background	1	.01	.09	.004	.03	.03	.52	.18	1.20	.35	3.59	.83	6.18	.09	.38
Sex X 1 Background	.01	.08	.12	.70	.02	.004	.05	.34	.14	1.45	.24	1.78	.34	1.40	
Error	151	.20		.17		.07		.15		.09		.14			.24

** Significant at. 01 level.

* Significant at. 05 level.

Discussion

This study was undertaken to see whether the perception of Feminine Worth has any relation to Fear of Success. The discussion of the obtained results are in two parts: the first part pertain to observations of Feminine Worth and Fear of Success and the second part deal with its relation to Fear of Success.

Sex differences in perception of feminine worth: The results of this study show overwhelming sex differences on Feminine Worth. Females by and large showed significantly favourable perception on overall Feminine North Scale as well as on 12 variables, as compared to males. These variables are birth of a girl-child, her education, her social status, marriage decision, marital adjustment, marital ethics, wife battering, widow remarriage, divorce, women and work, finance and flesh trade. Dowry was the only issue on which no sex differences were observed.

Females showed more favourable attitudes towards birth of a female child than the males. Similar results were obtained by Chaudhary (1988) in her study among the young women who strongly supported the birth of female children. Females also voiced significantly favourable attitudes toward education of the female children. Nowadays females view education as a means of economic independence (Chaudhary, 1988) and males perceive it as a threat of greater competition.

Females also have more favourable attitudes towards the social status of a woman than males. Though the conventional male-female social roles are changing (*Hindustan Times,* 1994) girls seem more supportive of improved status for women while males seem to be resisting this trend. Females also have significantly more emancipated attitudes than males towards the issues relating to flesh trade and female sexual exploitation. Bhogle, (1991) felt that social forces still promote sex stereotypes and male superiority and stressed the need to curb such discrimination against women. Females also show a better perception than males, of the issues relating to female work participation and financial independence for women. Mohan et al. (1991) too reported that the younger women in their study were emerging with more favourable attitudes towards economic independence. Females also had more favourable attitudes than males on issues relating to marriage, the role of the girl during marital negotiations, dowry issues, the onus of adjustment in marriage, marital ethics, wife battering, divorce and widow remarriage. Mohan & Nalwa (1993) found that even today in Indian society, males display greater dominance while females show more succour and abasement within the marital relationship. However, in the present sample, females seem to favour marriage on a more equitable basis.

Table 3

Correlation coefficient between fear of success and the 13 issues of feminine worth scale for males and females

Feminine worth scale and its variables	*Fear of success* *Males*	*Females*
Feminine Worth Scale (FWS)	.03	.012
1. Birth	.05	–.02
2. Education	–.17 *	–.004
3. Social	–.06	.14
4. Marriage	.03	.01
5. Dowry	.01	–.17 *
6. Marital adjustment	–.03	–.07
7. Marital ethics	–.08	–.05
8. Wife battering	.13	–.08
9. Widow remarriage	–.16	.09
10. Divorce	.02	–.01
11. Work	.12	–.19*
12. Finance	.20**	–.24**
13. Flesh trade	.03	.18*

** Significant at. 05 level

* Significant at. 10 level

In area of marital ethics, females favour the marital vow of fidelity more than the males. Mohan et al. (1991) reported that the younger women in their study were more favourably inclined than younger males toward the issue of marital ethics. There were marked sex differences in the area of wife battering, with females condemning wife battering more than males. Saheli (1986) stated that wife bettering is curbed by parents (Bhogle, 1991). Wang & Creedon (1989) reported that even in a structured society like China, despite equalitarian government policies, Chinese women, traditionally assigned to secondary roles, show higher Fear of Success than Chinese men.

Fear of Success and Feminine Worth

The coefficient of correlations between the scores of Fear of Success Scale and Feminine Worth Scale as well as each of the 13 variables were found to be insignificant for the total sample. But significant sex differences were found on all the 13 variables of Feminine Worth, and separate correlations were worked out for male and female groups for Feminine Worth and Fear of Success. These correlations show a different trend for males and females.

Among the female group significant negative correlations were found between Fear of Success and some of the issues relating to Feminine Worth, namely, dowry, work and finance. These are the core issues relating to a woman's struggle for dignity and self-respect as she attempts to carve a place for herself in society today. Social biases seem to reinforce attitudes that subvert a female's desire for independence and greater self-esteem. The relation between Fear of Success and each of these variables is discussed below.

There was significant negative correlations between Fear of Success and issues relating to dowry. According to Horner (1972), achievement-related anxieties arise when the traditionally prescribed social role is valued. The system of dowry is inextricable linked with the secondary status of women in a traditional society. Gautam and Trivedi (1987) have profiled the typical dowry victim as younger, less educated and dependent. Thus when the traditional role is valued regressive attitudes will remain in place.

Fear of Success among females will also lead to a poor perception of the worth of a woman in terms of issues relating to her working status and financial autonomy. When achievement is incompatible with the traditional feminine role there will not be much favour for participation by women in the economic sector and subsequently no financial autonomy for them. Stafford (1984) found that attitudes towards women's role were significantly correlated with the amount of labour force attachment, distinguishing home makers, job holders and careerists prevailing not only because of the social dependence of women, but also due to the cultural approval of violence for husbands on women. Females show more support than males for the idea of women to be endowed with the right to divorce. Chaudhary (1988) reported that most of the young female respondents felt that when there was a lack of faith between husband and wife they must seek divorce. Females showed more support than males for the idea of widow remarriage. Mohan et al. (1991) reported that the younger women in their study were more inclined towards widow remarriage than men. The only variable in which no sex differences were seen is the area of dowry. This may be because, despite legal sanctions, public attitudes towards this practice are still ambivalent. However,

Monan et al. (1991) report that younger women do express more emancipated opinions on dowry issues than older women.

In each of these areas mentioned above, favourable female attitudes reflect the young Indian women's desire to grow as an individual, to have freedom of choice and dignity. The male attitudes, on the other hand, do limit the choice of alternatives available to women today. Issues like birth of a girl-child, financial independence for females and anti-wife battering attitudes received high ranking from both males and females, whereas issues like marital ethics, and fidelity, divorced woman and her plight and flesh trade of women received low ranking front both the sexes.

Fear of Success: With regard to the fear of success the females showed higher fear of success than the males, but the difference is not significant. In the studies made by Dalsimer (1973) and Alper (1974) it was observed that fear of success was more prevalent among girls than boys where achievement was regarded culturally inappropriate to female. Most of the Western studies report little or no sex differences in Fear of Success (Singh, 1978; Pappo, 1983). This is because of the women's liberation movement that most of the Western women have come to regard achievement as females' appropriate behaviour (Pedersen & Conlin, 1987). But in the Indian scenario, despite social and political changes and an overall improvement in the position of women, the existing cultural practices reinforce the dependency status of women. Boys get more training for independence, social mobilisation and motivation than girls (Rai, 1991) and the originality and intellectual spark in daughters are systematically curbed by parents (Bhogle, 1991).

There was a significant positive correlation between Fear of Success and issues relating to Flesh Trade. Lower fear of success among females will lead to a poor perception of the worth of a woman on the issue of sexual exploitation of women. In the earlier works Mohan et al. (1991, 1994) found that females, who otherwise had high self-worth, ranked low on issues relating to Flesh Trade. Since times immemorial the sexual exploitation of women has been accepted. This acceptance is still reflected in present-day attitudes in the lower ratings given to issues relating to flesh trade.

Males in the present study have an overall lower perception of Feminine Worth as compared to females. We also see that males experiencing Fear of Success underplay the worth of a woman though the correlations obtained were only marginally relevant

However, this shows that enhanced status for women, especially in terms of education and economic independence, is seen as an ego threat in terms of greater competition. To meet this competition and to maintain the superior position assigned by the society, unfavourable attitudes towards female worth probably develop as a defence mechanism.

A significant negative correlation was obtained among the males, between Fear of Success and issues relating to educating the girl-child. In India today education for women is being increasingly emphasized as a necessity but males with fear of success show low acceptability for female education and probably want to sustain traditional roles for women.

A significant positive correlation was obtained among males between Fear of Success and issues relating to financial autonomy for women. Thus males with low Fear of Success will have a poor perception of the idea of financial autonomy for women and will not want the females to acquire financial independence. These chauvinistic attitudes ensure that the social order, where men are controllers of resources and the decision makers, will continue to prevail.

Thus we see that females are by and large developing a more positive attitudes towards issues that are intrinsically linked with their self-worth, identity and position in society. However, the male's attitude towards the status and worth of a woman in our society has not kept pace. Despite the judicial and constitutional guarantees and social rhetoric, our cultural environment seems to perpetrate traditional, servile and secondary roles for women. Girls are still socialised to accept male superiority and are caught in a vicious circle where the existing social bias reinforces the values which go against the interests of their gender group. The psychological barriers to achievement arise out of the valuation of the traditionally prescribed feminine roles and the fear of social disapproval which inhibit the performance of women in competitive situations. Thus females achieve less and even when they do achieve it, it is with one hand tied behind their back by social pressures to conform to set patterns.

Gender sensitisation, which stimulates the consciousness of the society towards the role, worth and dignity of a woman, is the only hope in the present scenario. The development of necessary skills and training in women alone can put up them to combat the dependency status. We can no longer be mute spectators to the subtle cultural throttling of feminine expectations and strivings. Any effort to remedy this situation has to involve mobilisation at all levels—the media, governmental and non-governmental agencies, the community and, most importantly, the family. The process of awakening consciousness among women must be the small beginning for the growth of a strong widespread awareness among the women's rights, liberty, equity, dignity and equality.

References

Alper, T.G., Achievement motivation in college women: a now-you-see-it-now-you-don't phenomenon, *American Psychologist,* 1974, 29, 194-203.

Ahuja, Ram, In marriage changes through the years, *Hindustan Times,* 1994, April 29, Vol. LXX, 17, New Delhi.

Bhogle, S., Evolving strategies for removing eliminating / minimising the unacceptability and discrimination against a girl child, Paper presented at UGC sponsored National Seminar on Psychological Aspects in the social acceptability of Girl Child, Kurukshetra, 15-17 March 1991.

Chaudhary, P.K., *Changing values among young women,* 1988, Amar Prakashan, New Delhi.

Dalsimer, Katherine, D.K., The Development, in Adolescent Girls, of Fear of Academic Success, *Dissertation Abstract International,* 1974, 34 (12B), 6207.

Gautam, D.N., and Trivedi, B.U., Unnatural Deaths of married women with Special reference to dowry deaths: A sample study of Delhi Police, *Research & Development,* Jan-Mar, 1987.

Hindustan Times, Friday April 29, 1994. Vol. LXX, No 17, New Delhi.

Horner, M.S., Sex differences in achievement motivation and performance in competitive and non-competitive situations, Unpublished Doctoral Dissertation, University of Michigan, 1968.

Horner, M.S., Toward an Understanding of Achievement-Related Conflicts in Women, *Journal of Social Issues,* 1972, 28 (2) 157-175.

Joshi, R.J., Contemporary change in the socioeconomic role of women in India: Its impact on family life, in Kamla Bhasin (Ed.), *The Position of Women in India,* Leslie Swahney Programme of Training for Democracy, Bombay, 1973.

Kumar, Usha, Indian Women and Work: A Paradigm for Research, *Psychological Studies,* 1986, 31 (2), 147-159.

Mohan, V., Is there hope for Battered Women? In Sushma Sood (Ed.), *Violence against women,* Arihant Publisher, Jaipur, 1990.

Mohan, V. & Kapur, B., *Role Conflict in Indian Working Women,* P.E.N., Nov-Dec, 1985, 5-8.

Mohan, V., Bali, M, Mohan, K., Perceiving Feminine Worth through Male and Female Viewpoint, Paper presented at UGC sponsored National Seminar on Psychological Aspects in the Social Acceptability of Girl Child, Kurukshetra, 15-17 March, 1991.

Mohan, V. & Nalwa, K., Needs and Marital Adjustment of Army and Civilian Couples, *Journal of Community Guidance & Research,* 1993, 10 (1), 11-25.

.... Bali, M. Mohan, K., The Perception of Feminine Worth by today's adolescents at the brink of the 21st century. Paper presented at National Seminar on Problems and Challenges before women in 21st century, Kurukshetra, Feb. 21-23, 1994.

Mukherjee, Nilanjana, The Working Mother, Femina, 1985.

Pappo, M., Fear of Success: The Construction and Validation of a Measuring Instrument, *Journal of Personality Assessment*, 1983, 47 (1.), 36-41.

Pedersen, D.M. & Conlin, T., Shifts in Fear of Success, in men and women from 1968 to 1987, *Psychological Reports*, 1987, 61 (1), 36 -38.

Punia & Punia, *Education and Changing Marriage Values*, P.E.N., Nov-Dec 1985, 12-13.

Saheli (1986) in Socio-Cultural Dynamics of Wife Battering by Dr. R.S. Bhatti in Sushma Sood (Ed.), *Violence Against Women*, Arihant Publishers, Jaipur, 1990.

Singh, Satvir, Motive to Avoid Success, *Asian Journal of Psychology and Education,* 1978, 3 (1), 39-45.

Stafford, I.P., Relation to Attitudes Towards Women's Roles and Occupational Behaviour to Women's Self-Esteem, *Journal of Counselling Psychology*, 1984, 31 (3), 332-338.

Rai, G.C., A study of the acceptability of girl child in terms of child rearing practices, Paper presented at UGC sponsored National Seminar on Psychological Aspects in the social acceptability of Girl child, Kurukshetra. 15-17 March, 1991.

Wang, T.H. and Creedon, C.F., Sex Role Orientations, Attributions for Achievement and Personal Goals of Chinese Youth, *Sex Roles,* 1989, 20 (9-10), 473-486.

Zuckerman, M.C. & Allison, S.N., An Objective Measure of Fear of Success — Construction and Validation, *Journal of Personality Assessment,* 1976 40, 422-430.

.........& Wheeler, L., To dispel fatasies about the fantasy-based measure of fear of success, *Psychological Bulletin,* 1975, 82, 932-946.

PART IV
PERSONALITY PROBLEMS OF ADOLESCENT PERIOD

The adolescent period is the crucial stage in the personality development of an individual. There are several factors involved in the development of personality of the adolescents. Personality generally means the qualities that form a person's character, the qualities that make someone popular and different from other persons. Psychologically personality is the unique organisation of fairly permanent characteristics that sets the individual apart from other individuals. Personality is not a single characteristic or trait. It is a unique organisation of several traits; each one is revealed in a particular situation. In the process of personality development, heredity and environment play equal importance, though the behaviourists attribute it only to the environment. The family is the primary social institution which shapes the individual right from the childhood period. The parents' love and affection, care and attention showered on the children and the interaction that takes place between the parents and the children, all influence the children to acquire some of the characteristics the parents exercise. Children go out and meet many persons of different type of characteristics. They slowly learn to adjust themselves with others. In schools, in playgrounds and are other recreational centres they meet many different peer groups. By moving with such boys and girls some new experiences are gained. By these means the adolescents develop various traits like, sociable versus independent, affectionate vs cold, friendly vs hostile, dominant vs submissive and so on.

CHAPTER 20

Root Personality Dimensions to Intelligence and Quality of Social Interaction among Adolescent Students

Sreekumar, E. and George Mathew V.

The objective of the study was to explore the extent of association that the personality dimensions have with intelligence and quality of social interaction in the case of adolescent students. A sample of 151 higher secondary students (including both boys and girls) were taken for the study I.A.S. Rating Scale, Mathew Test of Mental Abilities (verbal) and Facilitativeness Rating Scale were used for data collection. The data were statistically treated using the correlation coefficient method and t-test. The results show that Inertia has a significant negative correlation with Intelligence. Activation has a positive correlation with Intelligence only in the case of girls. Stability correlates positively with intelligence only in the case of boys. Stability has a positive correlation with Quality of social interaction only in the case of girls. Boys and girls differ significantly in Inertia and Activation. The results show that boys have more activation while girls have more inertia.

Introduction

The importance of personality increases as social life becomes more complex. A pleasing personality has a marketable value in a complex society and is highly prized and sought after. Individual differences in intelligence were observed and discussed at least 2,000 years before anyone attempted to measure this trait. In recent years, intelligence has become one of the most emotive topics in psychology. Intellectual skills have proven to be of great value in terms of survival. The quality of social interaction, another variable in this study, helps people to master the world, and it also helps people to find connectedness. The effort to find out the relationship of traits to major personality dimensions seemed to have greater value in a holistic approach to personality. The present investigation mainly attempts to study the relationship of root personality dimensions to intelligence and the quality of social interaction.

Inertia

Inertia is characterised by lethargy, laziness, fear, inhibition, anxiety, shallowness of emotions, low initiative, low self-confidence, low self-respect, etc. People having a large degree of 'I' lack energy. They are slow, late, not venturing, shy, withdrawn, weak-willed, suggestible, submissive, masochistic, intropunitive, and so on. They are unable to refuse, assert or argue individually, but are collectivistic and show hysteric collective aggression. They show blind conformity and inability to mix with strangers. They do not have strong emotional ties. The strong emotion they show is fear. They believe in fate and luck and superstitions.

Activation

This is characterised by restless overactivity, uncontrolled energy, high drive, and inability to remain alone or silent. Persons having high A are compulsive mixtures, hasty, risk taking, rash, adventurous, analytical, efficient in planning practical things for the future, competitive, assertive, aggressive, proud, egoistic, rebellious, dominant, individualistic, greedy, possessive, dogmatic, etc. Their predominant emotions are anger passion and possessive love. They have a high degree of practical intelligence and mechanical ability.

Stability

Stability is characterised by high self-awareness, freedom, flexibility, and control. Persons having a high degree of 'S' can be fast or slow, can work or rest as they choose or as the situation demands. They can be very sociable or alone with equal ease. They show metamotivation and are capable of detached action. They are wise, mature and intuitive. They are creative, self-actualising, holistic, balanced, even-tempered and dispassionate. They are relaxed, self-sufficient, democratic, tolerant, transcending and broad-minded.

Individuals are born with a certain personality pattern (I.A.S) as the starting point, which gradually undergoes a change as a result of interaction with the environment.

Intelligence

The study of intelligence establishes a domain of inquiry having high application value and theoretical concern. It has occupied a significant place in the practices of personal selection, training, placement, guidance, diagnostic tests, etc. Intelligence provides the person with the capacity to meet and solve the problems that adjustment to life requires. Intellectual capacities influence the kind of adjustment the person makes to his environment, to people and to himself.

Quality of Social Interaction

It refers to the degree of excellence of the social relations exists among persons. It is an interpersonal characteristic of behaviour.

According to Back (1977), social interaction refers to mutual influence between two or more persons or groups in which the behaviour of either one is the stimulus for the behaviour of the other. Poor interactions have ramifications for the development of social relationships in humans.

Objectives

1. To study the extent of association that the root personality dimensions have with intelligence and quality of social interaction.
2. To study whether there is any gender difference in root personality dimensions, intelligence and quality of social interaction.

Hypotheses

1. The root personality dimensions have positive association significantly with intelligence and quality of social interaction.
2. The root personality dimensions, intelligence and quality of social interaction have significant differences among adolescents.

Method

Sample: The sample of the study consisted of 151 higher secondary students (60 students from 'Plus one' and 91 students from 'Plus two' classes). There were 102 girls and 49 boys in this study. They belonged to the age level of 15-17 years. The sample was taken from different higher secondary schools in Thiruvananthapuram district. Students belonging to different socioeconomic status and from rural and urban areas were included in the study.

Tools: Three instruments were used to correct data:

1. I.A.S. Rating Scale (This scale measures the root personality dimensions; inertia, activation and stability)
2. Mathew Test of Mental Abilities (Verbal)
3. Facilitativeness Rating Scale

I.A.S. Rating Scale

This scale measures three pronounced behavioural tendencies (personality dimensions, inertia, activation and stability). These tendencies cut across cognitive, temperament and motivational modalities. This scale was developed by Mathew (1995).

Split-half reliabilities of 0.73, 0.89 and 0.86 for the three scales I, A and S respectively have been obtained. It has construct validity and many studies demonstrated concurrent validity in the scale (Mathew, 1995).

Mathew Test of Mental Abilities (Verbal)

This test has been prepared and standardised in the Kerala population, and found to be the best measure of general mental ability. The re-test reliability coefficient obtained for a group of tenth standard students with an interval of two months between the two occasions is 0.69. The verbal test correlated 0.43 with Bhatia's Battery of Performance test, 0.48 with General Mental ability test-Non verbal and 0.59 with standard progressive matrices. This test was designed and developed by Mathew (1993).

Facilitativeness Rating Scale

Facilitativeness Rating Scale measures the quality of social interaction of the subjects. Odd-even reliability of the scale was estimated to be 0.89 for males and 0.80 for females.

Procedure: The scales were administered individually by the investigator himself. Each subject was seated comfortably and the general instructions were given. At first, Mathew Test of Mental Abilities (Verbal) was administered. The test-booklet and answer sheet was given. The subject was asked to read the instructions and the examples were explained and the method of answering demonstrated. Then a starting signal was given in order to open the booklet and start doing the test. At the end of exactly 15 minutes the stopping signal was given and the answer sheet was collected.

Then the second test, I.A.S. Rating Scale, was given. The investigator read out the instructions, requesting the subject to follow the same in his / her copy. Then the subject was asked to start doing the test. There was no time limit for this test.

Finally, Facilitativeness Rating Scale was given. The subject was instructed to mark 0, 1 or 2 in response to each item on the basis of their dealings with other people. Each subject took about 30 minutes for the completion of the three scales. The school authorities provided the facilities for the administration of the scales.

Method of scoring: Mathew Test of mental abilities was scored by placing a scoring key over the answer sheet and aligning it properly. Then a tick mark was placed against each correct answer in the answer sheet. Then the number of right answers and wrong answers were entered separately. Then the correction formula (RW/4) was applied to get the corrected raw score. (Here 'R' represents the number of right answers and 'W' represents the number of wrong answers.)

LA.S. Rating Scaling was scored by adding the numerical weight in each column. For each subject, the total score of the first column gives the score of inertia, the second column gives the scores of activation and the third column gives the score of stability. Facilitative Rating Scale was scored by findings the sum of the scores given by the subject for all the 34 items. Answer sheets of all the three tests were scored separately for the 151 students. The scores were treated statistically.

Results and Discussion

The product moment correlation coefficient method was used to find out the inter-relationship among the variables. Table 1 shows that inertia is negatively correlated with intelligence (i.e., -0.34 for boys and -0.24 girls). The values are significant at 5 per cent level. Activation has a significant positive correlation with intelligence only for girls (r = 0.34, significant at 1% level). Stability correlates significantly with intelligence only for boys (r = 0.31, significant at 5% level). It is also found that stability has a significant positive correlation with quality of social interaction (r = -0.24) in the case of girls. The value is significant at 5 per cent level (Table 1).

Table 1

Shows the correlation coefficient of the root personality dimension with intelligence and quality of social interaction (Boys - N - 49, Girls - N - 102)

Personality variables		*Intelligence*		*Quality of social interaction*
	Boys	-0.34*	Boys	-0.15
Inertia	Girls	-0.24	Girls	-0.18
	Boys	-0.09	Boys	-0.07
Activation	Girls	0.34**	Girls	-0.14
	Boys	0.31 *	Boys	0:16
Stability	Girls	0.05	Girls	0.24

* Significant at 5% level

**Significant at 1% level

Table 2

Shows the correlation coefficient between intelligence and quality of social interaction for the boys and girls

Gender	*Correlation*
Boys (49)	0.15
Girls (102)	0.03

Table 3

Shows the scores of the adolescent boys and girls in the test of root personality dimensions, intelligence at quality of social interaction

	Root personality dimensions								*Quality of social*	
	Inertia		*Activation*		*Stability*		*Intelligence*		*Interaction*	
	M	*SD*	*M*	*SD*	*M*	*SD*	*M*	*SD*	*M*	*SD*
Boys N = 49	25.61	11.43	25.82	8.76	53.61	15.03	36.1	14.91	40.02	8.74
Girls N = 102	30.3	14.39	21.59	8.43	53.11	16.06	34.79	13.31	39.68	6.28
t	2.16*		12.70**		10.18		10.21		10.17	

* Significant at 5% level

* * Significant at 1% level

The results indicate that inertia has a significant negative correlation with intelligence, intelligence decreases with an increase in inertia. Inertia is characterised by fear and low adaptive capacity, and a negative correlation between inertia and intelligence is expected conceptually. Persons having high activation are more analytical and a positive relationship between activation and intelligence is expected conceptually. In this study activation has a significant positive correlation with intelligence only in the case of girls. Persons having high activation are compulsive mixtures, analytical, etc. Stability is associated with freedom and flexibility, and persons with a high degree of stability would have good relationships and better adjustment. In this study, stability is found to have significant positive correlation with intelligence only in the case of boys. Stability is positively associated with the quality of social interaction only in the case of girls (Table 1). Since the results did not support hypothesis, hypothesis 1 is rejected.

Gender differences in personality dimensions, intelligence and quality of social interaction were assessed and presented in Table 3.

The t-test was used to test whether there was any gender difference in personality dimensions, intelligence and quality of social interaction. The results given in Table 3 show that boys and girls differ significantly in their inertia scores (t = 2.16, significant at 5% level). The mean score of inertia for girls (30.30) is significantly greater than that of boys (25.61). The results given in Table 1 also indicate significant difference between boys and girls in 'Activation' (t = 2.70, significant at 1%. level). In the Activation dimension, boys scored higher (25.82) than the girls (21.59). Boys have higher activation than girls. There are significant differences among boys and girls in inertia and activation. There are no significant differences between stability and quality of social interaction among the adolescents. Girls are less aggressive and more passive compared to boys across several species. Girls have less of testosterone and other hormones which are linked to aggressive activity. Aggressive behaviour is part of male territorial behaviour. Therefore according to ancestral experience males are expected to show more activation in terms of aggressive activity.

Conclusions

1. The root personality dimension, intertia, is negatively correlated with intelligence for both boys and girls. Activation

correlates positively with intelligence in the case of girls and stability has a positive correlation with intelligence for boys. Stability and quality of social interaction are also found to have a significant positive correlation.

2. Boys and girls were found to have significant differences in their inertia and activation. Girls showed more inertia while boys showed more activation.

References

Back, K.W., *Social Psychology,* N.Y John Wiley and Sons, INC, 1977.

Mathew, V.G., *Facilitativeness Rating Scale,* Dept. of Psychology, University of Kerala, 1990.

.... *Manual of Mathew Test of Mental Abilities*, Dept. of Psychology University of Kerala, 1993.

........., *IAS Rating Scale,* Dept. of Psychology, University of Kerala, 1995.

........., *Integrative Psychology,* Dept. of Psychology, University of Kerala, 1997.

CHAPTER 21

Personality Profile of Adolescent Delinquents

Uma Devi I. and Mayuri K.

The investigation was taken up to study the personality development of adolescent delinquents who were staying in the observation homes at Hyderabad city of Andhra Pradesh. Forty-four adolescent delinquents (22 boys and 22 girls) who were in the age range of 13+ to 18+ years constituted the sample. The personality development of the sample was; assessed by using multi-dimensional assessment of personality series developed and published by Psy-Corn services, New Delhi, which covers 20 dimensions of personality. It is disheartening to note from the results that adolescent delinquents, both boys and girls, fell short of standard average mean scores in most of the personality dimensions like creativity, general ability, innovation, mental health, sensitivity and social warmth. It is interesting to note from the results that both boys and girls differed significantly in personality dimensions—guilt proneness, sensitivity, social warmth and maturity. It is noteworthy to mention that parental education and occupation were significantly related to important personality dimensions like academic achievement, creativity, guilt proneness, leadership, maturity, mental health, self-control and sensitivity. It is interesting to note that the majority of the personality dimensions were significantly related to each other.

Introduction

Home is everything for adolescents. All their intellectual, moral, physical, social, emotional, and educational needs are satisfied in the home. Behavioural problems are caused only when these needs remain unsatisfied. Adolescents to be well adjusted to parents, need to feel loved and emotionally secure. An adolescent is born in a definite family set-up. The home environment is important in developing the personality of the adolescent and also has prominent and lasting influence on the behaviour pattern of the individual. There are some homes where the parents are extremely authoritarian and lack democratic qualities. Parents also contribute to behaviour problems in their children. Wrong use of parental authority is a major source of maladjustment among adolescents. Thus the relationship between the parents and adolescents plays a major role during this difficult period of growth. It may be a source of conflict or of good adjustment.

When conflict arises, adolescents can become victims of delinquent, antisocial behaviours. Delinquency is a social maladjustment and a vital era of human concern. It is not a recent phenomenon. It has been a part of human behaviour since man started living in a society. The increasing rate of crime and delinquency in India and abroad has drawn the attention of social thinkers, psychologists, educationists, administrators and others towards this baffling problem of human society. The incidence of juvenile delinquency is rising in developing countries due to rapid social changes, economic development, rural urban migration, social disorganisation.

According to crimes in India (1992), National Crimes Records Bureau, the volume of juvenile delinquency was 3.1 lakhs in 1988 and in 1992 it was 0.7 per cent. Maharashtra contributes to the highest percentage of juvenile crimes (5,049), followed by Tamil Nadu (4,758), Madhya Pradesh (2,684) and Andhra Pradesh (1,055). In Punjab, Manipur, Bengal, Kerala and Karnataka the reported cases of delinquency are very less. The concept of viewing and dealing with juvenile delinquency was different from a criminal originated during the nineteenth century. The basic idea was to reform the juvenile without subjecting him to the deleterious effects of prisonisation or other punishments.

Most of the earlier studies have dealt with juveniles, more or less with adolescent offenders who may be quite different from the children in their personality characteristics, reactions to environmental forces and even in the expectations of others. Adolescence is a period of storm and stress and may be considered a very critical and a crucial one from the point of view of personality development. There is a need to understand these adolescents or youthful offenders separately with regard to their personality characteristics and casual factors for their state, so that separate corrective and preventive measures can be taken up.

Keeping the above theoretical background in view, the present study was taken up to study the personality dimensions of adolescent delinquents with the following objectives.

- — To study the personality dimensions of adolescent delinquent children.
- — To see the relationship, if any, between the personality dimensions and selected personal social variables of adolescent delinquents.
- — To see the relationship among different personality dimensions studied.

Method and Materials

1. *Design of Research:* Case study method with interviews and observation were adopted in the present study.
2. *Area of the Research:* As the study was on adolescent delinquents, an observation home for boys located at Chencalguda and an observation home for girls located at Nimbolia Adda, Hyderabad (Andhra Pradesh) were selected as areas of study. The observation home for boys is meant for short stay till the case is disposed and the observation home for girls is meant for long stay for girls of special home, juvenile home and also for short stay for observation home girls.

Sample: Twenty-two boys from the observation home for boys and 22 girls from the observation home for girls who were in the age range of 13+ to 18+ were purposefully selected. Hence, the total sample constituted 44 in number. The inmates were from various districts of Andhra Pradesh. The purposive random sampling method was adopted.

Measurement Tools: 1. Interview Schedule relating to (a) child's age, lender, class and ordinal position, (b) family back ground information, socioeconomic status information and details about parental status and adolescents inmates future aspirations was developed and used.

2. A wide range of personality dimensions that relate to adolescent delinquents were measured by using the Multi-

Dimensional Assessment of Personality Series (MAP Series). It is the test giving the fullest information in a shortest time about most personality dimensions developed and published by PSY-com services, New Delhi. This test measures personality dimensions, namely, adaptability, academic performance, boldness, competition, creativity, curiosity, enthusiasm, excitability, general ability, guilt proneness, individualism, innovation, leadership, maturity, mental health, morality, self-control, sensitivity, self sufficiency, social warmth and tension. In all 44 children's (22 boys & 22 girls) personality was measured across different age groups from 13 to 18 years. The raw scores on each dimension was converted into Sten scores for the purpose of analysis of data. Reliability of the test was determined by using 'test retest' and 'split half methods' and was reported as 0.63 - 0.74 and 0.64 - 0.75 respectively: The validity coefficients for each item was found out by using the factorial validity and it ranged from 0.77 to 0.85.

Data Collection Procedure: The observation homes for boys and girls were visited by the investigator after obtaining necessary permission from the authorities. Necessary rapport was established with the inmates of the homes. General information was collected by using pre-tested interview schedule prepared for the purpose. The adolescent delinquents' personality was assessed by rising MAP - Series form by interviewing them individually. The collected data were counter-checked and supplemented by unstructured interviews with observation home staff and by the information obtained from the child's case histories available in the home.

Analysis of Data: The data collected was scored and analysed in the following manner:

a) Multidimensional assessment of personality measure was presented in mean distribution across gender and discussed comparing gender means with that of the test manual's description of their corresponding standard means for gender; 't' test was computed to see the significant differences, if any, between boys and girls in personality dimensions studied.

b) Simple linear correlations were computed in order to understand the relationship of the selected personal social variables with the adolescent delinquent's personality development and also relationship among different personality dimensions.

Results and Discussion

Personal Profile of the Adolescent Delinquents

It is evident front the results that majority of the children were in the age group of 14+, 15+ and 16+ years age group. Thus it is in the period of adolescence that the incidence of delinquent behaviour is the highest. Shankar's (1958) study also confirmed the same.

It has already been documented by researchers that the ordinal position bears an important relationship to personality characteristics and behaviour. The first child is often overprotected or pampered. If he belongs to large family, he has to share the responsibility of the family from a very young age, which crushes down his traits, like tendencies, undeveloped and makes him mature untimely bringing him in contact with the people. A middle child is often neglected in the family, and falls easily in to bad company. In our present study 13 out of 44 were first borns, nine were second borns and 12 were third borns confirming the earlier research findings. Shukla and Kumawat (1988) found in their study that 67 per cent of the delinquents were either first borns or 311 borns and Visura and Jeyasingh (1983) found the same, saying that last borns had the chances to become criminals. In contrast, Venkateshamurthy (1989) reported that order of birth was not related to juvenile delinquency, but subsequent born children were more in delinquency group than the first borns. Educational status of the adolescent delinquents indicates that very few (8) had secondary education and 19 out of 44 had primary education and 17 were illiterates in 1994.

Out of 22 boys studied, two were orphans, one was a kleptomaniac. In the case of 22 girls studied, three were kleptomaniac, two were married and deserted by their husbands, one girl was married, two girls had love affair and one girl was an orphan; the parents of one girl were not willing to take her back from observation home due to disturbed family conditions.

Socio-economic Status Particulars

Out of 44 cases studied majority, i.e., 36 were from nuclear families and the remaining eight were from joint families. Bharathi Sharma (1990) also observed the same trend where she found 69 per cent of the delinquents studied were from nuclear families. The family size of majority of the respondents studied was medium in 50 per cent of cases followed by large (14) and small (8). The emerging profile of the present study suggests, and probably not altogether surprisingly in view of the prevailing social ethos, greater incidence of illiteracy of a delinquent's parents. Studies by Skankar (1956); Shukla and Kumawat (1988); Verma and Chawla (1989); Krishna (1993) and Haranath and Devi Prasad (1995) also confirmed the same.

Parental Status

In pursuing the consideration of family background of children, Figure 1 provides an insightful peep into yet another intimate, and in some ways the most critical, dimension of the family. The data in the figure conveys the parental status of families. It is revealing that among the adolescent delinquent group, nearly two-thirds of the delinquent parental status was not good either due to the death of both or any one parent or due to desertion. Findings of various studies, where the relationships are strained, is most susceptible to delinquency (Bharathi Sharma) 1990; Haranath & Devi Prasad, 1995; Jeayashankarappa, 1971; Muttaiah & Baskaran, 1964). Our results are not in line with Shankar's (1956) findings where he found no relation between delinquency and broken families.

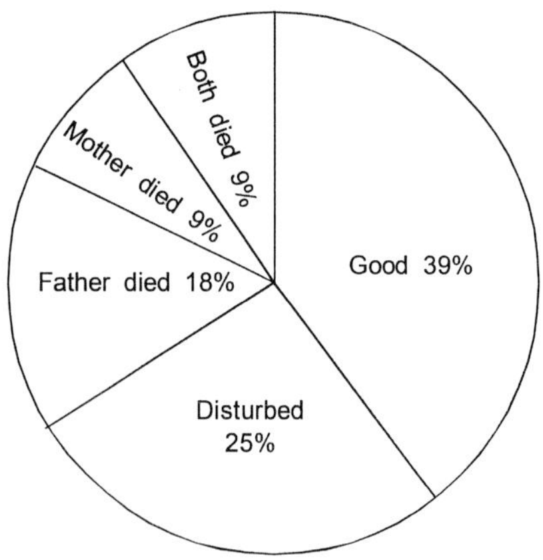

Figure 1: Parental status of adolescent delinquents

Personality Dimensions of Adolescent Delinquents

Carl Rogers (1951) has rightly said that "behaviour is basically the goal directed attempt of the organism to satisfy its needs as experienced in the field as perceived". Thus, the delinquent behaviour is the response to the need for recognition and resentment against the sense of insecurity and the feelings of being rejected and thwarted. Delinquents should be regarded as the maladjusted personalities and not as peculiar human beings with different kinds of needs. Their needs and desires are normal, only they are the victims of faulty upbringing and wrong treatment. It is clearly evident from the results (Figs. 2 & 3) that adolescent delinquents were superior in some dimensions of personality which include boldness, enthusiasm, maturity and self-sufficiency and were very low in personality dimensions like creativity, general ability, innovation, mental health, sensitivity, social warmth and tension. The inmates studied were nearing average in personality dimensions like self-control, individualism, adaptability, excitability, morality, etc. Krishna (1993) in his study found that high the delinquent group coming from urban areas scored higher on hostility, morality and guiltproneness. Delinquents possessed lower personality adjustment than non-delinquents (Prasad & Reddy, 1990). They had more guilt feelings, were more aggressive, dominant, rebellious and had a high degree of parent-child disturbances (Gaurmeet Singh, 1974).

In this study both boys and girls differed significantly in personality dimensions like guilt proneness, maturity, sensitivity and social warmth (5% level); where girls surpassed boys in maturity dimension, boys scored higher than girls in dimensions like guilt proneness, sensitivity and social warmth (Table 1). In the other six dimensions studied boys and girls did not differ significantly. Madhu Jain and Meghana (1998) in their study also found that male delinquents had better social adjustments than female delinquents because males were comparatively more outgoing, and they had more curiosity than females, therefore they were easily guided by the external demands of the environment.

Delinquents were generally low on abstract forms of thinking to see the problem as a whole and did not have maturity in expressing their feelings (Shankar, 1956). Socially- deprived children obtained significantly lower scores on concept formation tasks as compared to their non-deprived counter parts (Verma & Chawla, 1989). The investigations of Burt and others have clearly shown that delinquents are not mental defectives. But, it is also clear that the average intelligence of delinquent group is lower than the average intelligence of normal group — 85 according to Burt (1944) and 83 according to Shanker (1956). Our results also showed very low general ability levels which is equivalent only to 27 per cent of standard mean scores.

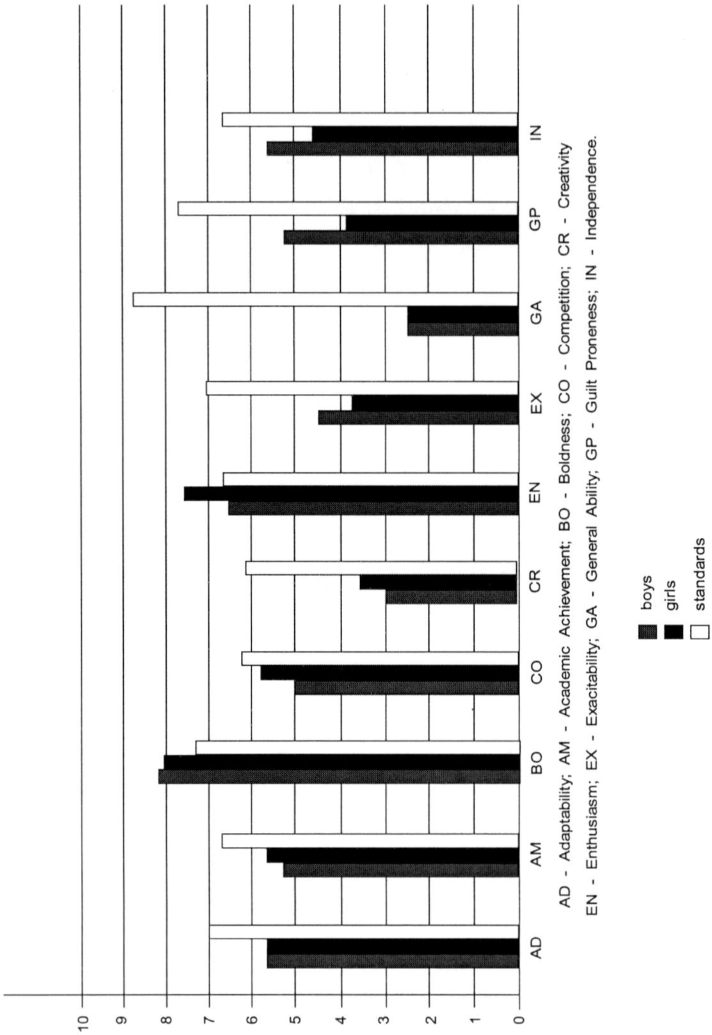

Figure 2. Comparison of personality dimensions of adolescent delinquents with standards

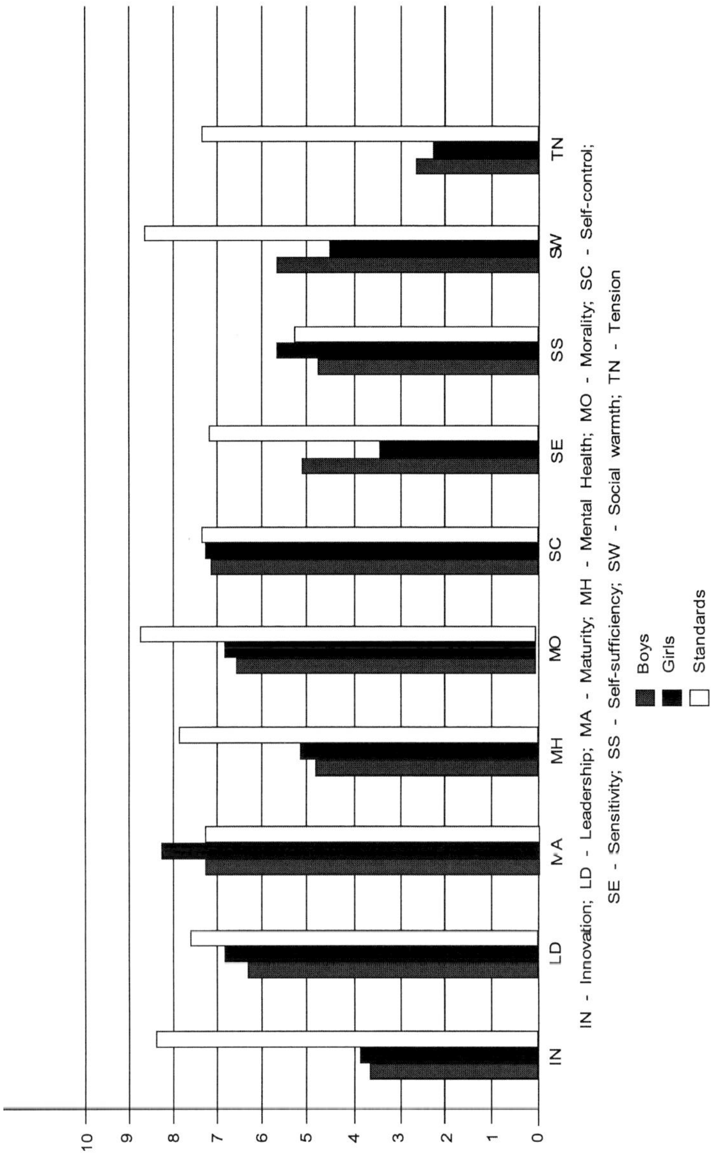

Figure 3. Comparison of personality dimensions of adolescent delinquents with standards

Venkatesha Murthy (1989) in his study found that delinquents and non-delinquents differ in their intelligence where non-delinquents over-power delinquents in this aspect.

It is known from the results that adolescent delinquent boys were consistently lower than standard average scores differing about 0 to 6.5 and show very low scores on personality dimensions like mental health, general ability; creativity, tension, innovation, excitability and social warmth. Boys possessed nearing average percentage standard scores for the remaining personality dimensions (Table 1).

The percentage possession of personality dimensions of girls indicate that they were very low on personality dimensions like general ability, tension, creativity, innovation, sensitivity, social warmth, excitability and mental health, and differed from standards which ranges from 0.4 to 6.5. They possessed above average percentage on personality dimensions such as boldness, enthusiasm, maturity and self sufficiency (Table 1).

In order to understand the relationship of the different personal social variables with the adolescent delinquent's personality dimensions simple linear correlations are computed and were presented in Table 2. The selected personal social variables include gender, age, class, ordinal position, parental education and occupation, caste, place of residence, parental status, hobbies, concept about home and observation home, stay duration, bad habits, stay frequency, etc. From the results it is clearly evident that the academic achievement is significantly and positively related to concepts about observation home at 5 per cent level. That means, those who scored better on academic achievement dimension had a good concept about observation home. Creativity is positively related to stay duration which means that children who stayed more in observation home exhibited better creativity than children whose stay was short. Guilt proneness is positively related to hobbies (5%) and negatively related to bad habits (5%) clearly indicating that the lesser the guilt proneness the higher the bad habits. Leadership dimension is positively related to father's occupation. It means that adolescent delinquents, whose father's occupational status was good, possessed good leadership qualities.

Table 1
Comparison of personality dimensions of adolescent delinquents with standard mean scores

Personality Dimensions	*Mean score Boys*	*S.D*	*Mean score For Girls*	*Standard S.D*	*% of mean scores*	*% standards Boys*	*of 't' standards Girls*	*value*
Adaptability	5.8	1.8	6.3	1.6	7.1	82	89	
Academic achievement	5.4	1.4	6.4	2.0	6.8	79	94	
Boldness	8.4	1.7	8.3	2.4	7.4	114	112	
Competition	5.0	2.4`	5.6	2.2	6.1	82	92	
Creativity	3.0	1.3	3.6	1.6	8.2	37	44	
Enthusiasm	6.6	1.9	7.5	1.9	6.8	97	110	
Excitability	4.8	2.6	3.9	2.1	7.1	68	55	
General ability	2.4	1.2	2.4	1.6	8.9	27	27	
Guilt proneness	5.2	2.2	4.1	1.2	.6.8	76	60	2.05*
Individualism	5.5	2.1	4.3	2.0	6.6	83	65	
Innovation	3.6	1.6	3.7	1.6	8.3	43	45	
Leadership	6.2	2:0	6.9	1.5	7.6	82	91	
Maturity	7.1	2.2	8.4	1.8	7.1	100	118	-2.19*
Mental health	4.9	1.8	5.3	1.9	7.8	63	68	
Morality	6.6	2.1	7.0	2.1	8.7	76	80	
Self-control	7.1	2.1	7.4	1.8	7.5	95	99	
Sensitivity	5.1	2.3	3.5	1.9	7.1	72	492.68*	
Self-sufficiency	4.8	1.7	5.6	2.7	5.2	92	108	
Social warmth	5.9	2.0	4.6	1.8	8.6	69	532.23*	
Tension	2.9	1.9	2.1	1.9	7.2	40	29	

*p > 0.05.

Maturity dimension is negatively related to mother's education, house type and stay frequency which means that the better the mother's education, the better the house type, and the greater the stay frequency, the lesser the maturity. Sensitivity is negatively related to gender. That is, girls were less sensitive compared to boys. Sensitivity is positively related to hobbies, i.e., the higher the sensitivity the better the hobbies. Self-sufficiency is positively related to stay duration. That means children who stay for long duration in the observation home showed good self-sufficiency scores. Socially warm children involved more in interpersonal interactions and therefore were low on pursuing hobbies.

It is interesting, to note from the results that none of the selected personal social variables were significantly related to the other 12 personality dimensions which include adaptability, boldness, competition, enthusiasm, excitability, general ability, individualism, innovation, mental health, morality, self-control and tension.

Table 2
Correlation of personality dimensions with selected personal social variables (N - 44)

Personality Dimensions	*Correlation with Personal Social Variables*
Academic achievement	Observation home concept (0.37*)
Creativity	Stay duration (0.40. *)
Guilt proneness	Hobbies (0.45*), bad habits (-0.38*)
Leadership	Father's occupation (-0.37*)
Maturity	Mother's education (-0.35*),
	House type (-0.39*),
	Stay frequency (-0.42*)
Mental health	Family concept (-0.37*)
Self-control	Family concept (0.36*)
Sensitivity	Gender (-0.38*), hobbies (0.36*)
Self-sufficiency	Stay duration (0.40*)
Social warmth	Hobbies (-0.45*)

*p>0.05,** p>0.01.

Inter Correlation among Different Personality Dimensions

After considering at length the relationship of adolescent delinquent's personality dimensions with selected personal social variables, we may now focus our attention on interrelationship of different personality dimensions studied. From Table 3, it is clearly evident that:

1) Adaptability is significantly related to competition at 1 per centlevel of significance, that means children who were more adaptable to situations were more competitive in nature.
2) Academic achievement is significantly negatively related to sensitivity at 5 per cent level which clearly explains that as children's academic achievement progresses they become less sensitive to situations.

3) Boldness is significantly related to competition only. Children who were bold enough exhibited more competitiveness than children who were less bold.

4) Enthusiasm dimension is significantly positively related to leadership, morality and self-control. Children who were more enthusiastic had good leadership qualities, possessed moral values and exhibited good self-control than less enthusiastic children.

5) Excitability dimension is significantly positively related to individualism (5%), tension (1%) and significantly negatively related to leadership and maturity at 1 per cent level. The higher the excitability, the higher the individualism, but the lesser the leadership qualities and maturity levels. At the same time the more excitable children were more tensedup.

6) General ability is related to leadership at 5 per cent level of significance. Maturity is related to enthusiasm and morality positively at 5 per cent level, which clearly indicates that better matured persons were more enthusiastic and also exhibit good moral values.

7) Morality is significantly and positively related to social warmth at 5 per cent levels indicating that moral values make the person more acceptable in the group as they will exhibit more social warmth.

Table 3: Inter-Correlations among personality dimensions: (N - 44)

Personality Dimensions	*Co-relations with personality dimensions details*
Adaptability	Competition (0.48 **)
Academic Achievement	Sensitivity (-0.37*)
Boldness	Competition (0.37*)
Enthusiasm	Maturity (0.44*), morality (0.37*), Self-control (0.39*)
Excitability	Individualism (038*), leadership (-0.50"*), Maturity (-0.45 *), tension (0.45 * *)
General ability	Leadership (0.36*),
Maturity	Enthusiasm (0.44*), morality (0.37*)
Morality	Social warmth (0.35 *)

*p > 0.05, ** p > 0.01.

Future Aspirations

A look at the future plans and occupational choices of these delinquent children (Figure 4), reveals their low aspiration levels which are probably the reflection of their parental family occupations. Most of the respondents did not have any future aspirations as they were confused and unclear about their future. The aspirations of boys include: to become a painter, mason, mechanic, labourer and to settle in unspecified jobs whereas girls wanted to settle as labourers, take up unspecified jobs, continue studies and settle in life with marriage. Boys had better aspirations than girls. Haranath and Devi Prasad (1995) in their study also reported low aspirations of the delinquents which included tailoring, agricultural labourer, hotel servicing, carpentry, cycle mechanical work and to pursue studies (10%). Shukla and Kumawat (1988) and Ganga, Ravichandran and Padmabhushan (1989) also confirmed the low aspirations of delinquents studied.

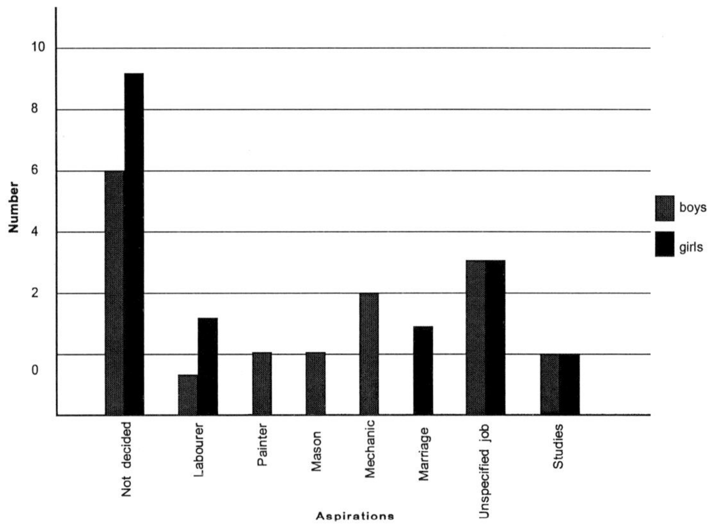

Figure 4: Future aspirations of adolescent delinquents

Conclusions

It can be concluded from the study that delinquent behaviour is an learned behaviour and the most important causes of antisocial behaviour are environmental and sociological in nature. The adolescent delinquents had very low personality characteristics and future aspirations which are mainly due to disturbed family background, lack of proper stimulation at home and also due to bad surroundings. As juvenile delinquency is one of the most critical social problems faced by the country, and the future of the country depends on its proper solution, it is essential that we should gear our energies for the purpose of protecting the greatest wealth of our nation, i.e., the children should develop them to develop in a socially acceptable channels, so that they become good citizens acid maintain the high traditions of the country.

References

Burt, C., *The Young Delinquent* (4th ed.), New York: Appleton, 1944.

Ganga, N., Ravichandran, P, & Padmabhushan, A.S. Delinquency in children, *Indian Journal of Paediatrics,* 1989, 56, 227-230.

Govindrajan, T.N., A study of juvenile delinquents position in the family, *Indian Journal of Applied Psychology,* 1966, 3, 56-63.

Haranath, S. & Devi Prasad, B., Juvenile Home Inmates: Background characteristics, *Indian Journal of Social Work,* 1995, LVI (3), 285-293.

Jain, M., & Meghana, B.N., Male and female and delinquents and their adjustment, *Indian Psychological Review,* 50(4), 1998, 181-185.

Jeyashankarappa, B.S., & Prasad Rao, D.C.V., A study of some aspects of psychosocial pathology of juvenile delinquents, *Indian Journal of Paediatrics,* 1971, 38(281), 215-271.

Krishna, U., Effect of sociological and psychological factors on adolescent delinquent behaviour, *Asian Journal of Psychology and Education,* 1993, 26(1-2), 28-31.

Multidimensional assessment of personality Series — Teenager form (MAP), Psycom Services: New Delhi, 1993.

Muttaiah, B. & Baskaran, A.S., Some factors of juvenile delinquency and sibling position, *Indian Journal of Applied Psychology,* 1964, 1, 116-119.

National Crime Records Bureau, *Crimes in India,* Ministry of Home Affairs, Government of India, New Delhi, 1992.

Prasad, P.L. & Reddy L.V., Personality adjustment and self ideal discrepancy among delinquents and non-delinquents, *Indian Journal of Criminology,* 1990, 18 (1), 1-5.

Rogers, C., Client Centred Therapy, Boston: Houghton & Mifflin Co. Shankar, U. (1956). Rorscharch responses of a group of juvenile thieves, *Indian Journal of Psychology,* 1951, 31, 15-20.

Shankar, U., *Problem children,* Delhi: Atmaram, 1958.

Sharma, B., *Juvenile delinquency and their social culture* (pp. 44-77), New Delhi: Uppal Publishing House, 1990.

Shukla, R.S., & Kumawat, U., A socio-psychological study of some convicted delinquents, *Asian Journal of Psychology and Education*, 1988, 21(1), 15-23.

Singh, G., A psychological study of delinquents and non-delinquent inmates, *Indian Journal of Psychiatry*, 1976, 18(2), 117-123.

Venkatesha Murthy, C.G., A comparative study of juvenile delinquents and non-delinquents, *The mind*, 1989, 39, 7-15.

Verma, S., & Chawla, S., Concept formation in socially deprived and non-deprived children, *Asian Journal of Psychology and Education*, 1989, 22(34), 18-28.

Visura, J., & Singh, T.J., Influence of family size, birth order and occupation on criminal behaviour, *Asian Journal of Psychology and Education*, 1983, 11(3), 19-23.

CHAPTER 22

Personality Traits of Adolescent Girl Students in Relation to their Parents

Swatantra Jain

This is an attempt to assess the personality traits of adolescent girl students in relation to their parents' acceptability. The sample consisted of 96 adolescent girls in the age group of 16 to 20 years, of which 50 were low accepted and 46 high accepted, screened out from 250 adolescent girls by administering the Family Relationship Inventory. They were drawn at random from high schools and colleges of southern Haryana state. The Cattall's 16 Personality Profile Inventory was administered on the sample. The results revealed that parents' level of acceptance had a definite influence upon certain traits of the girls. The low accepted group girls seem to be low on factors of reservedness (A), intelligence (B), and conservation (Q), higher in traits, apprehension (O) dominance (Q2) and tension Q4). The low accepted group also seems to be higher on traits of timidity (H), and sound follower (Q2).

Introduction

The humanistic psychology and the ego psychology are said to be the third force in psychology which stress the importance of the subjective unique experience of the individual. Recent theorists are associated with the psychoanalytic tradition, which laid more emphasis on social variables which are shaping the personality. The role of instinctive forces and genetic factors are not given any importance. The neo-Fredudians assert a 'Conflict free Sphere' of the ego (Hartmann, Kris and Loewenstein, 1947; Rapaport, 1951). Likewise, phenomenological theorists view the person as an 'experiencing being' rather than as a 'personality structure' or as a syndrome of 'psychodynamics' and long-term dispositions. It focuses on the individual's subjective experience, personal view of the world around and the self. Erikson's (1963) focus on psychosocial development also reflects the growing neo-Freudians' view on broad social and cultural forces, rather than instinctual drives alone. Erikson hypothesises a psycho-social crisis that arises from the person's efforts to solve the problem at that stage. For example, in infancy, the child must develop the right ratio of trust (forming intimate relationships) to mistrust (to protect himself) in a hostile world (Paplia and Wndkos, 1987, p.495). Erikson hypothesises that at this stage the child's relationship to its mother forms the basic attitudes about 'getting' and giving. If the crisis is properly resolved, the experience at this stage lays the foundation for later trust, drive and hope. The contrary would be true if the child experiences neglect instead of warmth and acceptance. A child's emotional acceptance, thus, has much to do in personality formation.

Harry Stack Sullivan also emphasized the crucial importance of interpersonal processes and the human relations for the development of personality traits. For Sullivan, the human's relationship of infancy, childhood and adolescence are of paramount concern. The individual can be understood only in his relationship to the significant people in his life (Whitaker, 1970, p. 474). Alfred-Adler also offered a somewhat similar view, when he focused on the person's lifestyle and his social interest or social milieu.

Karen Horney (1937), unlike Freud, views that anxiety grows in the child's relationship with his parents. She believe that the essential factor in personality development is 'the feeling a child has of being isolated and helpless in a potentially hostile world' (1937, p. 79). She had laid great emphasis on the home environment and the social structure within the family. The predominant reason that basic anxiety develops from parent-child relationship is the absence of genuine love and affection. "...the entirety of infantile experience combines to form a, certain character structure and it is this structure from which later difficulties emanate" (Horney, 1939, p. 9). She hypothesised that in attempting to find security, individuals use three types of behavioural pattern: moving toward, against or away from people (Horney, 1945). If the parents are rejecting, the child uses various means to cope with the anxiety, which develops into basic life attitude, complaint, aggression and detachment. The 'complaint' individuals relies upon other people being loving, kind and loyal, the 'aggressive' loves extreme independence and believes in 'Survival of the fittest' while 'detached' is perfectionisitic, uncreative and lacks inter-personal relationships. Horney believes the social factors to be of the preponderant importance. According to her, a secure and loving home always result in balanced healthy personality structure.

Erich Fromm (1941) also asserts that the character traits develop from a child's experiences with others. For example, the child develops self-respect and confidence through his early positive relations with the parents, while a negative attitude of parents may produce low self-esteem and lack of confidence, because the children's physical condition at birth and shortly thereafter makes their survival dependent upon their environment in general and upon their mother in particular. It was also stated by Ferenczi, that the warm relationship with the mother was missing in the lives of most of his neurotic patients (Jones, 1957; pp. 163-164).

Every child has the inherent urge to seek and experience intimacy in one's relationship. Bowlby (1965) has insisted on the biological mother-child bond as a necessary and sufficient condition for effective socialisation. Mohan and Singh (1981,1982), Sahney (1984) reported that thwarting of the need to be belonged, to be loved and security, consistently leads an individual to some form of maladjustment which may range from mild aggression to crime. Most of the child's attitudes are due to an induction and gradual taking over of the culture of the family, also, he develops a sort of positive or negative attitude towards them.

The girl is an unwanted child not only in India but also in many other Asian countries. In a culture that idolises sons and dreads the birth of a daughter, to be born a female comes perilously close to being born less than human and where the rejection of the unwanted girl begins even before her birth. From the day of her birth, a girl is viewed as a burden and a liability. Born into indifferences and reared on neglect, the girl-child is caught in a web of cultural practices and prejudices that divest her individuality and mould her into a submissive and self-sacrificing daughter and wife (Ministry of HRD). In view of the dearth of knowledge in the area of parental acceptability of girls in relation to personality development the present study was attempted.

Expectations from the present study: Every child has the inherent urge to seek and experience intimacy in one's relationship with other family members in general and mother in particular. Conceptual framework of neo-Freudians like Horney (1945), Fromm, Erikson, Sullivan and humanitarian psychologists like Carl Rogers and Maslow emphasize that the individual is more a product of social units and his interpersonal relationship within the family. It was hypothesised that the girls, who experience or perceive their parents to be having an attitude of neglect, low acceptance and more avoidance towards them, will grow with different personality traits as against those who experience an attitude of affection and acceptance.

Definition of the terms used: Roe (1957) hypothesised three types of parental attitudes, such as (a) acceptance, (b) concentration and (e) avoidance towards their children. As a result of these attitudes, which parents directly or indirectly, consciously or unconsciously express towards their children, they develop certain attitudes towards the low or high acceptability or avoidance of the parents. Sherry and Sinha viewed that the formation of attitude in the early stages of life plays a very significant role in the development of individuals.

Acceptance: It means that the parents consider the child as a full-fledged member of the family who needs a certain degree of independence and who has the capacity to assume responsibility.

Concentration: This refers to the attitudes of parents who devote a disproportionate amount of their time and energy to the direction and control of their children. They overprotect them through putting restrictions upon their efforts to explore the environment and place heavy demand upon them to perform beyond their capacities.

Avoidance: This characterises the disposition of parents who either neglect or reject the child. They withdraw when their child approaches them for affection and love; they fail to satisfy the child's physical needs or they openly abuse the child. In short, they do not manifest any positive interest in the child and give them the notion that the particular child is a burden to them.

Hypothesis: This is the study of the problems of the adolescent girl students in an Indian culture. Generally adolescent girls are very sensitive to their parents' expression of feelings and attitudes towards them. Parents' negative attitudes, like low acceptance, greater restrictions and avoidance, might become the cause of the development of unpleasant feelings and high acceptance, less restriction and affection and love may develop pleasant feelings among the girls. This becomes the basis for the development of certain personality traits in the individuals. Having these problems in view the following hypotheses are formulated:

1. If the adolescent girl students are low accepted (highly avoided) by their parents then they develop the traits like

reservedness (or detachment), low level of intelligence, emotional instability and unaccommoditiveness.

2. If the adolescent girl students get highly concentrated attention by their parents then they develop a weak ego, timidity and become highly imaginative.
3. If the adolescent girl students are neglected (or avoided) by their parents then they become highly depressive, conservative, will not be the followers and develop tension and frustration.

The independent variable in this study is parental acceptance and the dependent variables are the corresponding traits on the Cattell's 16 PF Inventory.

Method

Sample: The preliminary sample consisted of 250 adolescent girls in the age group of 16 to 20 belonging to Class C onward from the schools and colleges of three district headquarters of Karnal, Kurukshetra and Yamunanagar of Haryana. First they were administered with Family Relationship Inventory. Of the 250 answered inventories, 25 were rejected as they had high lie scores.

Target sample: Fifty low accepted / high avoidance and 46 high accepted / low avoidance girls were screened out on the basis of M ± 1SD. These two groups will be henceforth mentioned as LA and HA groups respectively. The dual criteria of standing above M+ 1 SD on Mother Acceptability (MA) and below M-1 SD on Mother Avoidance (MAV) for the high acceptable (HA) group and below M+SD on Mother Acceptability (MA) and above M ± 1 SD on Mother Avoidance (MAV) for the low acceptable (LA) group was strictly followed because the present study aimed at testing the hypothesis on only those girls who are high on acceptance but low on avoidance dimension (HA) vs those who are low on acceptance but high on avoidance dimension (LA). Regarding the acceptance there is not much difference between mother and father. The SDs for the groups are normal (Table 1). In the case of concentration there is some difference between father and mother. The mother concentration score (12.71) is higher than the father concentration score (9.51). The acoidance score between mother (.5.67) and father (6.31) did nor vary much (Table 1).

Materials: The following test materials were used in this study: (1) The Family Relationship Inventory. (2) Cattall's 16 Personality Profile Inventory.

1. *The Family Relationship Inventory:* This was designed and developed by Sherry and Sinha to measure the perceived parental attitudes of acceptance, concentration and avoidance. These two authors devised it on the basis of Brunken and Crites (Fri, 1964) in the Indian context. According to Sherry and Sinha this inventory discriminates the individuals who feel emotionally accepted, overprotected or rejected by their parents. The original inventory contains 150 items and six more extreme items were added for identifying the lie scores.
2. *Cattell's 16 Personality Profile Inventory:* This was originally designed and developed by Cattell. It consists of 16 personality factors such as (A) Reservedness, (B) Intelligence, (C) Emotionality, (E) Accommodativeness, (F) Soberess, (G) Expectancy, (H) Timidity, (I) Realism, (L) Trusting, (M) Practicality, (N) Straightforwardness, (O) Confidence, (Q1) Conservation, (Q2) Sound follower, (Q3) Indiscipline, (Q4) Tension. It is very widely used all over the world. It was adopted in Hindi by Kapoor (1970).

Table 1

Showing the scores of various dimensions of family relationship inventory (FRI) with which the low acceptance and high acceptance dichotomy was made

S.No.	*Dimensions*	*Mean Scores*	*SD*	*SEM*
1.	Mother acceptance (MA)	18.99	3.67	0.25
2.	Father acceptance (FA)	18.19	3.52	0.24
3.	Mother concentration (MC)	12.81	3.29	0.22
4.	Father concentration (FC)	9.51	2.61	0.17
5,	Mother avoidance (MAV)	5.67	3.69	0.25
6.	Father avoidance (FAV)	6.31	3.98	0.27

Procedure: The Family Relationship Inventory was first administrated on 250 adolescent girl students and they were classified into two groups as low acceptance and high avoidance group, high acceptance and low avoidance group on the basis of the three-dimensional scale. Then the Cattell's 16 Personality Profile Inventory was administrated on these two groups. The questionnaires were collected from the respondents and scrutinised to see whether they were answered properly. Then the scoring was made according to the procedure given by the authors of the inventories.

Results

The individual scores were obtained from both the groups on the Cattell's 16 Personality Profile Inventory and suitable statistical treatments were given to the scores and presented in tabular columns.

The hypothesis that girls with low acceptance by their parents develop the traits of reservedness or detached, low intelligence, emotionally instable and unaccommodative is verified in this study. The results of this study as given in Table 2 reveal that the low accepted girls scored low (8.88) in reservedness, intelligence (6.90), high in accomodativeness (12.42) (unaccommodative) in the Cattell's 16 Personality Profile Inventory. This is in contrast to the scores of high acceptance group. While comparing the scores of the two groups on these traits the 't' ratio is significant at. 01 level for reservedness. The mean scores differences are not significant in other traits. Therefore, the hypothesis is partially accepted (Table 2).

Table 2 Showing the scores on Cattell’ s 16 PF Inventory and the ‘ t’ ratios for the low accepted and high accepted groups

S.No		*Traits (N-50)*	*Low (N-46)*			*High*			*S.E. of diff.*		
			Mean	*SD*	*SEM*	*Mean*	*SD*	*SEM*			*SE*
1.	A.	Reservedness	8.88	2.47	.35	10.26	2.49	.37	0.51	2.68	0.01
2.	B.	Intelligence	6.94	2.32	.33	7.41	1.86	.27	0.43	1.05	NS
3.	C.	Emotionality	12.74	4.48	.63	12.15	3.55	:52	0.77	1.03	NS
4.	E.	Accommodativeness	12.42	3.05	.43	11.48	2.68	.39	0.58	1.62	NS
5.	F.	Soberness	11.80	3.97	.56	11.54	3.60	.53	0.74	0.05	NS
6.	G.	Expediency	13.28	3.03	.43	14.00	2.69	.40	0.58	1.24	NS
7.	H.	Timidity	13.80	3.41	.48	15.24	3.58	.53	0.72	2.01	0.05
8.	1.	Tough mindedness	10.82	2.76	.39	11.04	2.54	.37	0.54	0.41	NS
9.	L.	Trusting	9.30	2.69	.38	9.98	2.03	.30	0.48	1.42	NS
10.	M.	Practicality	11.32	3.38	.48	12.17	2.52	.37	0.61	1.41	NS
11.	N.	Straightforwardness	11.00	2.48	.35	11.20	2.66	.39	0.53	0.37	NS
12.	O.	Confidence/App	14.04	3.06	.43	12.00	3.66	.53	0.69	2.98	0.01
13.	Q_1	Conservative	9.16	2.35	.33	10.58	2.43	.36	0.48	2.96	0.01
14.	Q_2	Sound follower	9.86	2.72	.39	8.26	2.69	40	0.54	2.61	0.01
15.	Q_3	Indiscipline	12.26	2.82	.40	12.13	3.86	.57	0.66	1.83	NS
16.	Q_4	Tension	12.54	3.83	.54	10.96	3.62	.53	0.77	2.12	0.05

The second hypothesis that girls who get highly concentrated attention by their parents develop a weak ago, become timid, and conventional was verified and the results are given in Table 2. It is observed that these girls scored low in weak ego (G) (13.24), timidity (H), (14.80) conventionality (11.32). The mean score difference between the low acceptance and high acceptance, group is significant only in the case of timidity (H). In all other traits the differences are very small. Therefore the hypothesis is partially accepted (Table 2).

The third hypothesis that the adolescent girls who are avoided or neglected become highly depressive, conservative, do not follow instruction and become frightened and tense is verified in this study by using the Cattell's 16 PF Inventory. The data given in Table 2 reveal that the adolescent girls who are neglected by their parents were found to be scoring high in factor O, indicating that they are apprehensive, worrying and depressive and scored low in P, indicating that they are conservative, and scored high in factor Q2 showing that they are not sound followers and make their own decisions. The mean score difference between the low acceptance group and high acceptance group are highly significant for factors O, Q and Q2 at 0.01 level (Table 2). Therefore the hypothesis is accepted. The first two previous hypotheses which are partially accepted as the mean score difference were significant only in a few factors. But in the third hypothesis all the mean differences are varying significantly.

Discussion

This study has brought out certain results in the development of certain personality trait among the adolescent girls on the basis of the low and high acceptance attitudes of the parents.

The low accepted and high avoidance (LA) adolescent girls, scored significantly higher on apprehension Q, sound following (Q2) and tension and frustration (Q4) than the high acceptance (HA) group, while the same, i.e., low acceptance (LA) group scored lower on reservedness (A) conservation (Q) and timidity (H).

The LA group has come out to be more apprehensive, depressive, tense, frustrated, conservative, timid, reserved and shy while the HA group has turned out to be more outgoing, bold, relaxed, liberal and critical, placid, self-sufficient, confident.

Even though the differences are negligible between the mean scores of LA and HA groups with respect to certain traits, i.e., B, (intelligence), C (Emotionality), F (Soberness); G, (Expedient vs Conscientious), M (Practical vs Imaginative) and Q3 (Undisciplined vs Controlled), they are to be mentioned here as they are important factors. The tendency of the low acceptable (LA) girls towards being reserved, shy, tense, frustrated, restless or impatient, apprehensive, worrying and troubled can be explained in accordance with humanitarian, ego psychologists and neo-Freudians like Karen Horney, Fromm and Sullivan that anxiety develops out of the child's relationship with her parents. Karen Horney (1939) believes that the essential factor in personality development is 'the feeling a child has of being isolated and helpless in a potentially hostile world'.

The less acceptable girls imply that they perceive and experience a lack of warmth, affection and a feeling of lack of loving bent with their mothers in particular and parents in general. The lack of warmth and love, and a feeling of isolation generates in them a sense of pessimism, frustration, tension and makes them disinterested in people. The predominant reason that basic anxiety develops from parent-child relationship is the absence of genuine love and affection and according to Horney (1939) "the entirety of infantile experience combines to form a certain character and it is this structure from which later difficulties emanate" (1939, p. 9).

Such an affectionless child may lose interest in people and in life, as Horney puts it, in attempting to find security, individuals use three types of behavioural pattern: moving toward, away or against people. If the parents are rejecting, the child adopts various mean to cope with the anxiety which develops into a basic life attitude, i.e., complaint, detached or aggressive. In the present sample, the low acceptable girls seem to have adopted the middle way, i.e., detached attitude as they are higher on Factor A.

To conclude, social factors like interpersonal relationship, mother-child bond, are most important for a healthy personality development. Because the neglective attitude of parents may produce anxiety, low self-esteem, and low self confidence, seclusions, etc., a secure and loving home would always result in a balanced healthy personality of the girl-child. However the results of this study need to be verified in a wider area with a much larger sample. A sample with 50 low accepted and 46 high accepted from some part of Haryana state cannot be accepted as the generalised trait in the Indian context though the negative attitudes of the parents may become one of the causes of the development of unpleasant personality traits among the girls.

References

1. Adler, A., *Understanding Human Nature*, New York: Fawcett, 1954.
2. Bowlby, *In Essentials of Mental Health.*
3. Sherry and Sinha, *Manual of Family Relationship Inventory*, Brunken and Crites, 1977.
4. Erikeen E., *Childhood and Society,* New York: Norton, 1963.
5. Fromm, E., *Escape from Freedom,* New York; Holt, Rinehart and Winston, 1941.
6. Hartmann J. Kris E. and Loewenstein, R.M., Comments on the formation of Psychic Structure, In W. Mischel Ed., *Introduction to Personality,* 3rd Ed., Holt-Saunders International Editions, London; p.56, 1951.
7. Horney K., *The Neurotic Personality of Our Time,* New York: Norton, 1937.
8. __________, *New Ways in Psychoanalysis,* New York: Norton, 1939.
9. __________, *Our Inner Conflicts*, New York: Norton, 1945.
10. Kapoor S. D., *Manual of Cattell's 16 PF.* IPAT.
11. Maslow A., *The Farther Reaches of Human Nature,* New York, Viking, 1971.
12. Mohan V. and Singh, A., Sex differences in the adjustment of murderers, *Ind. J. Criminal,* 1982. 10(1) 53-55.
13. Papalia D.E. and Wndokos, S., *Psychology:* McGraw-Hill International Eds. 1987.
14. Roe, In Manual of Family Relationship Inventory, Sherry and Sinha, 1977.
15. Sahney J. S., *A Comparative Study of Personality,* adjustment in non-delinquents and delinquents — Ph.D. Thesis; Pb. Univ. chd., 1984.
16. Sherry G.P. and Sinha J.C., *Manual of Family Relationship Inventory,* National Psychological Corporation, Agra, 4. 1977.
17. Sullivan H.S. in: Whittaker's, *An Introduction to Psychology*, 2nd Ed. London, pp. 474-5, 1970.

CHAPTER 23

School Achievement and Personality: A TAT Study

N. Hota

An attempt has been made to find out the relationship between school achievement and personality traits of three subcultures of the State of Orissa.

The Indian version of 10 TAT cards were presented to 108 tribal school children, 100 rural school children and 92 urban school children. Among these subjects 162 were boys and 138 were girls.

Results indicated that a significant positive relationship was found between school achievement and conflict level, self-assertiveness and future outcomes of subjects. A high degree of positive relationship was found between school achievement and self- assertiveness in urban children, and aggressiveness and school achievement relationship in tribal children. Boys and girls do differ significantly in their conflict and school achievement relationship. It was also found that high achievers and law achievers do differ significantly in their personality traits except in 'affiliation' trait.

Introduction

Personality refers to the adjustment of an individual to the society in which his needs and demands can be met under the purview of the society. In other words, personality represents the sum total of everything about an individual that makes him adjust in his own way to his environment. Cattell expresses it as "that which enables us to predict a person's behaviour in a given situation". One is impressed by man's dynamic personality — that personality of the individual which has an irresistible and magnetic attraction. Such persons prove their assurance and confidence in their whole demeanour, speech and conduct. They are popular among their peers and in their society. Pielstick (1963) found that children who are academically competent, especially those who read well, are more popular than those whose academic work falls below par. Poor academic work, on the other hand, due to either low intelligence or poor study habits, adversely affect social acceptance. A number of studies have been cited to relate academic achievement to the personality of individuals Even a person's personality can be predicted from his scholastic attainment in schools. Cattell, Barton and Dielman (1972) conducted one study on 169 sixth Grade and 142 seventh grade children and administered personality (16 PF), motivation (MAT), and ability (CF I. Q) tests. Approximately three months later the same children were given standardised achievement tests (ETS) in the areas of mathematics, science, social studies and reading and their performances on these subjects were predicted from the personality, motivation and ability measures. It was concluded that personality, motivation and ability variables, each contributed independently and significantly to the predictions of school achievement but that the pattern of relevant predictors varied with the achievement area. Bhatnagar (1967) conducted a study of some of the personality variables as predictors of academic achievement of high school students keeping age, sex and intelligence constant. It was found that the need for achievement and aggression correlated positively and the need for affiliation correlated negatively to the academic achievement of the students.

Besides, Saxena (1972) found from his study that a positive self-concept was associated with higher academic achievement. Singh's study on 1965 revealed that academic achievement was significantly positively related to intelligence, concept formative ability and academic motivation and it was negatively related to personal relations and anxiety. Sarason (1960) reported that children who are low achievers or have behaviour problems are more likely responding to an excess of anxiety, rather than to its absence, although their behaviour frequently resembled that of the child who lacks sufficient anxiety. He found that bright children as well as slow learners are often highly anxious about tests and their classroom performances.

Sharma (1972) compared the over-achievers and under-achievers with some personality factors and his results showed that there were significant differences among the over-achievers, average-achievers and under-achievers with regard to their adjustment in the school, home, social and religious and miscellaneous areas, and the over-achievers had better adjustment than the under-achievers in all those areas of adjustment. Dhaliwali (1971) conducted a study of personality correlates of academic achievement. He concluded that high verbal ability, home, emotional and school adjustment, but poor social adjustment correspond with over-achievement whereas low verbal ability, emotional instability, assertiveness, happy-go-lucky temperament were associated with academic under-achievement. However, Misra (1962) and Muthayya (1965) compared the personality structure of high and low achievers; and found no difference between the two groups. But Misra found that high and low achievers do differ in anxiety and neuroticism and Muthayya concluded that those two groups differ in the need for achievement. On the other hand, Black's investigation in 1974 revealed that self-concept test performance was found to be significantly and negatively related to age, school, grade and each measure of achievements.

This brief review of literature indicates that there is controversy regarding the type and degree of relationship between academic achievement and personality traits.

The present study was aimed at exploring the type and degree of relationship between academic achievements and some of the personality traits of urban, rural and tribal children.

Method

Sample

The sample for the present study consisted of 300 school students of 12 to 15 years of age, among which 108 belonged to tribal school, 100 to rural and 92 to urban school children. Among the samples 162 were boys and 138 were girls. These Ss were divided into two groups: high achievers, those who had secured 55 per cent marks or B plus grade in their last qualifying school examination and low achievers, those who had secured less than 55 per cent marks or B minus grade, in their school examinations.

Test Materials

To find out the personality traits of the Ss, an Indian adapted and modified version of Thematic Apperception Test developed by Dr. Uma Choudhury was used. Ten cards of this test, Card No. 1, 2, MB 3, FG 3, MB 4, FG 4, 5, 7, 8 and 9 were used for this study. Ss last qualifying examination marks were treated as their academic achievements.

Method of Administering Test

The test was given in a self-administered written pattern. The instructions were given to each subject individually to tell a story for each card basing on its past, present and future outcomes and for which there would be no time limit or length limit. The instructions were presented to Ss to make them believe that their task was simply to describe the events leading up to the perceived situation and to tell what was going on in each picture card. However, questions were encouraged to clarify the instructions.

Scoring the TAT

Stories obtained from the Ss were judged for "need achievements", "aggressiveness", "affiliation", "self-assertiveness", "conflict level", and "pessimistic" or "optimistic attitude" of the central character.

Results and Discussion

The data were subjected to Pearson's Product Moment Correlation to find out the degree of relationship between personality scores and scores of school achievement. "Z" score was computed to infer the role of sex on the personality-school achievement relationships. To infer the association of high achievers and low achievers as regard to their personality variables, chi-square tests were computed.

The results of the investigation establish that a positive relationship is found between school achievement and different personality variables taken for this study. Table 1 shows that the relationship between school achievement and need achievement, future outcomings of students is significant at. 05 level (r=. 21 &. 23 respectively and P <. 05), whereas the relationship between academic achievement and conflict level, self-assertiveness of Ss is positive and significant at. 01 level (r. 39 and. 25 respectively & P <. 01). Other personality variables, i.e., aggressiveness, and affiliation are positively related to the Ss scholastic attainment. It means that there is a direct relationship between school achievement and personality variables. In other words personality and academic achievement move in same direction. Bhatnagar (1967) confirmed the result by finding out a positive relationship between academic achievement and aggression of individuals. However, he found a negative relation between academic achievement and need affiliation which opposes his present finding. Singh's (1965) study also opposed this present view. On the contrary Misra (1962) and Muthayya. (1965) found no relationship between high achievers and low achievers with their personality traits. But Black (1974) found a negative relationship between academic achievement and self-concept of individuals.

Table 1

Correlation between school achievement and personality factors

	Need achievement	*Aggression*	*Affiliation*	*Conflict*	*Self-assertion*	*Outcome*
School achievement N-300	.21*	.18	.14	.39**	.25**	.23*

* Significant at. 05 level

** Significant at. 01 level

Table 2

Correlation between school achievement and personality factors of different area children

Group	*Need achievement*	*Aggression*	*Affiliation*	*Conflict*	*Self-assertion*	*Outcome*
Urban	.33	–.01	.02	.42*	.69**	.11
Rural	.12	–.01	.40*	.23	.19	.14
Tribal	.32	.53**	.004	.28	.20	.33**

* Significant at. 05 level

**Significant at. 01 level

Taking the samples of different sub-cultural groups separately, it is evident from the result in Table 2 that all the personality variables understudy are directly related to academic achievement of tribal children, whereas both in urban and rural children negative insignificant relationship is found between school achievement and aggression. It is also revealed from the result in Table 2 that such relation is highly significant and positive in tribal children (r = 53, P <. 01). Direct and significant relationship was evident between school achievement and need achievement, future outcomings of tribal area children (r=.32 &. 33 respectively, & P <. 05), school achievement and conflict level, self-assertion in urban area children (r =. 42 &. 69 respectively, P <. 05 & <. 01 respectively) and between school achievement and affiliation in rural area children (r =. 40, P <. 05). In toto it can be said that when high achievers have greater aggressiveness among tribal children, in rural and urban children high achievers have low aggressive tendencies. In urban area, high assertiveness is associated with high achievers. Dhaliwali (1971) supported such findings. In rural area children having high affiliation are overachievers in school grade. Singh (1965)'s view, however, opposed it.

Table 3
Relationship of boys and birls in regard to their school achievement and personality factors relationship

Group	*Need achievement*	*Aggression*	*Affiliation*	*Conflict*	*Self-assertion*	*Outcome*
Boys (162)	.27*	.17	–.13	.15	.10	.21
Girls (138)	.31*	.16	.48*	.71**	.37**	.16
/Z/	.20	.06	.90	3.70**	1.45	.25

* Significant at. 05 level

** Significant at. 01 level

So far as the sex role is concerned, the result revealed the fact that a highly positive and significant relationship between personality traits and academic achievement is present more in case of girls than in the case of boys. Table 3 shows that in the case of girls the correlation between school achievement and affiliation conflict, and self-assertiveness are. 48,. 71 and. 37 respectively and they are significant at. 01 level. It means that the high achiever girls are more affiliated to others, have more conflicts and are more self-assertive, whereas, low achiever girls are less affiliate, low self-assertive in nature. It is also inferred from the result that the correlation between school achievement and need achievement of boys is. 27 and of girls is. 31 and both of them are significant at. 05 level, which means that in both boys and girls academic achievement is directly related to the need achievement of the Ss. It is also found that a negative significant relationship exists between school achievement and affiliation in the case of boys. It indicates that high achiever boys are less affiliated to parents, family and other members of the society.

Fisher's 'Z' transformation formula was adopted to find out the sex role on such correlations. Table 3 shows that only in one case, the correlation between conflict and school achievement, the 'Z' is significant at. 01 level. It means than boys and girls do differ significantly in respect of their academic achievement and conflict level relationship.

The analysis of the result shows that there is some association between school achievement and personality traits of Ss. Interpreting the result (Table 4) it can be stated that except in case of affiliation, other traits are associated with scholastic attainment of Ss. Muthayya

(1956)'s result partly supports this finding. Since the cell frequencies of low achiever's high need achievement, high achievers' low aggression, and high achievers' pessimistic attitudes were less than 5, they were pulled up and the chi-square test was computed. It was found that there were high degree of association between need achievement, aggressiveness, conflict level, self-assertiveness, future outcomings and title school achievements of Ss (X^2 = 25.728, 21.614, 12.33, 22.53, 13.565 respectively and P <. 01). Sharma's (1972) experimental investigations have supported this view. But scholastic attainment and affiliation traits are unrelated or independent (X^2 = 0.26, P>.05). In other words, it can be said that high achievers and low achievers do differ significantly in their need achievement, aggression, conflict level, self-assertion and future outcome and not in affiliation trait.

Table 4

Comparative scores cf personality factors between high achievers and low achievers

Personality	*Variables*	*High achievers*	*Low achievers*	*Pulled frequencies*		X^2
Need	tow	32	151	32	151	
achievement	Medium	43	62	52	65	25.728**
	High	9	3			
Aggression	Low	3	9	52	186	
	Neutral	49	177	32	30	21.614**
	High	32	30			
Affiliation	No aff.	9	24			
	Medium aff	56	149			.26
	High aff	19	43			
Conflict	Low	9	51			
	Medium	45	124			12.33**
	High	30	41			
Self-	Unasst.	27	100			
assertion	Med. asst.	43	111			22.53**
	High asst.	14	5			
Outcome	Pessimist	3	22	54	181	
	Neutral	51	159			13.565**
	Optimist	30	35	30	35	

** Significant at. 01 level

References

Bhatnagar, R. P., A study of some of the personality variables as predicators of Academic achievement, Doctoral dissertation in Education, Delhi University, 1967.

Black, F. W., Self concept as related to achievement and age in learning—disabled children, *Child Development,* 1974, 45, 1137-1140.

Cattell, R. B. Barton, K., & Dielman, T. E., Prediction of school achievement from motivation, personality and ability measures, *Psychological Reports,* 1972, 30, 35-43.

Dhaliwali A. S., A study of some factors contributing to academic success and failure among high school students — Personality correlates of academic over, under-achievement, Doctoral dissertation in Psychology, Aligarh Muslim University, 1971.

Kundu, C. L., *Personality Development: A critique of Indian Studies*, Vishal Publications, University Campus, Kurukshetra (Haryana-India), 1971.

Misra H. K., Personality patterns of the high and low achievers in Engineering Education, Doctoral dissertation, Indian Institute of Technology, Kharagpur, 1962.

Muthayya, B. C., Some correlates of achievement motive among high and low achievers in the scholastic field, *Journal of Psychological Researches,* 1955, 9, 89-91.

Pielstic, N. L., Perception of mentally superior children by their classmates, *Perceptual and Motor Skills*, 1963, 17, 47-53.

S. Rason, S.B., *Anxiety in Elementary School Children*, New York, John Wiley & Sons, Inc, 1960.

Sexena, P. C., A. study of interests, need patterns and adjustments problems of over and under achievers, Doctoral dissertation in Education, Allahabad University, 1972.

Sharma K. C,. A comparative study of adjustment of over and under achievers, Doctoral dissertation in Education, Aligarh Muslim University, 1972.

Singh, B. N. K., Some non-intellectual correlates of academic achievements, Doctoral dissertation, Patna University, 1965.

CHAPTER 24

Effect of Inhabitance on Personality Traits of Scheduled Tribe and Scheduled Caste Adolescents in Comparison with Upper Caste

Kalpana Jain and V.L. Chouhan

The purpose of the study was to observe effect of inhabitance on scheduled tribe and scheduled caste students in comparison with the upper caste. Hindi version of Cattell's Higher Secondary Personality Questionnaire developed by Kapoor, Srivastava and Srivastava (1985) was administered to 900 adolescents of scheduled caste, scheduled tribe and upper castes belonging to urban and rural areas of Udaipur district. Results showed that inhabitance affected four personality factors, B, G, Q_2 and Q_3 of the students of different castes (scheduled caste, scheduled tribe and upper caste) in different ways. However a similar effect was observed in the study with regard to personality factors A, C, D, E, F, H, I, J, O and Q_4 in these three castes. The significant interaction effect of caste and inhabitance was discussed in the light of development of scheduled tribe and schedule castes.

Introduction

The personality pattern of a person is highly affected by the region and environment in which he lives (Cattell; 1968). The needs, requirement and available sources of urban and rural areas are quite different which lead to different patterns of life and thinking.

Lack of culture is variably susceptible to the changes in personality patterns. How the urban scheduled tribes (ST) and scheduled castes (SC) differ from their rural counterparts and from upper caste will help in identifying new, variables and in suggesting new strategies for the development of these backward classes. Therefore the present study is concerned with the effect of inhabitance on personality traits of SC and ST in comparison with the upper caste.

Some studies have been reported regarding the effect of ecology. Robert (1971), Ahluwalia and Kalia (1984), Chatterjee and Ray (1986), Itangari (1987) found urban students more intelligent than rural ones. Chatterjee and Bhaskar (1981) and Chatterjee and Paul (1983) observed no difference in anxiety due to area of residence. Ahluwalia. & Kalia (1984) reported urban adolescents to be self-opinioned, suspicious and practical. Jitendre & Sharma observed urban students to be extroverted and less neurotic. Chouhan and Jain (1987) reported urban disadvantaged students (SC & ST) to be more reserved, shrewd, undisciplined and group dependent than rural students. The review clearly reveals that though many studies were done on the effect of ecology on the general population yet negligible studies are available on scheduled tribe and scheduled caste students.

Method

Sample

The sample consisted of total 900 students (150 respondents of each scheduled tribe urban STU, scheduled tribe rural STR, scheduled caste urban SCU, scheduled caste rural SCR, upper caste urban UCU, upper caste rural UCR). The age range of subjects was from 12 to 18 years studying in sixth to ninth classes. The sample was drawn from the city and villages of Udaipur district.

Apparatus

The Hindi version of Cattell's HSPQ (Higher Secondary Personality Questionnaire) developed by Kapoor, Srivastava and Srivastava (1985) was used. The test measures 14 primary, functional, independent and psychologically meaningful dimensions, which gives almost complete coverage of personality traits possible in a short time.

The short term reliability of the Form A varies from 0.72 to 0.91 and stability coefficient, i.e., retest after a long interval ranges from 0. 44 to 0. 69. The direct concept validities vary from 0. 58 to 0.77 for

Form A which is used for the study out of four parallel forms, viz., A, B, C and D.

Procedure

The test was administered in group situation in the classrooms. Instructions were given according to the manual of the test. Subjects took about an hour to complete the questionnaire. After administration of the test, the answer sheets were scored using keys provided for the purpose.

The mean values were worked out for each of the six groups of the study. Analysis of variance was applied for each personality factor to find out the significance of difference between mean values.

Results

The analysis of variance (Table 1) reveals that the interaction effect of caste and inhabitance was not significant with regard to personality factors A, C, D, E, F, H, 1, J, O, Q4, namely, reserved vs outgoing, egostrength, obedient vs assertive, sober vs enthusiastic, shy vs adventurous, tough-minded vs tender-minded, zestful vs circumspect individualism, self-assured vs apprehensive, uncontrolled vs controlled and relaxed vs tense. It indicates that effect of inhabitance was the same for the three castes of the study on these personality factors, whereas the significant effect was observed with regard to four personality factors, viz. B-less intelligent vs more intelligent, G-expedient vs conscientious, Q_2-sociably group dependent vs self-sufficient, Q_3-uncontrolled vs controlled. It means that inhabitance had effect on these personality traits in various ways in these caste students.

The critical difference (CD) and means values from Table 1 show that upper caste urban adolescents were more intelligent, bright, intellectually adaptable and inclined to have more intellectual interests than rural subjects. But in scheduled tribe and scheduled caste no effect was observed. The conscientiousness of ST was not changed because of urbanisation but UC and SC of the urban area were found more conscientious, responsible, consistently ordered, emotionally disciplined, determined and concerned about moral standards and rules than their rural counterparts.

Table 1
Means, F-Ratios and critical difference values of tribe, scheduled caste and upper caste urban and rural students on 14 personality factors

Personality		*Urban*			*Rural*		*F. Ratio*		
Factors	*ST*	*SC*	*UC*	*ST*	*SC*	*UC*	*(Caste x Area)*		*C.D.*
A	9.85	10.17	10.24	10.18	10.37	10.35			
B		4.88	4.97	5.79	4.82	4.99	4.77	5.76**	0.32
C	11.12	12.09	13.05	11.03	12.39	11.27	1.75		
D	10.59	10.19	9.78	10.39	9.82	10.09	1.56		
E		8.72	8.95	8.69	9.43	9.21	9.87	2.46	
F		9.75	9.95	9.51	9.51	9.42	9.43	1.91	
G	12.21	13.92	12.73	11.83	12.37	11.14	5.43**	0.58	
H	10.67	9.89	10.95	11.10	10.71	10.55	2.37		
I		11.83	12.35	'12.24	11.01	11.59	11.42		
J		10.09	9.89	9.63	10.55	10.00	10.31		
O	10.16	10.12	9.60	10.41	10.23	10.29			
Q2	10.55	11.23	11.48	10.81	11.07	10.71	2.91*	0.49	
Q3	12.53	11.59	12.01	11.32	11.99	10.89	4.23*	0.57	
Q4	9.55	9.71	8.96	10.41	9.11	9.91	2.11		

Significant at 0.05 level
Significant at 0.01 level

Further data in Table 1 reveal that SC of urban inhabitance were self-sufficient, resourceful and prefers their own decisions than their rural counterparts but the mean of ST and UC of urban and rural areas was not significantly different on this factor Q2. The urban adolescents of ST and SC were found to be more controlled, socially precise and compulsive than rural students but no difference in urban and rural subjects of UC was observed in the present study.

Discussion

The present study provides evidence that urbanisation affects some personality traits variably in different culture. However, the present study should be taken as an indicator of some differences only. Gereralisation for this will be unwarranted without replication on another sample which consisted of more tribal and scheduled caste groups.

The intelligence score of ST and SC did not increase in urban environment. Though it was observed in the present and other studies (Robert, 1971; Ahluwalia and Kalia, 1984; Chatterjee and Ray, 1986; Rangari, 1987) urban students are more intelligent than their rural counterparts. The absence of a similar trend in SC and ST may be because of the fact that students of these castes might not have taken the advantages of better environment available in urban areas for intelligence development. It implies that it is better to provide facilities to SC and ST students within their own surrounding and setting to get better results for their development.

Scheduled tribe communities basically live near forests and hills, i.e., this caste is isolated in comparison to other ones. No change in conscientiousness in rural and urban students of this caste can be attributed to this fact. The SC of urban area were found to be more self-sufficient than their rural counterparts. It may be because of the fact that the feeling of untouchability is negligibly present in cities, whereas in rural areas it is still present. The feeling of indifference with others may lead to SC of urban area to be more self-sufficient and resourceful than those living in rural areas. No such type of feeling was found for tribes, therefore no difference on this factor was observed between rural and urban ST adolescents. So it can be suggested that a feeling of equality and integration should be emphasized in rural areas.

The ST and SC of urban areas were more controlled and socially precise than those of rural adolescents. This can be due to familiarity of rural areas to them which make them free and comfortable.

From the above discussion it can be concluded that the effect of inhabitance was there, but it varies from culture to cultures—scheduled tribe, scheduled caste and upper caste.

References

Ahluwalia, S. P. and Kalia, A. K., An investigation into the urban-rural differencies on values, adjustment, personality and intelligence, *Journal of Institute of Educational Research,* 1984, 8 3, 21-25.

Cattell, R. B. and Cattell, M. D. L., *Handbook for the Jr. Sr. High School Personality Questionnaire,* The HSPQ for ages twelve through eighteen years, The Psycho-centre. New Delhi, 1976.

Chatterjee, R. G. and Bhaskar, P., Impact of schooling, urban-rural differences and trait anxiety on field independence, *Italian Journal of Psychology,* 1981, 8 (3), 235-242.

Chatterjee R. G. and Paul, B., *Ecological differences trait anxiety and field independence,* Bombay, Psychologist. 1983, 5, 1, 78-83.

........., and Ray, G., *Environment impact on cognition and intelligence, Paper presented at the Indian Academy, of Applied Psychology,* Varanasi, 1986.

Chuhan V. L. and jain, K., A study of Personality of Socially disadvantaged students in relation to their ecology (urban-rural) and Sex, *Personality Study and Group Behaviour,* 1987, 7, 1, 25-31.

Kapoor, S. D., Srivastava, S. S. and Srivastava, G. N. P., *Manual for the HSPQ,* The Psycho-Centre, New Delhi, 1985.

Rangari. A., Caste affiliation, sex, area of residence, and socio-economic status as sources of variation in intelligence of students, *Indian Psychological Review*, 1987, 32, 5-6, 43-49.

Robert, J., Intellectual development of children by demographic and socio-economic factors, *Vital and Health Statistics Series,* 1971, 11, No. 110.